BLACK AND WHITE:

Reflections of a White Southern Sociologist

THE REYNOLDS SERIES IN SOCIOLOGY

Larry T. Reynolds, *Editor*

by **GENERAL HALL, INC.**

BLACK AND WHITE:

Reflections of a White Southern Sociologist

Lewis M. Killian
The University of West Florida

Introduction By
Julius Lester
University of Massachusetts at Amherst

GENERAL HALL, INC.
Publishers
5 Talon Way
Dix Hills, New York 11746

BLACK AND WHITE:
Reflections of a White Southern Sociologist

GENERAL HALL, INC.
5 Talon Way
Dix Hills, New York 11746

Copyright © 1994 by General Hall, Inc.

Publisher: Ravi Mehra
Editor: Alan Gold
Composition: *Graphics Division,* General Hall, Inc.

LIBRARY OF CONGRESS CATALOG CARD NUMBER: **93–79475**

ISBN: 1–882289–12–9 [cloth]

Manufactured in the United States of America

DEDICATION

To those much beloved and well-remembered people who, although we were born of a different hue, still accepted me as a friend: Butler, Belvin, Ophelia, Pearl Easley, "Saint" Chrysler, "Doc," Bill Hale, Frank Edwards, Tilman Cothran, Harry Walker, Mozell Hill, Hylan Lewis, Bonita and Preston Valien, Victoria Warner, Charles Key, Mike Thelwell, James and Martha Faison, Julius Lester, Ruel and Patricia, Chuck and Louise Stone, Les Humphrey, and, most of all, Charles U. Smith, William J. Wilson, and Henry Burrell.

Contents

ACKNOWLEDGMENTS

Black and White was twenty years in the writing, competing with many books and articles which demanded my attention in the short term. During those two decades my patient wife, Kay, was my constant support and comfort. I must express my thanks to her first, last, and always.

I have often felt that since I do not qualify as a celebrity, hubris was required for me to write an autobiography, even a focussed one dealing primarily with my professional life. During the early stages of the writing I sorely needed assurance that the project was worth doing. I received such assurance from diverse sources, and I am grateful to those people. One is my grandson, Kevin McHugh,Jr., who as a teenager read the first chapter and told me, "Grandad, that's interesting — I want to know the rest of your story." Julius Lester, a prodigious writer, took time to read some early chapters. I took heart from his comment, "Your story shed light for me on the white South as nothing else I've read has done."

As I reached the end of the manuscript and began to believe that publication was a possibility, others gave me much appreciated encouragement. Gideon Sjoberg, of the University of Texas, did so when he enthusiastically accepted Chapter 7, "Working for the Segregationist Establishment," for publication in a special issue of *The Journal of Applied Behavioral Science* which he edited. This chapter is reprinted with permission from NTL Institute, from pp. 487-498, *The Journal of Applied Behavioral Science,* Vol.25, No. 4, copyright, 1989.

After I submitted the manuscript to General Hall, Inc., Larry Reynolds, editor, became my advocate with the publisher. I was further heartened by positive reactions from Bernard Meltzer, a classmate at the University of Chicago and now a senior faculty member at Central Michigan University, and Richard Martin, a former student at the University of Massachusetts and today a highly effective editor himself. After the work had been accepted for publication, Mrs. Pat Salem of the University of West Florida (an exemplary learning environment) assisted, with great diligence and wonderful good cheer, in getting it ready for the printer.

There is no greater debt than the one I owe to the late Charles H. Page, my friend and colleague for sixteen years at the University of Massachusetts, Amherst. After reading some early chapters he urged me to continue with the project and offered to be my editorial adviser. Over many years he read each chapter, edited it with superb skill, and asked for more. He edited the last three chapters when we both knew that he was dying of cancer and daily was growing weaker. Despite his infirmity he kept writing, "Send me the next chapter — I want to know the ending!" I will always be profoundly indebted to Charles and his wife, Leonora, for their willingness to help me even *in extremis.*

Lewis M. Killian

INTRODUCTION

By Julius Lester

This is not an autobiography which reviews the accomplishments of a lifetime. It could have been. As a teacher and sociologist Lewis Killian has accomplished much. He has authored and co-authored works that have become standards in sociology. In the sociological tradition pioneered by W.E.B. Du Bois, he has used information gathered as the basis for prophetic reflections on history. *The Impossible Revolution?* and *The Impossible Revolution: Phase II* are express truths so revealing of the black condition in America that many blacks have been stunned to learn that Killian is a white southerner. Killian has been the model of the politically-engaged scholar who maintained his intellectual and spiritual integrity, never succumbing to the Siren call of ideology of the Right or Left.

Autobiography is a difficult form because it compels one to do what is almost impossible: to see oneself-truly. Such a feat requires that you stand outside and look at yourself with disinterest while, simultaneously, writing about yourself with passion. Such a feat can be undertaken successfully only if one is impelled to write by the need to know who he is.

The autobiography which recounts a life of public achievement is based on the premise that the individual is synonymous with the public persona, that the person is the sum of his or her achievements.

However, most of us are painfully aware that we are in some ways more than our accomplishments and in others, less. There are instances, too, when there can be an almost unbridgeable chasm between public and private. Autobiography becomes the arena in which one attempts to bring the two into harmonious relationship. This requires asking and attempting to answer that most fundamental and unanswerable of questions: Who am I?

Killian has chosen to answer the question with one word: *Cracker.* It is at once affirmation and affront, a statement of class solidarity so provocative that the reader is required to examine his and her own prejudices. In the two syllables of the one word, the reader is challenged to do what Killian does - confront his prejudices. To do so is to learn who one is.

Lewis Killian was born in Georgia in the first year after the end of World War I, only fifty four years after the end of the Civil War. Thus he was born and raised in a world where ex-slave and ex-slave owner still lived, a world where the power ethic engendered by slavery still prevailed between blacks and whites, and would for almost another half century.

Killian grew up with the prejudices of the time and place into which he was born. To his credit he has not insulted us by writing a self-serving story of "How I Grew Up A Racist But Learned To Love Negroes." The story he writes is far more complex and thereby more honest.

It is the story of our time and the story of our country. At the center of our nation's history lies the black presence, a presence with which the non-black majority has never found the means to be comfortable. An important component of America's story in the twentieth century is the effort made by whites to come to terms with that black presence.

Lewis Killian's story, then, is more than an individual one. It is the story of one person's interaction with history. And is that not the story of each of our lives?

Each of us is born into a particular place at a particular time. We inherit traditions, mores, a regional culture, idiosyncrasies of speech and accent. Our encounter with history begins and unfolds as we decide, in large ways and small, to accept this of our inheritance but reject that. Who we become as human beings is determined by what we choose and what we reject.

Through Lewis Killian's autobiography we see graphically that social change may be set in motion by an overarching event like the 1954 Supreme Court decision against segregation in public education. But how social change evolves is the direct result of the choices made by individuals.

There is no big dramatic moment in Killian's life when he begins to break with the white southern heritage bequeathed. There is no epiphany, no conversion experience from which he emerges with a soul redeemed from racism. Instead, there are choices, those moments when he chose to relate not as a white man but as a man.

Killian understands, however, that one does not choose once and the matter is settled. Living with integrity and decency is a matter of having to choose, again and again, and one of the virtues of *Black and White* is that Killian has the courage to record those moments when he did not choose in accord with his ideals. The "cracker" his environment raised him to be remains part of him and sometimes shames him.

It is this uncommon honesty that makes Killian's autobiography exceptional. He wonders if his understanding and sympathy for Black Power did not come from a sense that Black Power was a restatement of racial separation, the milieu in which he had grown quite comfortably. He is never able to answer definitively.

He gives us portraits of relatives and friends with whom he grew up, and while acknowledging that their allegiance to the "southern way of life" did not change, Killian's affection for them does not abate. Part of me would have preferred if he had denounced them for being racists, etc., etc., etc. Part of me is grateful he did not. The key to our humanity lies in our ability to accept and even love that in ourselves and in others which is morally unacceptable.

Although Killian is a sociologist, in his reflections he writes as if he were sitting on your porch or in your living room telling a story. There is no academic jargon. He is a man telling a story in language that is direct and simple. He has a good eye for detail which enables us as readers to feel that we, too, are there - be it in the Georgia of his childhood, the Florida of the 1950s, or New England in the 70s.

While this is not a confessional, it is deeply personal. He writes about his near-suicidal depressions, his hospitalization in a therapeutic community, his present despair that his life has not amounted to much.

The worth of our lives depends on the standards we use to measure them. At age 54, I am 19 years younger than Killian, but I think I perceive that it is not ours to know the meaning and worth of our lives. It is ours to simply live with as much decency and courage and simple honesty as we can muster from one day to the next. If we can manage that (and that is a lot) our lives will have made a difference.

Here is one man's story of the effort to live decently and honestly and with courage, to live in a rhythm of an ongoing dialogue with history, knowing that we cannot overcome the history we are born into but neither are we compelled to live as history's puppet and plaything. We say yes and we say no, and when we say which, and what we say yes and no to eventually shape and mold us until we have that mysterious thing called character, or we don't.

Lewis Killian does not know it, but in telling us of his struggle to know when and to whom or what a yes or no was addressed, he has given us a measure of instruction in what it means to be decent, in what it means to be fully human.

This book reminds us that there is a "cracker" in each of us, attitudes and emotions of which we are ashamed but of which we can never wholly divest ourselves. If we try to deny its existence, if we pretend that it is not there, the "cracker" within will make us unworthy of respect and trust. There is no alternative but to turn and face it, to acknowledge its existence. In so doing, we accept ourselves in our imperfection, accept ourselves in our utter fragility. And in that moment of acceptance, we become whole men and whole women.

In an age when human possibilities are being narrowed by religious and political ideologues of the Right and Left, when an increasing emphasis on ethnic, gender and racial identities threatens to obliterate the sanctity of the individual soul, this autobiographical reflection on a life and its dialogue with history serves as a needed reminder of the beautiful complexities we human beings are.

Julius Lester is Professor of Judaic Studies at the University of Massachusetts at Amherst.

A CRACKER BOY

Chapter **1**

The Heart of Georgia—Black Friends, White Enemies—
Genteel Prejudice—to High School in Uniform

A bright Georgia sun, hot sand in a backyard dappled with cool, dark spots where trees and the house cast shadows; two very small boys, one black, one white, sitting in the yard playing together—this is a picture of my early childhood that often flashes into my mind. I was the little white boy. The black boy was Minnie Carter's son, Tom. Minnie, our maid, would have been watching us from the back porch as she worked. She was a genuine "mammy," fitting the stereotype even to being fat like Aunt Jemima. Like many black domestics in the South of the early 1920s she brought her toddler to work with her, and he became one of my earliest playmates.

Our friendship did not last long. For some reason that I was too young to know, Minnie found employment with another white family. She and her son disappeared from my life. The friendship would not have lasted long anyway, for the etiquette of race relations would not have permitted an older black child to run around our neighborhood and become part of my white play group. I had forgotten Tom when, a few years later, my mother pointed him out as he bicycled down our street delivering groceries.

I cannot even vouch for the fact that I really remember the scene I have portrayed; perhaps I reconstructed it from my mother's accounts of how Minnie used to bring her small son to work with her. But my earliest memories—those glimpses of childhood that all of us retain like still pictures from a movie that we cannot fully reconstruct—contain many black characters. There was a young and pretty nurse who cared for me after Minnie left, and there was Sylvester, a man who worked as a mechanic's helper to my uncle and always went with him when he changed employers. Then there were the vegetable women who walked down our street in the early morning balancing huge baskets on their heads, and the iceman who drove a wagon drawn by a team of mules. Black people were always an element in my environment, and my early memories of them are warm and pleasant. I have to look to a later time in my life to recall fearing or disliking blacks.

1

I was born in the small town of Darien, Georgia, but my childhood was spent in Macon, promoted by the city fathers as "the heart of Georgia." A sign on the outskirts of town marked the geographical center of the state.

When I celebrated my first birthday in 1920, Macon had a population of 53,000, of whom 30,000 were white and 23,000 black—or "Negro" then. There were 698 foreign-born whites in the city; the ones I knew included a Jewish cobbler from Russia and an Italian clarinet player who also ran a music store. The four people enumerated as "Other" in the census must have been the Chinese family that, again stereotypically, ran a laundry downtown on Walnut Street. Macon was a very typical southern city at the time. Its economy rested on a base that included several large cotton mills and the farms that surrounded the city. Peaches were important; Macon was then at the center of the largest peach-growing area in the world.

Racial segregation was both law and custom, and black workers were terribly exploited. Few white households outside the mill villages could not afford a black domestic, for wages were incredibly low. The lower-class whites who worked in the cotton mills were also exploited, their lives as strictly regulated by the mill owners as were those of blacks. The two groups did not make common cause, however, and whites were guided in their thinking and feelings about blacks by southern demagogues, many of whom were Georgia politicians.

Although I grew up in the Deep South at a time when segregation was firmly entrenched and lynchings were the scandal of the region, I was not taught to hate "nigras," or "colored people," as my family called them. The prejudices I acquired were of the genteel variety, as socially significant but not nearly as vicious in content as the stereotype of white southern racism would lead one to believe. In contrast to psychopathological prejudice, mine was the normative or conforming type of prejudice which sociologists Robert Merton, Pierre van den Bergh, and Muzafer Sherif have pointed out as central to problems of intergroup relations. As genteel as my bigotry was, however, it was powerfully resistant to change, and the attitudes and behavior of the "gentle people" of the South, including my family, were the bulwark of racial inequality until the Black Revolution at midcentury.

I grew up in a "Christian family," although our Methodist and Baptist neighbors had some doubts about what kind of Christianity was propagated at the Episcopal church to which we belonged. When we moved to Macon, the family consisted of my widowed mother and me, my mother's bachelor brother, my grandmother, and my grandfather, a retired Episcopal priest. Although no family member had ever graduated from college, ours was an educated family by the standards of the time and place. Grandpa had read for the Anglican ministry in England, where he grew up, and in Canada, where he was ordained. Mother had attended two years of normal school and had been a schoolteacher since she was eighteen or nineteen years old. My father had finished two years of junior college at Gordon Military College, worked as an accountant, earned a commission in the army, and then died during the flu epidemic of 1918, before I was born. Serving God, raising me to be moral, successful, and worthy of my father in heaven, and supporting the family were what my mother lived for. We were never affluent enough to reach beyond the lower limits of the upper middle class, and the neighborhood in which we lived was inhabited primarily by working-class families. This would be a significant influence on my life. Years later, I recognized our marginality in the neighborhood and Macon society. Although our income was no higher than that of most of our neighbors, our tastes and aspirations were those of a better social class. Yet we did not have a "good" address.

The neighborhood was marginal. Holt Avenue, where we lived, stretched for about eight or nine long blocks. At our end lived people who, for the most part, owned their own homes and worked in such jobs as retail store clerk, railroad engineer, city fireman, police officer, and building superintendent. At the other end was a mill village, a collection of cottages owned by a cotton mill and rented to the hands. The "mill people" were the "poor whites" of the industrial South—the "lintheads." I learned at an early age to be careful to let people know *which* end of Holt Avenue I lived on. The situation was complicated immeasurably when a most atypical family of mill people bought a house directly across the street from ours, having sold their small farm outside Macon. The father, a skilled mechanic, obtained a job in the nearby mill, and his wife and older daughter worked as hands; all could walk to work from our end of the street. But the family was not to remain "mill people" forever. Its members were upwardly mobile, and two of the younger children eventually graduated from college. These two became my closest friends within days after they moved on the street.

I was about four years old and I found these new neighbors fascinating. They moved in with a horse-drawn wagon and a cow that they pastured in their big backyard, no doubt to the consternation of the neighbors. Joe and his sister, Louise, were both close to my age. They became constant playmates and remained so until high school activities drew us apart.

Yet it was as a result of my relationships with mill people that I developed my first full-blown prejudice. My mother could hardly stop me from playing with my new friends, but she soon let me know that I should not imitate them because they were not "our kind of people." Their dress, food habits, use of the English language, and religious beliefs set them apart from our style of life. My mother's explanation—more to her satisfaction than to mine—was that they were "all right," but they were "common." Even within the bonds of friendship, I developed an attitude of social and intellectual superiority. Although Joe was a year older than I and much tougher physically, I read more and had a more active imagination. He let me take the lead in many of our games, and I became the dominant one in our activities.

When I began school, fear and hatred of "common" people (my friends excepted) were added to my sense of superiority. "Mill kids" went to the same school, and they were mean! The boys were tough and quick to start a fight at the slightest pretext. After a few encounters resulting from such trivia as jostling someone in the lunch line, I learned to fear and dislike them. One traumatic incident taught me how they felt about me. On my way to school one morning, a "mill kid" taunted me. When I protested, he dared me to do something about it. Before I could react, he let me know that he didn't think I would do anything. "Rich kids can't fight," he said. I had never thought of myself as a "rich kid," but now I began to grasp what a gulf existed between his end of the street and mine.

Thus my social world began to be structured at an early age. It was a white world, even though individual blacks moved in and out of it regularly. At the center were my family and a few close friends in the neighborhood, particularly Joe, whom I thought of almost as a brother. Then there were "my kind of people"—the kids who went to my Sunday school, were invited to my birthday parties, and would become my best friends when I started school. They didn't live on my street but in Cherokee Heights, one of Macon's newest suburbs. Our church was located there, so this section was also an important part of my world. I was there every Sunday and often on other days, for such events as Boy Scout meetings.

I was also learning far more about race relations than I can remember being deliberately taught. The perceptive sociologist, Olive Westbrook Quinn, herself a southerner, could have been writing about my indoctrination when she wrote in "Transmission of Racial Attitudes Among White Southerners, "For the most part the South does not teach attitudes to its white children. Such teaching is not necessary; in establishing practices, by precepts, by example, and by law, which separate the races and make distinctions between interracial and intraracial behavior, the South has established a way of life which can have but one meaning for those who diligently practice it." Images, beliefs, and practices that I would later question, and even abhor, seemed natural then to me.

Some of the earliest stories I remember having read to me are considered racist today. I loved them. There was the heroic figure Little Black Sambo outwitting the tigers. I liked the story of Epaminandous even more, perhaps because my mother told it in dialect. It conveyed the image of the little black boy who was lovable but dumb. When his "mammy" cautioned him, in the folk expression, "You be careful how you step on those pies," he carefully stepped in the middle of each of the freshly baked pies sitting on the front porch to cool! The most durable and beloved character was Uncle Remus, the kindly old black man sitting by the fire in his cabin spinning wonderful tales for the little white boy from the big house. Many people's knowledge of Joel Chandler Harris and Uncle Remus is limited to the story of Br'er Rabbit and the Tar Baby. Somehow my family had acquired two full volumes of tales of Uncle Remus written in the dialect of the ex-slaves Harris knew in Georgia. My mother would read me these stories in her version of this dialect.

The genuine, original Uncle Remus myth presented nothing of the saccharine, paternalistic image of the Old South conveyed by Walt Disney's *Song of the South*. To me as a little boy, Uncle Remus was simply a wonderful storyteller; his characters and their exploits were of first importance. Br'er Rabbit, Br'er Fox, Br'er B'ar, Br'er Wolf, and others were semihuman figures portraying human virtues and frailties.

If old Uncle Remus conveyed the stereotype of the black man as Uncle Tom, I was not aware of it. "Uncle" was a term of affection, not of inferiority: the only real people associated with it were much loved relatives or close adult friends— and old black men. Only the dialect as a form of "black English" conveyed any suggestion of black difference and inferiority.

Br'er Rabbit, the hero of the stories, was no inferior being, however. His character and maneuvers against his enemies were far more complex and profound than my child's mind could have grasped, and more than most people who confuse "Remus" and "Tom" would believe. As Joel Chandler Harris knew, his stories represented an important part of the African heritage of blacks in the Americas. Their themes were found in African folktales and in stories told by blacks in Caribbean and South American countries. More significantly, they often carried a veiled protest theme. Br'er Rabbit was the wily black constantly winning a struggle for survival against Br'er Fox, the stronger but not as clever white oppressor. But these themes were as far beyond my comprehension as was the notion that Uncle Remus might be a symbol of the subservient black and the little boy a "role model" from whom I would learn that I could call black men "uncle," but not "mister."

In day-to-day interaction with both black and white people, I acquired the perceptions and behavior patterns that made up the "etiquette of race relations" in the segregated South. I saw that blacks did not go to the front door of a white home—our cleaning women didn't, and neither did Annie, who had worked next door for many years. I learned that separate dishes were kept for them and that they never ate their lunch in the dining room but always in the kitchen or on the back porch. Somehow it came to seem natural that black folks had no last names, that whites did not shake hands with them, and that they did not sit next to white people when traveling. This resulted in the ridiculous practice of having a black cook or maid sitting in the back seat of an automobile while her white employer chauffeured her to and from work.

Yet these degrading symbols of white supremacy were not accompanied by feelings of fear, hatred or superiority towards blacks. This anomaly is illustrated by Butler, our mail carrier, whom I knew as far back as I can remember. As an employee of the U.S. Post Office in the early 1920s, Butler was certainly a member of the black middle class of that era. He was a dignified man—tall, dark brown, and with high cheekbones. Mother was sure he was part American Indian. Nevertheless, he was still a "nigra." Courteous, efficient, and well-spoken, he was liked by all the white people on his route—but he was still just "Butler." I have never known whether that was his first or last name. It was probably his surname, for many black men told whites only their last names to avoid the insult of being addressed by their first names.

Butler became one of my favorite people. He delivered our mail until I was in senior high school. Then a young white man who lived in the neighborhood obtained an appointment as a mail carrier and requested that he be given Butler's route. There was nothing my mother and other neighbors could do about it without offending the new carrier's family and running the risk of appearing to be "nigger lovers." Yet they did "love" Butler, and there was genuine resentment against the young white man who caused him to disappear from their lives. Disappear he did, for without his job he no longer had a place among us. "His place" was on his new route, wherever it was, and in the black neighborhood where he lived. He had never been a whole person to the whites he served so well, not even as much as a white tradesman might have been. Yet it would be wrong to assume that those white folks did not really love and respect that part of Butler the system allowed them to know.

Nurses, cooks, maids, icemen, postmen—the black people I knew as a child were kind, nurturant figures. The people who aroused bad feelings in me were white. I disliked some of my white schoolmates because they were bullies, or so I assumed. I was afraid of policemen because adults said they'd "get you" if you misbehaved. I was terrified of "mill kids" because some of them threatened to beat me up—no black kid had ever made such a threat! When my "lint-head" tormentor said, "Rich boys can't fight," he was half right as far as I was concerned—I wasn't rich, but I sure couldn't fight. In fact, I was a timorous child, gravely deficient in aggressive impulses. And the person I feared most was my own mother. It was not so much the spankings or "switchings" (literally with a peach-tree switch) which she did not hesitate to administer that inspired terror in me. It was her stern looks of disapproval and her expressed disappointment in me that made me fear that if I were not good, she would no longer love me.

Although she was an old-fashioned puritan in her standards of personal behavior (despite her Episcopalian heritage), she still believed in a simple and absolute way that "God is love." She taught me by precept and example to be kind to all living things. My first pet, a puppy named Toby, she took away from me because I pulled his tail and hurt him. More than once I was required to apologize to one of my playmates for my part in some childish altercation—to be at all aggressive came to make me feel guilty. At an early age I learned about giving a nickel each Sunday out of my meager allowance, to be sent to help our little red, brown, and yellow brothers and sisters whom we read about in Sunday school. Our charity was not limited to dropping money in the alms basin or filling our mite boxes during Lent. It included going into the homes of cotton-mill families adopted by our little parish, delivering food and clothing to them, especially at Thanksgiving and Christmas. On these occasions I saw and smelled the poverty experienced by exploited *white* people.

For all her "schoolmarm" sternness, my mother truly loved and nurtured the children she taught year after year in the sixth grade. Some of them were not easy to love. There were no "social promotions" in those days, and some of the "big boys" in her classes were larger than the teacher and had already spent time in reform school. Tears came to her eyes when she would learn that a boy whom she hoped would straighten out ended up instead in the state penitentiary at Milledgeville. I am convinced that she gave of herself so much as to hasten her death from a heart attack the year she was to retire. Although she taught in a totally segregated public school system and did not question the "Negro's place" as defined in the South in which she had grown up, I never saw her do an intentionally cruel thing to anyone, white or black. Puritanical, stern, conventional, she was nevertheless a loving person, and she taught me that the highest virtue was to love all God's creatures.

Where, then, was the dark side, the "white racism" that it has become fashionable for guilt-ridden white southerners to confess and lament? I certainly was not taught to hate black people, and I was taught that it was wrong to hurt them just as it was cruel to hurt animals. But what I was not taught was how the whole structure of white supremacy, manifest in the complex etiquette of race relations, led whites to hurt blacks when they did not intend to. So I had no way of knowing that when I joyfully greeted the mail carrier with "Hey, Butler, what do you have for us today?" I was reminding him of the Negro's place which permitted a small white child to so address him. For my mother and other white ladies to give castoff clothes and leftover food to black servants while paying them the customary low wages black domestics received was seen as kindness, not exploitation.

To the white people I knew best, the daily indignities heaped on blacks seemed natural; to a black or a white not imbued with the system they would have appeared terribly cruel. The insensitivity is evident in the story of another of my childhood black friends, "Black Lewis." He was known in the neighborhood by this name, although I don't know how often he was so addressed directly. At some point in my childhood, when I was graduating from a "coaster wagon" to roller skates, a shabby black man appeared soliciting yard work. He proved to be a good yardman and soon had enough regular customers to bring him to the street two or three days each week. My mother gave him my little wagon, which he used to pull his tools. I always felt close to Lewis, partly because it was my wagon that became his trademark.

He presented a problem, however, since there was already a "Lewis" in the neighborhood. Me! So if a housewife wanted to know if he were working in the neighborhood, she might ask, "Have you seen *Black* Lewis this morning?" and so he came to be referred to by almost everyone, including me and my playmates.

Black Lewis had steady employment but at cruelly low wages. These were supplemented by hearty lunches provided by his employers. I can remember many summer days when my friend Joe and I would talk with Lewis while he ate his lunch—sitting on the back steps, of course. He was almost as entertaining as Uncle Remus, but his stories were personal, not allegorical. On Sunday he was a preacher; I remember seeing him walking through the neighborhood with his black coat, white shirt, and necktie. He got into fights with other men sometimes, and there was a woman with whom he maintained a not entirely harmonious relationship. It turned out that he did have a last name, which apparently my mother had known all along. A time came when Black Lewis stopped appearing to take care of the yards. Several weeks later, Mother announced, "I guess we won't be seeing Black Lewis or his wagon anymore. There's a story in tonight's paper that a Lewis Walker has been given a life sentence for stabbing his girl friend to death!" It was a sad day in my life. I knew I'd miss Lewis, and Joe and I had long ago concluded that his woman didn't treat him well. I couldn't think of him as a criminal, and that he should be locked away seemed cruel.

That nobody ever called him anything but Lewis and that he sat on our back steps to eat his lunch seemed perfectly natural to me and reflects the white view of the world that I and other Georgia boys had. Such countless symbolic acts made up the etiquette and fit neatly together, like pieces of a jigsaw puzzle, to present a uniform picture of black difference and inferiority. Although it has often been described and analyzed, the etiquette was never codified or made formal. It was primarily custom, even though it rested on laws, including the "separate but equal" doctrine of the Supreme Court. Many aspects of segregation that people believe were specified in Jim Crow laws actually were not. As blacks knew better than whites, many local variations existed in the specifics of Jim Crow, and blacks always had to be on the alert. What I learned was only one version, but still a many-faceted one.

I learned the "rules of naming." No black was ever addressed or even referred to as "mister," "missus," or "miss," but except for very small children, all whites had to be accorded an honorific title by blacks. At some point in my childhood I became "Mister Lewis" to whatever black domestic happened to be employed at the time. Yet I learned that some black adults might be given titles, although never "mister." For example, when the people of our parish made an annual pilgrimage to the Episcopal college for Negroes at Ft. Valley, the black president, the father of Julian Bond, was addressed as "Dr. Bond." On one occasion, southern customs clashed with Episcopalian notions of propriety for the good ladies of St. James. The women's auxiliary accepted as a speaker a black missionary to Africa who was touring the country under the auspices of the national church. He was an ordained Episcopal priest, but in low-church

Georgia, Episcopalians addressed their priests as "mister." This wouldn't do, however, for the man was black. They couldn't address him as "Reverend Jones" because this was grammatically incorrect, and they would sound like Baptists or Methodists. Reluctantly they decided to call him "Father Jones," even though this high-church usage grated harshly on their low-church ears!

One of my most direct lessons in naming came when a black woman came begging at our front door. Still a very small boy, I rushed to the door and then hastened to the back of the house to tell Mother, "There's a lady at the door." When Mother returned, she said sharply to me, "You should have told me that was a colored woman. Ladies are white!"

There were also the norms regulating physical contacts and spatial relationships, such as the "back door rule," the "back of the bus pattern," and the "blacks eat in the kitchen" protocol. In later years I learned how illogical the whole system appeared to outsiders when I tried to explain to northerners why white southerners did not object to eating food prepared by blacks but would be distressed if a black person ate at the table with them—unless it was at the kitchen table. The system could be understood in terms used to describe it by the sociologist Robert E. Park: It permitted minimal physical distance while preserving maximum social distance.

The whole complex of taboos against any contact that might symbolize equal social status was so powerful as to produce physical reactions in whites. I remember a sociology student who, intellectually liberated from her south Georgia background, still became nauseated the first time she actually sat next to a black person in an auditorium. After I overcame my early indoctrination and began to shake hands with blacks, I found that it was easier to change my mind than my feelings. For years I would be intensely conscious of my right hand, almost as if it had been burned, for minutes after the touch of a black hand.

I was also imbued with the more brutal implications of the principle "White is right." In the contacts between whites and blacks that I witnessed, whites were clearly dominant, just as adults were in relation to me. I learned that whites were therefore free to discipline blacks as if they were children. For example, in my early teens I had a regular appointment with an orthodontist. One day he explained that he couldn't adjust my braces because his right hand was in a cast. "A nigger 'boy' at the filling station got smart with me and I had to hit him. I didn't mean to hit him that hard, though!"

I am thankful that I never backed my exercise of white supremacy with physical force. To do so would have run counter to my general fear of violence as well as to my mother's teachings of love. I do remember with shame occasions when I verbally abused blacks, using epithets such as "nigger" or "black boy." In these cases I felt I had some justification, as when I thought a porter had misplaced my suitcase at a bus station. But I recoiled at what appeared to be unwarranted cruelty or injustice. Two incidents stand out in my memory.

For a few months, a family living across the street from us kept an unattractive little dog that had taken up with them. The mongrel received little care and usually lay in the front yard, getting up to bark at every passerby. One summer morning, a small black boy walked by. The dog charged at him viciously, barking and snarling. The boy veered off the sidewalk into the street, picked up a rock, and threw it at the mutt. At that point, the "lady" of the house appeared at the door and screamed, "Nigger, what are you throwing rocks at my dog for?" He replied, "He were about to bite me!" Her rejoinder shocked even my white ears: "You're not supposed to walk on this street anyway. Why don't you walk on Blackburn?" Blackburn Avenue, which paralleled our street, was an unpaved back road with no sidewalks.

Another incident occurred when I was thirteen or fourteen years old and a member of a high school Junior ROTC unit. One day, our battalion was marching near the school grounds. As we passed, two small black boys innocently gaped at us. A cadet several ranks ahead of me snatched the cap from one boy's head and "continued the march," cap in hand. The little boy stood watching helplessly, on the verge of tears, as I in turn marched by, feeling sick at the cruelty I had witnessed but doing nothing.

The perpetrator of this bit of pure meanness was a boy who was frequently in trouble, as were his brothers. They were known in our school as "mean," and the family was regarded by my mother as "poor white trash." So I was not greatly surprised that one of them would do such a thing—they were the kind of low-class white folks who were mean to colored people. They, not blacks, were the sort of people I feared and disliked.

But the monstrous evil of the system was that we—Christian people—could not see the cruelty of our daily behavior or our complicity in the deliberate acts of whites whom we disdained. My inaction as a cadet marching by the disconsolate black boy symbolized this complicity. I would not "break ranks" to challenge the cruelty when it became obvious.

Thus I came to adulthood as a typical genteel bigot with prejudices so deeply ingrained that I could not recognize them for what they were. I have never been persuaded that it was a need to hate that animated that bigotry. The *feeling* part of our attitude toward blacks was benign; it was the *cognitive* portion that was warped and distorted. Our daily behavior was guided by a set of beliefs that defined "the Negro's place" in our world and taught us that "our colored folks" were happy in that place as long as we were not mean to them. So being unwittingly cruel seemed natural and not mean at all; to avoid such cruelty by violating the etiquette not only required a conscious effort but would also arouse severe feelings of discomfort. Hence to change, to break out of the cage of white supremacy, required more than intellectual learning. It also required practicing new patterns of behavior and coming to terms with the feelings that doing so aroused.

It was from such a cage that I, like many other renegade "Crackers," eventually escaped. I am convinced that studying "liberal" writings about race relations and having different contacts with blacks do not fully explain the process of breaking out. Experiences *within* the bounds of my white world were equally important. They may, indeed, have been essential phases of my progress toward becoming a "white liberal" or, in the words of some of my compatriots, a "nigger lover." Some of these experiences were a consequence of my transfer from one segregated grammar school to another when I was nine years old and in fifth grade.

That year, 1928-1929, was full of conflict for me, occasioned by the clash of a variety of southern biases. The Democrats, then the party of the South, had nominated for the presidency a Catholic from the sidewalks of New York. Alfred E. Smith was not only a slave of the pope but also a "boozer" who wanted Prohibition repealed—or so my Methodist and Baptist friends proclaimed. But I understood that my mother was going to vote for him. When I defended her choice in childish but heated political arguments, I was asked if I knew that guns were stored in St. Joseph's church so the local Catholics could take over after Smith was elected. Even though Herbert Hoover was a Republican, did I want the pope to run our country? Bewildered, I asked my mother why she opposed Hoover. The answer I remember getting still shocks me: he would put Negroes to work in the Capitol if he were elected! This was the defense that southern Democratic loyalists had devised to counter Protestant bigotry in this vicious campaign.

Even now it is my guess that Mother used this weak argument, uttered abruptly as if reluctantly, because of the cross pressures she felt. I doubt that she agreed with Smith's support of Repeal, and she may have felt some discomfort about his Catholicism. Yet she had been a lifelong Democrat and, as an Episcopalian, was too close to Catholicism to believe the scare stories propagated by the Protestant "yahoos," who even suspected us because our minister wore his collar backward. The strength of her feelings for the Democratic party was indicated by her dismay when the "Solid South" split in the election. I remember her reading aloud a news story of how citizens of Richmond draped a statue of Thomas Jefferson with black crepe to mourn that state's defection to Hoover. It was evident that her sympathies were with them.

Despite conflicts of this sort with my friends and occasional frightening encounters with "mill kids," I was happy in the school to which I walked every morning. My friends from the neighborhood and from Sunday school went there. The latter, all from upper-middle-class families, gave the school an elitist quality that the school where my mother taught, located in a large blue-collar section with a tough reputation, lacked. There were three or four schools like this in the city, one of them being in the district next door to ours.

In midyear I was greeted with the devastating news that my school was becoming overcrowded and that I would have to transfer to the school in the adjoining district. But Mother felt that even her school was better than this one, so she arranged for me to transfer to "South Macon," even though this meant I would have to ride to school with her every day. So one February morning I found myself sitting in a classroom with a totally new group of kids, some of them two or three years older than I was because they hadn't been promoted.

The official name of my new school was John W. Burke, but it was generally called South Macon after the district it served. Blacks lived in this area but went to school elsewhere—I still do not know where their school was located. In the white neighbor-hoods in South Macon, blue-collar workers far outnumbered white-collar workers; the one teacher who actually lived in the John W. Burke district was an exception. Unemployment, poverty, adult crime, and juvenile delinquency were everyday realities, not abstract social problems.

That many of the children with whom I attended South Macon were poor was obvious from their clothes. That many were "problem students" was evident from the age range in this elementary school—some would be fifteen or sixteen by the time they completed seventh grade. Some of the boys had been slowed down by trips to reform school. I learned from Mother that one boy often fell asleep in her class because his bootlegger father kept him up late making deliveries. This was a strange world, and I, as a teacher's kid, was an outsider. Each day after school, I returned to a part of Macon "on the other side of the tracks" that was as little known to my classmates as South Macon was to my friends at Winship School in Cherokee Heights. I was terrified by the toughness of some of the "big boys," as the teachers referred to the overage, outsized underachievers. I was shocked by the sexual precocity of both boys and girls.

Yet, my two and a half years there turned out to be one of the most enjoyable as well as enlightening periods of my youth. Quickly overcoming my initial homesickness for my friends at Winship, I not only made new friends but came to appreciate the virtues of South Macon. Largely because of the iron hand of the principal, the school had a remarkable esprit de corps. Mrs. Weir, already a white-haired lady by the time I arrived, had been at John W. Burke for so long that she had become an institution in the community, and a highly valued one. Sometimes, when a belligerent father would complain that she had punished his child unjustly she would remind him that she had applied her razor strop to *him* when he was a student and could not be intimidated now. Undaunted by the quality of the human material with which she had to work, she held a vision of excellence before the students, rewarded individual achievement, punished transgressors firmly and often physically, and unceasingly cultivated pride in the school. There was a school song—"South Macon is Rolling Along"—sung to the tune of the Caisson Song. Each day, at the end of "big recess," the whole student body formed in lines before the front entrance, joined in the Pledge of Allegiance to the flag, sang a stanza of "My Country 'Tis of Thee," and then marched into the classrooms to the rhythm of a piano accompanied by an excessive number of drums loudly pounded by little boys. At this daily ceremony, noteworthy accomplishments, academic or athletic, were recognized. For weeks before the annual citywide track meet in the spring, which South Macon usually won, the ceremony turned into a pep rally. I had never seen such school spirit at Winship.

In this milieu I became acquainted with the "common people" in ways that I had never known before. The really tough kids didn't like me and tolerated me only because I was Mrs. Killian's son; I knew better than to try to get too close to them, because I was suspected of being a snitch. Some of my best friends were poor, however, and were making impressive progress in overcoming their handicaps. One of them, Barney, was a boy I can never picture as wearing anything to school but bib overalls. Often, even on quite cold days, he was barefoot—and he walked two miles to school. Barney was strong but gentle, and his grades were always as high as mine. Another friend and academic rival, Ena, came from a problem home in which not only poverty but violence must have been familiar. If there had been federal welfare programs in those pre-New Deal days, I am sure that hers would have been a welfare family. Even in South Macon, Ena's clothes stood out as ill-fitting hand-me-downs. She would flare up at the slightest insult or challenge and pour out a stream of invectives that she was ready to back up with fingernails and fists. We respected her not only for her intelligence but also for her temper.

Through these friendships and my happy experience at South Macon, I began to get an inkling of how the attitudes of my friends in Cherokee Heights, of my mother and her friends, and of myself were snobbish and class based. Years later, I learned that one of the ladies of St. James' Church had grown up in near poverty in South Macon but had been "rescued" by marriage to a prosperous business-man. She carefully concealed her background from her neighbors and friends. I myself learned to say little about South Macon and my new friends to old acquaintances from the "right" side of the tracks because I could never be sure how they would react. Class prejudice was as real as race prejudice in Georgia, and I learned to recognize it.

I learned little during these two and a half years that would directly influence my attitudes toward blacks. I did get to know two more beautiful black people, the only ones who ever set foot in John W. Burke School. Belvin—probably his last name—was the janitor, and Ophelia, his wife, was the school maid. They were essential cogs in the smoothly operating machinery of the institution. They were deeply loved, southern style, by Mrs. Weir, my mother, and all the other teachers. They presented strong, dignified images even while "staying in their place." The white children all knew that they had the weight of Mrs. Weir's authority behind them. Belvin, the only adult male in the school, was the first choice to go into the boys' toilet in case there was a disturbance inside. Ophelia performed many tasks other than helping to keep the school clean. among them functioning as the principal's intelligence agent and messenger. A periodic source of anxiety for the whole teaching staff was the unannounced visits of the supervisors from the superintendent's office, who would drop in to check on what the teachers were doing and to evaluate them. When one appeared in Mrs. Weir's office, Ophelia would start out on a visit to every classroom to deliver a cryptic note. It read, "The cat is on the mat." South Macon's teachers usually got excellent ratings from the dreaded supervisors.

Indirectly, on the playground, I learned more about the complexity of southern race relations. The *machismo* of some of the older, tougher boys led them to boast loudly of their nocturnal visits to "niggertown." Whether their exploits were real or imagined, I first heard from them the myth that "black pussy is tighter than white." This revelation was added to my store of folklore about blacks, such as the myth that you couldn't hurt one by hitting him in the head but that a well-placed blow to the heel would surely kill him. (I have never known how black kinship to Achilles was supposed to have been derived.) Several years later, I became acquainted with the belief in the very large size of the sexual organ of black males, a belief that I found to be held even by some doctors. But the playground discussions of blacks and race relations were apt to be abstract, for it would be many years before a black child would enter John W. Burke School.

It was the humanity of lower-class whites, of "common people," that I learned to appreciate at South Macon—the same people who were as prejudiced against blacks as I was against them. But I also learned a bittersweet lesson, which grows more bitter in retrospect, about the unearned rewards that high status may bring. I'm sure that at the time I felt some guilt and discomfort, which I tried very hard to repress. This feeling reached its high point at my moment of glory at South Macon, when honors were handed out at our little graduation ceremony. In Macon, as in most other cities, the American Legion offered a medal for the outstanding boy graduating from each elementary school. In the years following World War I, this was a highly cherished honor. From the time I entered school, my mother, motivated by her ambitions for me and loyalty to the memory of my father, buried in his army lieutenant's uniform three months before I was born, was determined that I should win this medal. When I transferred to South Macon, I soon became aware that not only Mother but Mrs. Weir and all the teachers assumed that I would win. The pressure on me was tremendous. The most harmless misconduct, the slightest deviation from academic excellence, would be discussed and bewailed in the teachers' lounge. My mother did not have to wait for the monthly report card; she received a report every day.

Not that I didn't want the medal. I did. Not only did I know that it would please Mother; I also knew that I would be the first boy in Macon whose father had died in the war to receive this honor from the veterans organization. But there was a problem: I knew in my heart that Barney, my barefoot friend, deserved the medal as much or more than I did. This would not have been a problem in any other school; we both would have gotten the award. At one upper-class school that year five boys were chosen "the outstanding boy!" But Mrs. Weir believed that tough choices had to be made, and she was iron willed—she had never allowed her teachers to name more than one recipient. So I received the medal. I don't think I ever doubted that I would; worse yet, Barney probably never doubted it either.

Lanier High School for Boys was a new segment of my white world. Not only was it all white, it was all male, and although it was a public school, its tone was that of a military academy. It combined both junior and senior high school grades. All the boys in the tenth, eleventh, and twelfth grades wore ROTC uniforms to school Monday through Thursday; on Friday we were supposed to have the uniforms cleaned for Monday inspection in ranks. Outside the classrooms, all the discipline was military, and a guard of cadets was posted in the corridors daily to maintain order. A senior was cadet Officer of the Day. During the five years I was at Lanier the professor of military science and tactics was a regular army officer, Philip R. Dwyer, a graduate of West Point; he attempted to reproduce the atmosphere of the Military Academy as closely as possible.

One of the major dimensions of stratification in the school was rank in the cadet corps—it was the very first entry under a graduate's picture in the yearbook. Each year there was a colonel, three lieutenant colonels, several majors and captains, and a host of lieutenants, sergeants, and corporals. The least distinguished entry under a boy's name would read "Private Eternal." Once again my mother's ambition was clear to me: I should be the regimental commander, cadet colonel. This goal, like that of winning the American Legion medal, was enhanced by the fact that my father had died in uniform and my favorite uncle was still an active army officer. Hence I was willing to do whatever was necessary to reach the top of the military hierarchy. Making the Honor Roll—achieving a straight-A report card—was the easiest part. The military requirements during the daily drill period were not too difficult, nor were the extracurricular activities, such as working on the student newspaper. But proving that I was "all-round" by taking part in athletics was pure torture. Quite correctly, I felt very incompetent in "subvarsity" football and basketball. But I endured enough of the torture to earn a sufficient number of points under the heading *sports*—and more than some of my rivals for the highest rank.

The other dimension of stratification was purely academic, but it reflected the class system of white society in the county. Each boy registered for a "course" (today called a "track") leading to a diploma based on a particular combination of subjects. The A course was the agricultural program; most of the students taking it were "bus boys" brought in daily from the rural parts of the county and generally viewed as "hicks." The E course was the "shop course"; it was generally assumed that boys who took it lacked either the intelligence or the ambition to go on to college and therefore took a vocational curriculum. The B (for "business") course was another vocational program, but one with greater prestige, since the students in it had to take elementary accounting and some typing and shorthand. The D course was a catch-all curriculum—I never knew exactly what it was. The prestige course was C, obviously standing for "college." If a boy who would be expected on the basis of his family's income and social standing to go on to college did not take this course, some explanation was in order.

Despite the rigor and sometimes intellectual excitement of the subjects, what I learned in classes during those five years of high school did not change me nearly so much as what went on in my social life and in the larger world. Those were momentous times, even for a teenager. I remember the bank failures of the early 1930s, for I lost my first small savings account when the Fourth National Bank closed its doors. The crash and the Great Depression reached into my own life when my mother's brother lost his job and couldn't find another. A skilled bookkeeper, he had to do pick-and-shovel work on a Works Progress Administration project to support his family. In November 1931 my mother suffered none of the doubts that tore her four years earlier when Al Smith was the Democratic standard-bearer. Like the majority of her fellow southerners, she looked to Franklin D. Roosevelt as a savior. Even without television, the magic of his radio voice made him a leader who appeared to be very personal and at the same time larger than life.

The poorly informed quality of many people's belief in his seemingly magic powers was manifest in Macon during the famous ninety days, following the passage of the National Recovery Act (NRA). The Blue Eagle appeared in store windows all over the city, and these same stores, even small, family-operated grocery markets, began to close at five in the afternoon. Roosevelt had called for a forty-hour week, and even though they could not see what it would accomplish, the loyal Democrats of Macon complied. It took less than a week for word to come from Washington that FDR meant that employees should be paid time-and-a-half for *extra* hours of work, not that overtime should be eliminated for "Mom and Pop" in their own store.

There was excitement in Macon over the fact that the Indian mounds outside the city were to be excavated by workers employed with funds from the Federal Emergency Relief Administration and later the WPA. It was there that my uncle obtained "work relief." The verdict of history that the New Deal did not really put an end to the depression notwithstanding, the many novel relief measures gave the impression that Roosevelt was leading the nation out of the desert into which Hoover had allowed us to wander. Long before I was old enough to vote in my first presidential election, I became a devout New Deal Democrat, southern style.

But cross-pressures existed to temper my nascent liberalism. White southerners were the most conservative element in the coalition that Roosevelt put together, and I too remained conservative. Jim Crow remained unchallenged; Eleanor Roosevelt was explained by most southerners as a homely misfortune borne by Franklin, like his polio. The South also remained staunchly anti-communist and militaristic. Roosevelt's call for recognition of the Soviet government was as hard for his white southern supporters to excuse as were Eleanor's criticisms of racial segregation. There was nothing in New Deal liberalism to shake my complacency about the "American way of life" or the traditions of the South. The fact that the Little White House was in Warm Springs, Georgia, made FDR an honorary southerner in spite of his patrician New York heritage.

A new, conservatizing pressure came from within my family. In 1931 my father's brother, Calhoun Killian, moved back to Georgia after being forced into early retirement from the army by a combination of a cut in the size of the armed forces and his own physical disability. Only thirty-eight when he retired as a major, he had been in uniform for twenty years. After two years of military college, he joined the newly formed Philippine Constabulary in 1912 and left the United States, not to return until 1921. He had taken up the "white man's burden" in America's imperialistic venture in the Far East, acquiring a conservative political outlook and an intestinal parasite, both of which remained with him the rest of his life. In 1917 he obtained a commission in the U.S. Army and in 1919 took part in the nation's first anti-Soviet venture, the Siberian Expeditionary Force. As part of the 27th Infantry Regiment, he saw combat protecting the Trans-Siberian Railroad from Bolsheviks and bandits.

Uncle "Coon," as I called him from the time I first tried to say "Calhoun," was a veteran anticommunist and a vicious Roosevelt hater. His diatribes against the president were so fierce that my mother would blanch when the dinnertable conversation veered into politics. A lifelong registered Democrat because of the one-party system in Georgia, I doubt that he had ever voted for a Democratic candidate for president. This arch conservative was as close to being a father to me as anyone ever was. He taught me a great deal, most of which was wrong, about politics, but even more about love. As I grew older—I was sixty-two when he died at the age of eighty-seven—the philosophical differences between us grew more evident, despite my attempts to avoid arguments that might alienate him. As I look back, however, I believe that he loved me so deeply that he could have overlooked anything I might have done short of joining the Communist party. After two years as professor of military science and tactics at his alma mater, Gordon Military College in nearby Barnesville, he moved to Sarasota, Florida, in full retirement for the rest of his life. We saw each other frequently. He took me on my first fishing trip, taught me how to swim in the surf, and did much else to offset my mother's feminizing influence. When the time came for me to enter college, he paid for most of my expenses even though he would have been much happier had I chosen a military career and gone to West Point. In his latter years he was like a grandfather to my children, who learned to love him in spite of ideological differences.

Just as these cross-pressures were shaping my strangely inconsistent political philosophy, other influences were producing a growing disaffection with my own background and peer group as I approached graduation from high school. In my career at Lanier High School, I had met all my mother's expectations. Except for one or two months during the eighth grade, I was on the Honor Roll every month. I was editor-in-chief of the school paper. Best of all, I was cadet colonel during my senior year.

But my success proved bittersweet. For one thing, I took my duties as a cadet NCO and later colonel too seriously. When I took my turn on guard in the halls and locker rooms, I actually reported fellow students for sneaking forbidden cigarettes in the corners. As an officer, I reported them for wearing the uniform improperly, even off the school grounds. According to the military regulations of the school, I was doing my duty; according to the informal code of the student body, I was a rat! I paid for my devotion to duty with a great deal of unpopularity and a black eye received in a fight behind the gym. Ironically, the fact that I was willing to give my victim revenge helped lessen my unpopularity with his friends. All of this contributed to making my senior year a less than joyous one in spite of my several honors.

To achieve these honors I had to win out over boys who constituted far more serious competition than had my classmates at South Macon. None were like Barney. There were few of his social class in the entire school by the senior year. My rivals were the sons of bankers, lawyers, business executives, boys whose families belonged to the country club and lived in the most prestigious parts of town, not on the same street as a mill village. But I beat them all and won not only the military honors but also a social position I had never enjoyed before. The girl I asked to be my "sponsor" and I were like a queen and king as the end of the school year approached. Our attendance at parties and dances was virtually mandatory; I went into homes I had seen only from the outside. Yet through all the exciting commencement season, I still felt myself to be an outsider. I harbored a deep-seated suspicion that my social acceptance had been forced on my elite classmates and their friends from the girls' high school. An incident that reinforced such doubts occurred early in the school year at a dance. A boy from a socially prominent family, a friend but not a close one, took me by the arm and said, "Lewis, there's a girl over here I want to introduce you to. Now that you are cadet colonel, you should know people like her."

So I finished high school with a great sense of relief. My mother did not know how much unhappiness lay beneath my sense of triumph, nor did I realize at the time how much anger against her I had repressed over the years. Yet from a little boy who suffered terrible homesickness whenever I was separated from her, I had grown into a young man eager to shake the dust of my home town from my feet. The prospect of going to Athens, a completely strange town, to attend the University of Georgia held no terrors for me.

Chapter 2

WHITE COLUMNS AND CONVERSION

*Life as a KA—Encounter with Sociology—Conversion of
A Cracker—Entering the Race Relations Industry*

The University of Georgia and the town of Athens were a different South from the one I had known in Macon. Athens was smaller, and the antebellum mansions, many of them now occupied by fraternities and sororities, gave a sense that the hand of history still weighed on the community. On the campus, the white columns of the old chapel dominated the greensward that began at the Georgia Arch, under which no freshman was allowed to walk. In front of the chapel a sundial marked the site of the Toombs Oak, under which "Fighting Bob" Toombs, later vice-president of the Confederacy, delivered an unauthorized valedictory address after having been expelled for drunkenness and fighting just before commencement. The Phi Kappa Literary Society still met in the hall in which other generations of students had debated nullification and secession. It was easy to transport oneself back to the days of *College Life in the Old South* as described by Georgia's foremost historian, E. Merton Coulter, whose course on the history of Georgia was a privilege, not a requirement.

Nor were those golden days so late in time that the faculty could not constitute a link to the Old South. My Latin Professor enlivened his classes with stories of his youth, when he was a telegrapher with one of the best "fists" on the railroad line, and we were fascinated by the deftness with which he could slip a plug of tobacco into his cheek in the midst of a translation of *Caesar's Gallic Wars*. Professor Bocock, who taught Greek but from whom I took a course in international relations, never chewed tobacco in class, but he countenanced it. During the first meeting of each course, he laid down the following rule, among others: "If any young gentleman wishes to chew tobacco during class, he will find that there is a window in the back of the room with a pane missing. I ask that he sit there so that he can expectorate. Of course, no gentleman would chew gum in class."

The figure who most visibly embodied the link to the past was T.W. Reed, the registrar. He lived in Reed House, located on valuable land near the center of the campus, but not to be demolished as long as he lived. Every morning he walked across the green to his office, always clad in a black suit, a white shirt with winged collar, and a black string tie. He was even more fascinating to a wide-eyed freshman because of the legend that in his youth he had seen Robert E. Lee.

Yet the social structure of the university community reflected a new, changing South, and I became acquainted with types of people I had not known before. Of course, the few blacks on campus were janitors, maids, or "institutions," like Clegg, who had worked for the Athletic Department for many years and was known to everyone who attended the football games. Part of the community, but on the periphery, were the butlers, houseboys, and cooks employed in the fraternities and sororities. Some of them later came to play an important part in my education. The whites I was to become acquainted with mirrored complexities of class and ethnicity altogether new to me. Despite the low esteem in which the University of Georgia, like most southern state universities, was held in the academic community, it was considered a prestigious school by the people of the state. Within it was a white Protestant elite: the sons of rich Atlanta families, such as the Candlers; Atlanta society girls, who were for some reason called "pinks"; children of the "first families" in numerous small towns—some, like "Weetie" Tift, of Tifton, bearing the name of the town. There were also political types, headed for law school and careers in Georgia politics. "Hummon" Talmadge had just graduated from law school, and the campus still abounded with stories of his riotous nights on the town. His Sigma Nu brothers never seemed sure whether to be embarrassed or to boast about having the governor's son as an "alum." One of my classmates was Ernest Vandiver, who was to become governor in time to be confronted with the applications of the first blacks to be admitted to the university. Charlene Hunter Gault, now a television celebrity, was the first black woman to enroll.

Nearly all the members of the WASP aristocracy, plus some rare Catholics who were not Yankee football players, joined the leading fraternities and sororities, as we who belong to them ranked them. The independents constituted a lower stratum set aside by their not having at least one of the qualifications for top status: money, family, or high grades. Many of them lived in one of the older, less commodious dormitories nicknamed "Buckingham Palace," which is how the residents answered the phone. Another significant stratum included those agriculture majors who lived in Camp Wilkins, on "Ag Hill," some two miles from the main campus. Living in Camp Wilkins was spartan but cheap; a farm boy could even pay his rent "in kind," with foodstuffs for the dining hall.

I believe that Jewish students outnumbered Catholics at Georgia. I learned about differences among the Jewish population I had never known before. Several of my friends at school in Macon were the sons and daughters of affluent Jewish families who were segregated only when it came to marriage. The only Jews I knew who were targets of ethnic jibes were the children of a family who ran a grocery store on the edge of the mill village. The boys in the family were all fat, and the cruel mill kids called the younger one "Jew baby."

Many of the Jewish students were from the North. Quotas in many northern schools may have driven them to the South. Lower costs and lower admission standards may have attracted others, and a few were on athletic scholarships. At any rate, for the first time I met urban, eastern Jews. I don't remember knowing any of them well; my Jewish friends were from the Jewish elite.

A few were from families I had known in Macon, others from their counterparts in Atlanta, Augusta, Columbus, and Athens. In my dormitory I got to know a Sephardic Jew. From Savannah, he was descended from one of the Spanish families Oglethorpe had invited to his colony. Like most of my friends from Savannah, he spoke with a "Geechie" accent, similar to the Gullah speech of the South Carolina coast.

Some of my friends were from the Jewish community in Atlanta, of the type of family portrayed years later in *Driving Miss Daisy*. Others were from small towns in which their families constituted a minority of two or three. Morris Abram, from Fitzgerald, was one of them. An outstanding debater and a frequent speaker on inter-faith programs, he went on to become nationally known for his defense of the civil rights of black Americans, but also for his opposition to affirmative action quotas. The social position of all these people was very insecure on campus and back home, however. In Atlanta, for example, there was a Jewish country club partly because of the exclusionary policy of the Piedmont Driving Club. On campus, the same separation was manifest by the existence of several Jewish fraternities and sororities. They, too, reflected differences within the Jewish student community, some being more selective than others. The fraternity Phi Epsilon Pi was the outstanding example of Jewish elitism. The chapter was small but well financed. Moreover, it always led all other fraternities in grade-point average. For a Gentile fraternity to run second to it was considered an honor; we Kappa Alphas prided ourselves on the fact that we were frequent runners-up. It was widely believed among other fraternity men that the "PhiEps" did not have to compete for pledges during rush week. They were said to select new members in advance on the basis of "recs" and hand them pledge pins when they arrived on campus, confident that none would refuse.

These were some of the facets of the new social world into which I arrived in Athens, a scared freshman determined to do whatever was necessary to become "Joe College." I bought a "rat cap" and wore it faithfully, particularly after the night a group of football players caught me on the street and shaved my head. I acquired a new name after that—"Goon"—which stuck with me long after my hair grew back. I took part in the annual "shirttail parade" before the first football game. This barbaric ritual followed a pep rally at the football field. As soon as the rally ended, all the freshmen with any school spirit took off their trousers and started a march of about five miles to another campus where women students lived during their first two years at the university. We marched at a dog trot most of the way because we were flanked and pursued by upperclassmen who lashed any buttocks within range with a belt or paddle. At the end I was proud that I had endured this ordeal and happy that I had been fast enough to escape without a bloody butt.

In my dormitory, one of the choice residences for men, I was exposed to situations I had never encountered at home. Residents sometimes came in after midnight and vomited cheap whiskey on the bathroom floor. The dormitory was named "Joe Brown" after a civil war governor of Georgia. Anonymous wits would come through the courtyard at 1 A.M. shouting, "Joe Brown! Wake up and piss! The world's on fire!"

My fraternity was one of the most important things in my new life. Years later, it gained notoriety for flaunting the Confederate battle flag in the midst of the desegregation crisis and was accused of being the headquarters of the resistance on campus. Kappa Alpha (KA) was a "southern fraternity" in that it had no chapters north of the Mason-Dixon Line, although it had spread west to California. We had a picture of Robert E. Lee in the living room, as did every chapter, and we celebrated the founding of the fraternity on his birthday. We never flew a Confederate flag, however, nor did we boast of being a southern organization. Rival fraternities that had also originated in the south would have ridiculed us for claiming to be distinctive in this respect. At least three other fraternities, like ours, had originated at Washington College in Virginia when Lee was the school's president. Only ours had made him our patron saint, and our tradition emphasized his gentlemanly, even knightly qualities, not his loyalty to the Lost Cause. During "rush," the fact that we had no chapters in the North was not something we paraded as proof of southern patriotism; we came near to apologizing for it, particularly if we were rushing an occasional Yankee freshman. Our carefully contrived explanation was that while the fraternity had started in the South, we could have expanded to the North, but chose not to. By the time the opportunity arose, we said, it was evident that northern fraternities were becoming very different from those in the South and West. Some even had "open rush," inviting anyone who passed by the house to come in and be considered. Then we would point to what had happened to one of our major rivals, Sigma Alpha Epsilon. It had been founded at the University of Alabama but had made the mistake of trying to be the biggest, geographically and numerically. Now, we charged, there were so many SAEs from so many parts of the country that they could not possibly have much in common. On our campus they had the largest chapter in the Interfraternity Council; we called them "Sigma Alpha Everybody."

Thus, in 1936 Kappa Alpha was less visibly and self-consciously southern than it was twenty years later, not only at Georgia, but throughout "the Order," as we called it. One of the main reasons I chose this fraternity was the national leader, the knight commander, was the Episcopal bishop of the Diocese of Atlanta, Henry Judah Mikell, who had confirmed me. He was a tremendously dignified, but very caring man; and he was quite liberal by the standards of the pre-1954 South. His name sounded Jewish and indeed was—one of his grandparents was from a Savannah Jewish family. He believed, and the witness of his life led me to believe, that Kappa Alpha stood for the ideals of love and reconciliation that Lee urged on his students after the war.

I moved into the KA house my second year and lived there until graduation. Life there was fun, but it did not interfere with my studying. The fraternity contributed to my socialization, however, for I was under great pressure to attend dances ranging from "house dances" to grand balls at Homecoming and Little Commencement. One of the large affairs held annually in the college gym, the KA's big dance, illustrated how little being "southern" was on our minds in those years. My freshmen year, the brothers decided to have a costume ball instead of an evening dress affair. There was a formidable obstacle to this idea in the dean of women. She had banned costume balls since the last one held on campus, when a coed had ridden a white horse into the gym as Lady Godiva. We were able to persuade the dean to relent; she agreed to approve a costume ball if we specified a theme for the costumes. In later years, the "Old South" or "Confederate Ball" became a trademark of KA chapters everywhere. But we decided to have a "Wild West Ball." The affair was the talk of the campus that year, and we repeated it in succeeding years. We did shift to an "Old South" theme before I left Georgia, but I accept the theory that such events became popular after the premiere of *Gone With the Wind* in nearby Atlanta. Ferrol Sams, a KA at Mercer University and author of *Whisper of the River*, contends that Atlanta costume suppliers, stuck with an overstock of Confederate uniforms, unloaded them on our fraternity brothers.

The libations that most of the brothers consumed before the dances or during visits to the parking lot were supplied largely by another fixture at the fraternity house, "Saint," our butler. Like all fraternity house butlers, he was a bootlegger, but we thought that our versatile retainer was something special. He was a big, handsome, still youthful-looking brown man who had worked for the fraternity for more years than any of us could remember. Gray-haired alums would stop by the house to see Saint, who remembered each one. I learned that what we called him was no nickname, but his middle name. One day I saw an envelope addressed to him as "Tar Saint Chrysler," obviously a corruption of "Toussaint."

Mr. T.S. Chrysler was a superb butler who supervised the work of "Doc," the houseboy, and whoever happened to be the cook at the time. The housemother, a poor widow of good family, thought she managed all of them, but she was like a company commander who doesn't know that the first sergeant really runs the outfit. Saint was also an entrepreneur with many enterprises beside his bootlegging, including the operation of a dance hall on Saturday nights. He cared for and looked after the brothers, and suffered with tremendous patience and dignity the cruel insensitivity of southern white boys, who often hurt him without intention.

He and Doc were my friends, too, but before I left Athens our friendship reached a different level from the dependent-paternalistic basis on which it had begun.

It was the symbol of the end of an era when, in 1942, Saint forsook the Kappa Alphas of Georgia for the Detroit ghetto as defense industries beckoned him and thousands of his brothers and sisters. The fraternity butlers point up the paternalistic aspect of southern race relations in those days. They were intensely loyal to the "boys" who employed them and whom they took care of as faithful menservants. A story from the University of Alabama illustrated their identification with "their" fraternities. Some butlers allegedly decided to form a fraternity of their own, limited to black fraternity house employees. Their organizational meeting was attended by a butler from one of the Jewish houses, but he was told that he would not be eligible for membership!

Loyalty flowed the other way, too. The men from each chapter were sure that their butler was the best; we KAs were confident that Saint was a dean among butlers. How far-reaching such paternalistic loyalty could be was illustrated after one of the butlers killed his estranged wife, a cook for another fraternity. It seemed a simple case of second-degree murder. The two had met one morning as they were walking to work and had argued violently. He picked up a large stone and bashed her head in. Each fraternity numbered among its alumni a prominent local lawyer, each with considerable influence at the courthouse. The trial became a struggle between two white factions in Athens to determine which could win for "its Negro."

The informal education provided by this kind of world did nothing to make me any less a conventional, orthodox white southerner. Neither did the courses that I took at first. I began my university career as an education major, since my ambition was to be a high school history teacher. Because all freshmen were in a basic college regardless of major, my academic adviser was from neither education nor history. He was a chemistry professor. One afternoon, between sips from a series of beakers containing a concoction he hoped would one day rival Coca-Cola, he informed me that I should major in history if I wanted to teach the subject. Totally unaware of what a profound conflict in educational philosophies his advice reflected, I trotted over to the Registrar' Office and changed my major.

This made little difference in my schedule of courses for that year. All freshmen had to take the three social science survey courses that had replaced the freshmen history requirement. The first two were little more than unimaginative world and American history courses, taught by graduate assistants or instructors from the history department. But the third required course, Contemporary Georgia, was vastly different.

A huge lecture section was taught each year by a sociologist, the first I had ever encountered. He was Walter Coutu, a Yankee from Minnesota with a Ph.D. from the University of Wisconsin. The Georgia we learned about had no magnolias or white-columned mansions. In our readings we wandered down unpaved roads past sharecroppers' shacks with cotton growing up to the front doors. We learned how many Georgians, white and black, suffered from pellagra and hookworm. The masters of the mansions I had known in Macon were exposed as the owners of the cotton mills and the exploiters of the poor whites I had seen in the mill villages. I learned how much the county unit system of representation in the legislature contributed to the hegemony of the rural landlords and "Ol' Gene" Talmadge. This was the most disturbing and yet exciting kind of education I had ever experienced. It fitted well with my admiration for Franklin D. Roosevelt and my sympathy for the underdog.

Coutu was not to last long at the University of Georgia; he was constantly under fire from both politicians and timorous administrators. He changed my life during that course on Georgia; at the beginning of my sophomore year, I became a sociology major. Henceforth I would take, in addition to the history courses I loved, courses in social problems, theory, demography, social statistics, and social psychology. The members of the tiny Sociology Department who had the greatest influence on me were Walter Coutu and Joseph B. Gittler, who was still working on his dissertation at the University of Chicago under William F. Ogburn, a native Georgian. Joe was Jewish and had grown up in New York City. Both he and Coutu were staunch New Deal liberals. In addition, Joe was concerned about the road that Germany was following under Hitler in a way that most Americans were not. This was at a time when some exchange students returned to Georgia from a year in the Third Reich full of praise for what the Fuehrer was doing for that nation.

While I cannot remember any explicit teaching about race relations in my sociology courses, I was slowly but surely imbibing the reformist attitudes of my professors. There was no course in race relations in the sociology curriculum—such courses were rare in those days. I am sure that even such a crusader as Coutu felt that he must handle the topic cautiously. Yet I must have been exposed to facts and ideas that prepared me for my later conversion from southern ortho-doxy. My actions during an episode that took place during my senior year, when I was Kappa Alpha treasurer and house manager, convinces me of this.

In the spring of that year we had a large house dance, one for which we needed help in addition to Saint and Doc. Doc recruited a young friend of his named Eddie to work for the evening. I first encountered Eddie, a small, almost boyish black man, after he had put on his white waiter's jacket and was distributing hors d'oeuvres to the guests. There was a sudden commotion at the back door and when I got there, a police car was driving away, with Eddie in it. One of our alumni who was serving as a chaperone accompanied me to the police stations, and we posted bail for Eddie so that he could come back to work—our main concern.

The next day I learned from Saint and Doc that Eddie had taken a taxi to get to the house because he was about to be late for work. (In Athens, white cab drivers would take black fares.) There was a second white man in the front seat with the driver. During the ride to the house, some words were exchanged, and Eddie said something that for the driver constituted "getting out of place." After Eddie had been deposited and had paid his fare, the driver went to the police station and reported his version of the incident. Two policemen came to our fraternity house, walked in the back door, grabbed Eddie, and dragged him to their car, beating him as they did so.

My reaction to this story was quixotic, and it led to my first real appreciation of the cruelty of southern white supremacy. First, I naively went to the desk sergeant at the police station and asked if the officers had a warrant to enter our house in pursuit of their victim. I was told curtly and firmly, "You don't need no warrant in a city case." Undaunted, I consulted a young alumnus who was now practicing law in Athens and asked him how much he would charge the chapter to defend Eddie. Patiently and with some amusement, he informed me that the worst thing we could do for Eddie was to fight the case. He said, in effect, "Just let him forfeit the bond and you take the loss. If he goes into city court with a lawyer, the judge will get mad and throw the book at him." We forfeited the bond, Eddie left town to stay with friends in the country for a few weeks, and the case was closed. But not for me. I made an appointment with the father of one of my KA brothers who was supposed to be a highly knowledgeable constitutional lawyer. He seemed to agree that Eddie's constitutional rights had been violated, but he proposed no remedy. Furthermore, he didn't seem to care. But some of my brothers cared a great deal when they found out that I had been trying to stir up trouble that might involve the fraternity, and all because of an "uppity nigger." They told me to forget it, but I continued to tell the story whenever I found a possibly sympathetic audience. One white lady who seemed sympathetic to Eddie stated that she still thought the city judge was a good man because he was hard on drunk drivers.

This event was only the prelude to my deeper involvement in race relations, which commenced shortly afterward. By the beginning of my senior year, the year during which the Nazis invaded Poland, I was firmly committed to a career in sociology. Being a high school teacher now seemed a very limited goal; I hoped to earn a Ph.D. and to teach sociology at a university. When an incoming faculty member and chairman-to-be of the Sociology Department asked me in what area I was interested, I replied, "Social problems." I was still so innocent that I believed that sociology was a real science and that sociologists could solve social problems through their research. After all, one of the works over which I had labored with both desparation and fascination was *Recent Social Trends*, the report of a presidential commission. W.F. Ogburn, a sociologist dedicated in his faith in sociology as a science, had directed the work of the commission and edited the lengthy report. It had revealed to me that there was a sufficiency of social problems, particularly in the South, to challenge an army of do-gooders like myself.

There was, however, the personal problem of how to finance further years of education. My mother could not back me, and I could not expect my uncle to continue his contribution of $500 a year, which had financed my first four years of college.

A New England family of abolitionists made it possible for me to undertake my first year of graduate study. The Phelps-Stokes family had left funds for a foundation that subsidized a fellowship for graduate study in the social sciences at two southern institutions, Georgia and the University of Virginia. The stipend was $500 a year. The surprising condition of this fellowship, established about 1910, was that the research should focus on the life and condition of blacks. I applied for the fellowship and won it. In later years, when I became more cynical about both social science and social reform, I sometimes said that the reason I went into race relations was that $500. Certainly, at the time I became a Phelps-Stokes fellow I had no more concern about problems of race relations than about other social problems. My deep commitment was to emerge the next year.

With the general area of my master's research defined for me, during my senior year I plunged into the literature about blacks and their relationships with whites. Two books stand out in my memory: Edwin Embree's *Brown America* and *The New Negro* by Alain Locke. The former book had been declared subversive by Governor Eugene Talmadge, who ignorantly charged that it advocated "mongrelization" to produce a uniformly brown American population. *The New Negro* was a far more explosive volume, containing selections by some of the fiery writers of the Harlem Renaissance, such as Langston Hughes. Apparently "Ol' Gene" had never heard of it or did not find the title alarming. I was both shocked and intrigued by the bitter, angry literature of protest.

During the summer, after commencement, I embarked on an even more mind-shaking experience for a young Cracker. The Phelps-Stokes fellow the previous year had been another sociology student, M.W.H. Collins, Jr., a good friend of mine. Before he left for the University of Wisconsin to start work on his doctorate, he offered to introduce me to the black community of Athens. This community had been described in 1912 by the first Phelps-Stokes fellow at Georgia, T.J. Woofter, who later became a sell-known rural sociologist. Bill Collins had just completed a follow-up study over a quarter of a century later.

All that summer, Bill and I went on excursions into a world I had lived near but had never known. He introduced me to black men and women who had been helpful to him in his research; we went into their homes and sat down and drank coffee with them. We went to services at black churches—usually we were ushered to seats of honor in the front pew. I heard black preachers chanting their sermons and marveled at the unrestrained responses from the "amen corner." As the summer wore on, I became bolder and went places without Bill. During two of these "solo flights," incidents occurred that changed forever my self-conception in relation to black people. The first incident prepared the way for the second. Bill had urged me to be sure to talk with a doctor who was probably the most militant black in Athens. His hostility to white people was so thinly veiled that it is a wonder he had been able to remain in the town. One reason he could do so was that he isolated himself from whites as much as possible, even to the extent of hiring his own pharmacist so he would not have to send his patients to white drugstores. I managed to arrange a short appointment with him, probably because he knew Bill. Still feeling some trepidation, I went to his office in the heart of the small black business section. I sat in his waiting room surrounded by black patients and waited and waited until it suited his convenience to see me. My thoughts and emotions were in turmoil: I felt out of place, I was a little bit afraid, and perhaps a little indignant that here I was, for the first time in my life, waiting subserviently for a "nigger." When the doctor finally saw me, I encountered a handsome, dignified professional man who spoke to me almost aggressively, with no hint of subservience on his part. I cannot recall the content of our conversation, but I do remember that at the end of the interview I felt both humbled and exhilarated. It was a cleansing experience; I had been baptized in the waters of a river I had never entered before, and the first layer of years' accumulation of feelings of white superiority had been washed away.

After that episode, associating with blacks came easier to me. There was a Methodist church that I particularly enjoyed attending. One of the elders, the patriarch of a large family, was named Killian. One night after the service, he asked me if by any chance I came from Madison, Georgia. When I told him no, he said, "Well, the reason I asked is that my grandfather was an Irishman who had a big plantation near there." This black man was suggesting that we were related. I didn't mind—in fact, I was pleased that he had enough confidence in my goodwill to ask if I might be his cousin. As I thought about this encounter, I was certain that something drastic had happened to me. My world, particularly my "white world," would never be the same again.

Other people noticed a change in me. Like many other KAs I enjoyed sitting around "shooting the bull" with Saint and Doc. Sometimes they'd have a visitor, one of Mr. Killian's sons who was a student at Howard University. One day, Saint said to me, "Mr. Killian, there's something different about you. You don't talk to us the way you used to. You're friendlier." Doc added, "You know, that Killian boy you see around here—he says you're different from the other white boys that know him. He says you're the only one that will speak to him if you see him up town instead of here at the house."

Their perceptions were correct. As a result of my reading, my research, and the changes in my behavior that exploring the black community had forced on me, I had begun to see blacks as fully human, as potential equals. No longer could

I act toward them in the sometimes paternalistic, sometimes arrogant, but always insensitive manner with which I had grown up.

Although my forays into the black community during the summer of 1940 constituted only a preparation for systematic research, I probably could not have carried out the survey for my master's thesis without that experience. During my first year of graduate study, I interviewed 110 black female domestic servants and their employers, under a wide variety of conditions. At times the servant and I were conspirators, for many housewives made it clear that they did not want me talking to their "nigger maids" unless they were present. One of their greatest fears was that I might tell a neighbor how much the servant was paid and set off a bidding war for her services.

My thesis topic was "The Training in Domestic Service of Negro Women in Athens, Georgia." Why such a narrow focus? As an apprentice sociologist, already possessed of the illusions of the profession, I wanted my research to be very scientific. Therefore I chose to study something that was manageable, specific, and quantifiable. Thus I attempted to relate the training domestics received to their wages, their working conditions, and the attitudes of their white employers.

Although I did find enough servants with some training to make statistical comparisons, my major finding was that having training other than "on-the-job training" by the housewife had no significant relationship to other variables. The mean hourly cash wage of all servants was a miserable 7.5¢. Most servants worked a 48-hour week, and so the man cash weekly wage was $3.68. When I added an estimate of "payment in kind," including the meals the servant ate while at work, the total was $7.72 a week. Even in 1941, this was slave labor indeed. As for training, housewives cared little. The relationship between employer and servant was typically paternalistic, exploitative, and oppressive. It was expressed in the attitudes of "Miss Annie": "Mandy is *my* maid; I trained her and she does things my way; I look after her and she's very happy; how much I pay her is nobody's business but hers and mine."

The education I received doing these interviews was worth far more than the sociological training I was supposed to receive through the research exercise. I observed directly the exploitation that white supremacy permitted. My mother had engaged in it, but now I recognized it for what it was. I heard repeatedly the accounts with which white women deceived themselves that they were "good to their colored people." I was amazed at how little bitterness or hostility was expressed by the black women; they seemed grateful for the pittance the whites regarded as largess. I became even more conscious of the two worlds that white and black southerners inhabited as they moved in each other's presence.

During my last year at the University of Georgia I also saw first-hand the terror of the system of white supremacy. Governor Eugene Talmadge suddenly declared that he wanted some administrators and professors in the university system fired forthwith because they were advocating "race mixing." He told the Board of Regents that if they wouldn't fire them, he'd "redline" them in the budget. There were ten intended victims, but the one I knew was Walter E. Cocking, dean of our College of Education.

Cocking had been at the university for only two or three years, but in that time he had made vast improvements in the college. He had garnered foundation funds and attracted high-quality faculty and graduate students. He had also refused to renew the contracts of some faculty members. It was rumored that one casualty of his administration, a teacher in the Laboratory School, was a cousin of "Ol' Gene" and had provided him the information on which he based his attack on the dean. The governor charged that at a workshop for public school teachers, Cocking had remarked that at some time in the future white and Negro teachers might meet to discuss their common problems. On this basis, Talmadge ordered the regents to get rid of him.

The Board of Regents was Talmadge's creature. He had appointed the majority of its members, including the chairman. But during a football game, the latter tipped off the president as to what was coming. President Harmon W. Caldwell is reputed to have replied, "If Cocking is fired without a hearing, I will resign." As a result, the stage was set for a public hearing in Atlanta, not only for Cocking but also for the other targets of Talmadge's assault.

During the months before the hearing, I saw both protest and terror on a university campus. Dean Cocking was popular with faculty members and students. Many of us rallied to his support with protest meetings and petitions. Such was the power of "Ol' Gene," however, that some erstwhile faculty friends deserted the dean. One was my department head, who regularly enjoyed an after-lunch pool game with him at the faculty club. This association came to an abrupt stop. Furthermore, my frightened professor suggested that since my thesis was on race relations, perhaps I should send it to the governor's office for "clearance" before submitting it officially. I immediately let him know that I did not like his idea, and fortunately he did not press me. I was prepared to burn the manuscript rather than submit to Talmadge's reign of terror.

There was reason for the timorous to be fearful. Operating in Athens during these months was an undercover employee of the governor who looked and acted like a thug. On one occasion, he abducted Dean Cocking's black butler for several hours and tried to frighten him into providing personal information that might be used against his employer. I saw this man on campus several times, always at night. Through the sort of arcane maneuver of which university administrators are capable, Cocking's disgruntled predecessor as dean had been given an office in the Sociology Department. Since it was next to the room in which the calculators were kept, I was nearby on many nights. To my dismay, I observed that the governor's agent was using the ex-dean's office as his base of operations in Athens. Needless to say, I avoided any contact with him.

When the hearing was finally held, in the chamber of the House of Representatives in Atlanta, I was in the student delegation that trekked to Atlanta to see the kangaroo court in action. Students from universities in the area were there too, aroused by the attack on academic freedom. So outrageous were some of the questions directed at the "defendants" and some of the distinguished witnesses appearing on their behalf that some spectators could not suppress cries of protest. This proved dangerous, for the rostrum was flanked by the governor's agents, including the thug I recognized, and they were obviously spotting protestors in the audience. After I returned to Athens, I received a letter from Bates Block, a Princeton student from Atlanta. I had struck up an acquaintance with him during the day. He told me that after the hearings he had been assaulted by one of the spotters in the corridors of the state capitol. Fortunately, Bates was an amateur boxer. He wrote, "My coach would have been proud of me!"

The outcome of the hearings was a foregone conclusion. Cocking and the others would be dismissed. By the time I entered the University of North Carolina in the fall, the ax had fallen, and the entire university system of Georgia had been suspended from accredited status. The martyrdom of the academics was not in vain, however. So enraged were college students throughout Georgia that even though most were not old enough to vote, they campaigned vigorously for Talmadge's opponent in the fall primary, Ellis Arnall. I was proud of the fact that he was a Kappa Alpha. A prototype of the southern liberal politicians of whom President Jimmy Carter became the most famous, he won the election and led Georgia to be the first state to lower the voting age to eighteen.

By the time I had finished my thesis, I had been awarded a teaching fellowship for graduate study at the University of North Carolina at Chapel Hill. The University of Wisconsin had accepted me but had failed to give me a fellowship because I held a commission in the army reserve and was subject to call at any time. I left Athens with two degrees in sociology, the gold bars of a second lieutenant, and a radically different view of race relations from the one I had brought there five years earlier. The gold bars would influence my fate most during the next five years.

Chapter	**3**	THE WAR YEARS AND THE VETERANS

UNC Under Howard Odum—Finding a Wife—Jim Crow
in Khaki—Peace and Northern Bigotry

When I entered on what proved to be a short but rewarding sojourn in Chapel Hill, I became part of yet another South. The village (it still had few sidewalks) and the University of North Carolina constituted a unique island of liberalism in a conservative region. Frank Porter Graham was president of the university. Through his leadership and his life he fostered a democratic spirit in this state-supported institution. He staunchly defended the exercise of freedom by faculty and students when challenged by conservative legislators. One of the major manifestations of "Tarheel liberalism" was the Institute of Social Research, established by Howard W. Odum as the research arm of the department of sociology. Odum's term "the Southern Regional Laboratory" referred not only to a room full of data, maps, and charts, but also to the whole southern region, which he had defined, described, and analyzed in *Southern Regions.*

I was privileged to study for one academic quarter under this great prophet of southern regionalism and liberalism. A Georgian himself, Odum held up a great but unrealistic goal for me. I was to complete the Ph.D. in sociology, return to Georgia, enter politics, and someday become governor of the Peach State! Fortunately, I was flattered rather than tempted by his vision. As did all new graduate students, I sat in his course on contemporary sociology one night every week. He was so critical of the work in sociology being done at the University of Chicago that it is a wonder I clung to the hope that I might one day study there.

The influence of Guy B. Johnson, a Texan who became one of the most insightful white southern students of race relations, was far greater. He possessed a profound knowledge of the culture and psychology of southerners, both white and black. It was he who taught me about the significant connection between the Uncle Remus stories and the folktales of the African slaves. Although I took only one course from him, I sought in my subsequent work to emulate his humane but realistic approach to the dilemmas of black-white relations in the South.

I spent most of my time with graduate students. They were not all Southerners or all liberal; some were left-wing radicals. From them I heard, much to my surprise, criticisms of the great Odum for being mystical, overly optimistic, and

33

in some respects, more conservative than his public image suggested. We even sang a bawdy song about his ideas, a Freudian parody on regionalism as a theory and Odum's proposition that the South was "the seedbed of the nation." At parties we sang labor songs and even the "Internationale". The range of opinions about the war in Europe was wide. Although everyone despised and feared the Third Reich, there were some isolationists in our group. They agreed with Senator Gerald Nye, who came to the campus to speak in favor of American neutrality just a month before Pearl Harbor. Others, like myself, were ready to fight if we entered the war, while a few were dedicated pacifists already in contention with draft boards reluctant to grant conscientious-objector status.

One experience that both surprised and thrilled me occurred on a beautiful October afternoon on the campus of North Carolina College in Durham. Several of us piled into an old car jointly owned by Donald Calhoun and Harold Garfinkel, later of ethnomethodological fame, and drove to the black college to hear a speech by the famous but controversial singer and scholar, Paul Robeson. The state university, even under Frank Graham, was not so free that Robeson could have been invited to speak in Chapel Hill, although he surely could have sung on the campus. Instead, he was spending the day on a segregated black campus. His visit must have escaped the notice of conservative politicians, for he was traveling under the auspices of the National Negro Congress, which had been heavily infiltrated by communists during the "popular front" of the Roosevelt era. Robeson was speaking to the campus chapter of the Negro Youth Congress. The white supremacist watchdogs in North Carolina should have been alarmed, but who cared what transpired within the confines of a black institution in those days?

Robeson's short address was the most radical attack on segregation, economic discrimination, and capitalism I had ever heard. My naive image of this brilliant man as just a talented performer, satisfied with the plaudits of white audiences, was shattered. In later years I was quick to sympathize with him when I learned of the countless insults he endured because of the principle that while he was talented, he was still "just a nigger." Nor was I any longer surprised when he bitterly and publicly denounced the United States for its racism and its capitalist system.

My lectures in the social problems course that I taught under the terms of my fellowship began to reflect my new critique of American society. One of several very attractive "Carolina coeds" in my class evoked my special attention because she would agree with my most liberal ideas, point for point. I remember the day when I tried to shake her up by pointing out that an idea she had presented in class discussion sounded socialist. She snapped back, "What's wrong with socialism?" The combination of her beauty, her intellect, and a certain openness in her relations with people overpowered my sense of propriety as a fledgling teacher.

I started dating her surreptitiously and decided quickly that she was the woman I wanted to marry.

I had known a little about Katharine ("Kay") Goold before we met in class. While attending an Episcopal conference at Kanuga Lake, a conference center in the North Carolina mountains, I had stayed in the cottage with her older brother, Edgar. I learned from him that their father was an Episcopal minister in Raleigh, but it was not until I knew Kay that I learned that he was president of St. Augustine's College, a church-supported college for blacks.

"St. Aug's" had been established just after the War Between the States as a normal school. Later it developed into a liberal arts college, somewhat out of the pattern of black "A and M" colleges. It numbers among its graduates many lawyers and doctors and three Episcopal bishops. Kay and her brother and younger sister, Margaret, were all born on this campus. They grew up surrounded by black people, faculty and their families, students and staff, skilled and unskilled.

Edgar Hunt Goold, Kay's father, was a graduate of Amherst College, Columbia University, and the General Theological Seminary in New York, and had studied at Oxford. He went to St. Augustine's in 1912 as chaplain and professor of philosophy and ethics. Within a year or two, he became president. There he took his bride, Katharine Birdsall of East Orange, New Jersey; for thirty-five years, they lived a life unknown to most white southerners.

They were, of course, "Yankees." When I met Kay she could hardly understand my central-Georgia "flat" speech. Perhaps the fact that the family lived in such isolation from the white people of Raleigh kept her from picking up their speech patterns. The campus was situated in what the Raleigh locals would know as "niggertown." Despite her father's professional standing and near-aristocratic background, the family was ostracized by most of the whites in Raleigh. As Katharine and her brother and sister grew up, most of their playmates were the children of the new black faculty members; many of the older faculty were white New England spinsters. The white children whose parents would allow them to visit the Goold home could be numbered on one hand. The Goold children met other white children at school and in the downtown Sunday school they attended, but their association with most of them ended there.

Kay, an adventurous child, had good times with her black play-mates. Once, while waiting in an airport, I fell into conversation with a well-dressed black man and learned that he was a member of the Delaney family, prominent at St. Augustine's for many years. When I told him who my wife was, he answered, laughing, "Oh, I used to play with her. We'd slide down the fire escape outside the women's dormitory; President Goold didn't like that at all!" My future wife was also popular with the college students. I wondered why a girl who was of the "jitterbug" era was a virtuoso in dancing the Charleston until she recalled how she learned the dance. As a child, she was taught by the black students, who would stand around her applauding and laughing at the sight of the little white girl dancing for *them.*

Given this very unsouthern upbringing, the etiquette of race relations never came naturally to Kay, as it did to me. In fact, she became aware of it only when she evoked reproofs off campus by violating such taboos as not referring to adult blacks as "mister" or "miss." This even happened to her at the Episcopal church where she attended the Young People's Service League as a teenager.

Most impressive to me, a convert from southern orthodoxy, was the casual, easy way in which Kay experienced socializing with blacks. Whereas I had gone from feelings of discomfort to a sense of elation when I interacted with them without the barrier of the etiquette, she could feel perfectly natural even if we were the only whites in a group. The first illustration of the difference between us came during the autumn of 1941 when she was still my student. Our class, along with some others, made a field trip to Raleigh to tour several institutions, including an all-black public housing project. When we reached it, Kay said, "Let's go see if my friend Julia Margaret is at home. She lives here." We broke away from the guided tour and spent our time in the apartment of a young black woman whom Kay had known since childhood; her mother had worked for the Goolds. Despite the hours I had spent interviewing blacks in Athens, a purely social visit in a black home was a new experience for me.

As she had grown up, Kay had acquired firsthand knowledge of black society that I knew only through books. "St. Aug's" had "black" students of all shades of pigmentation; they came from many states and from the West Indies. Kay was aware of the disdain with which many of the West Indians viewed American blacks. She knew about the status distinctions made by blacks themselves on the basis of color; she knew tragic stories of family conflicts that erupted when a son or daughter failed to "marry light." She had witnessed the trouble to which black women went to straighten their hair. And she knew how arbitrary the color line was, for many of the "Negroes" she saw on the campus, sometimes in her home, were light enough to "pass."

One, in particular, had known Kay since she was born. Mrs. Hall managed the college laundry and served as matron for a women's dormitory. The first time I saw her, I assumed that she was one of the white staff members. Kay soon straightened me out and told a fascinating story. When Mrs. Hall left the campus, she usually passed as white, not because she wanted to, but because it was easier than convincing bus drivers and clerks that she was "really a Negro." She must have experienced great anxiety while playing such a dangerous game, similar to that described by Walter White, the blond, blue-eyed secretary of the National Association for the Advancement of Colored People, in *A Man Called White.* The other salient fact about Mrs. Hall was that she made no bones about her dislike of darker blacks. Knowing that she herself accepted her definition as a Negro, I recognized the presence of self-hate, something I had read about. My impression was confirmed by a remark she made to Kay when she learned that I intended to study race relations. With a sad expression, she said, "Oh, Katharine, what a shame! Your father has always been involved with Negroes and now your husband will be too."

This was before we were married. Events moved swiftly that autumn of 1941. Scarcely had I realized that I had found the woman I wished to marry someday when the attack on Pearl Harbor made the future appear foreshortened. By Christmas, I had given Kay an engagement ring; in February, I was called to active duty and assigned to Fort McClellan, Alabama. In April, we were married during my first three-day leave. Kay returned to Chapel Hill after our one-week honeymoon to finish her senior year. I returned to my miserable one-man tent and canvas cot. She did not come to live with me in a furnished room in Anniston until June 1942.

I was an officer in a Jim Crow army. During my in-processing at Fort McClellan, I requested that I be assigned to serve with black troops. The army ignored my request, in spite of the fact that there were five battalions of black trainees on the post. I learned later that there were many white officers in the black regiment who would gladly have changed places with me. Those of us in the six white replacement training regiments saw little of the First Regiment, although we would encounter their officers at the Officers' Club—excepting the chaplains, who were black. During my one-year stay at this post, more black troops came. The Headquarters and Division Artillery of the 92d Infantry Division, the "Buffalo Division," were stationed at Fort McClellan for training, while the remainder of the outfit trained at Fort Huachuca, Arizona. I never knew how many black officers there were, for, again, only white officers from the division frequented the club. These included the division commander, Major General Edward Almond of Virginia. He was the brother of J. Lindsay Almond, who, in 1956, as governor, would lead the Old Dominion in massive resistance to school desegregation. The record of the 92d in combat under Almond's command would be mixed and controversial. Many blacks believed that the poor performance of some of the black soldiers was a consequence of the attitudes of the white officers who were supposed to lead them. This was a believable explanation. I served four years on active duty, officially segregated from black officers and soldiers and seeing more of the evil results of segregation. My orders to go overseas took me to an area remote from the fighting, the Persian Gulf Command, which stretched from Teheran to the gulf ports of Khorramshahr and Bandar Shahpur, Iran. The only time in four years that I put on my steel helmet for actual protection, the "enemy" were black soldiers at Camp Reynolds, Pennsylvania. This was where our shipment of replacements staged for overseas movement in July 1943, a few days after the Detroit race riot of June 20-21. There had also been some violence between whites and blacks in Youngstown, Ohio, an hour away from Shenango, as Camp Reynolds was then called. Thus there may have already been some racial tension in the camp when, late one afternoon, some black soldiers entered a branch PX in the white section of the camp. They were threatened by some white soldiers who were drinking beer and were told by the manager to go back to "their own PX." They did, spreading the story of their rejection to fellow customers. While they were still there in the early evening, some white soldiers entered "their PX." A fight developed and the MPs were called; one of them was killed, and two black soldiers were severely injured by a shotgun blast. The outnumbered MPs fled from the black area, and the frightened blacks retreated, carrying their wounded, to the section most remote from the white barracks—the area in which the camp arsenal was located. They raided it, armed themselves with M-1 rifles and ammunition, and prepared to withstand attempts to take any of their number into custody. The camp commander, who was later relieved of his command, hit the panic button. He ordered an impromptu force of white soldiers, armed with baseball bats, axes, and other tools, to cordon off the black area. The frightened and angry blacks, fearing an assault, started firing at anyone in the white area silhouetted on the skyline. The camp was blacked out, and we were ordered to wear our helmets anytime we left our quarters.

This dangerous standoff was ended the next morning when a courageous young white MP lieutenant from our shipment volunteered to walk into the black area and persuade the soldiers to give up their arms and allow their wounded comrades to be taken to the hospital. He succeeded. We who knew him were very proud of him, and our contempt for the officers of the "permanent party" increased.

I never learned the rest of the story, for shortly after this episode our shipment entrained for San Francisco, where we boarded a troopship headed across the Pacific. Among the 5000 passengers were not only our "veterans" of the Shenango episode, but also a black antiaircraft artillery regiment. Their white officers spoke highly of their skill as gunners. The regimental chaplain was a black Baptist minister, who had been pastor of an interracial church in Connecticut. I came to know him well and found that he carried in his gear an extra canteen, which he intended to fill with water from the river Jordan if we ended up in the Middle East. Unfortunately, his unit went to Burma after we finally reached India, while I was the one who continued the journey to the west.

After a boring, month-long voyage from San Francisco our ship, the *Brazil*, made its first stop in Hobart, Tasmania. There we docked for three days to take on fresh food and water. Still appalled by the narrow escape from a race riot at Camp Reynolds, I held my breath for fear that violence might erupt in the Australian port. At the end of our first day of shore leave, black soldiers could be seen at the foot of the gangplank kissing white girls they had picked up during the day. Rumors were circulating that the blacks were telling the Aussie girls that they were American Indians. My fears of racial conflict proved unfounded, for there was never an incident during our three days ashore. I had not had enough faith in the simple measure our commander-of- troops devised; he announced that if a single incident was reported, he would immediately cancel all passes for the shore. I have remembered this occasion as a practical lesson related to the much-debated "actions versus attitudes" issue.

During the two years I served in Iran, most of the time at the rail terminal in Teheran, I had little contact with black troops, for none were stationed in the area. The military railway service to which I was assigned reflected the structure of civilian railroads in all but one respect. We had no black firemen or track hands, traditional jobs for blacks. Our white American noncoms supervised low-paid Iranian civilians—"wogs," not "niggers." We Americans picked up the former epithet from our British allies.

Most of the black troops in the command were members of port battalions in the Southern District. There they unloaded ships in temperatures that sometimes reached 130 degrees, and it was even hotter in the holds where they worked. As usual, all their officers were white, many of them tough Irish or Italian longshoremen.

During my entire wartime service, I witnessed only one instance of real integration in the army. While headquarters company commander in Teheran, I provided transient quarters for visiting details such as athletic teams. On one occasion, a boxing team including white and black soldiers came from the Southern District. Automatically I started to set up a separate barracks for the black members. The coach, a white lieutenant, firmly objected. "My men are a team," he said. "They box together, eat together, and sleep together." I was happy to accede to his request, but was chagrined that I had so easily accommodated to the racial etiquette of the army.

Later, when I was adjutant and personnel officer for the Third Military Railway Service, I processed the paperwork on a case that I have often used to impress on my classes how arbitrary racial classifications are. A soldier in one of our units submitted a request to have his racial designation changed from "white" to "Negro." He and a brother were both very light, but while his brother had been drafted as a Negro, he was drafted as white. He felt uncomfortable in a white unit, and found that his "whiteness" was questioned frequently enough to frighten him. Higher headquarters approved his request, and he was transferred to a black unit.

I was still in Iran when V-E Day marked the end of our mission of hauling supplies to our Russian allies. Before I could be transferred to the Pacific Theater in 1945, the war ended. Now, with the aid of the GI Bill, I had more resources than ever to continue my graduate work in sociology. My immediate goal was the University of Chicago; Joe Gittler had convinced me that it had the greatest sociology department in the world. I had no trouble being accepted, but there was a serious problem of finding housing for me, Kay, and our daughter, Kit, who was two and half years old before I ever saw her. What would I do until I could find a place for us to live? Gittler came to my rescue, steering me into an instructorship at Iowa State College, where he was teaching. Thus I could be employed while awaiting veterans housing in Chicago. Hence, my introduction to the North was in Ames, Iowa.

I knew well the white world of the segregated South. In Ames, I encountered a town that was almost "lily-white." There were only a few black students and two or three black families in Ames. I never got to know any of these blacks, but I did learn something about bigotry, northern style. In good white liberal fashion I joined in defending the rights of blacks, uninvited by them.

Still aglow with idealism after helping to defeat Nazi racism, I joined the Iowa State College chapter of the American Veterans Committee (AVC), the newest and most liberal veterans organization. We wanted nothing to do with the reactionary mossbacks of the American Legion, the heroes of my childhood. Although not many joined us at Ames, we welcomed women, blacks, merchant seamen, and communists into our ranks.

The one project the chapter undertook was a campaign to get the operators of a privately owned swimming lake on the edge of town to admit black patrons. Our representatives approached the owners of the "club" and got one of the standard excuses for discrimination: "We don't have anything against them, but our white customers wouldn't stand for it." This was the North, which was not supposed to be segregated. Our response was to try to prove the operators wrong. We started tramping the streets with a petition asking whites to state that they would have no objection to having blacks sharing the town's only swimming hole. I found that some of the people I approached said they *would* object. Yankees or not, they were staunch segregationists. One, some kind of fundamentalist minister, even recited the old southern biblical account of how God had ordained white supremacy when Noah shouted to his youngest son, Ham, "Cursed be Canaan [Ham's small son]: a servant of servants shall he be unto his brethren." The preacher did not note that it was Noah, not God, who cursed Ham, presumably so fiercely that it turned him black on the spot, and that the old man was suffering from a severe hangover and a fit of shame when he uttered the curse (see Genesis 10:20-27). From the first time I ever heard it, I have thought that this story is a most degrading justification of white supremacy—degrading to whites, not to blacks and their mythical "Hamitic" ancestor.

Our little campaign had no effect on the owners of the lake. The only other memorable experience I had as a member of the American Veterans Committee was attending the national convention in 1946 in Des Moines. It was an interracial gathering, and one of the featured speakers was Brigadier General B.O. Davis, Jr., the first black to fly in the U.S. Army Air Corps and the first black general in the U.S. Air Force. The other featured speakers were Walter Reuther, then at the peak of his power in the labor movement, and Franklin D. Roosevelt,

Jr. This was an exciting, inspiring event—a liberal revival meeting. Sadly, the next national convention saw the beginning of the decline of AVC as a result of the communist members' "rule or ruin" tactics and the inability of the liberals to cope with them. After I left Ames, I attended only one meeting of the Chicago chapter. There I witnessed the machinations of a small clique that dominated the proceedings and shouted down anyone who disagreed with them.

My stay in Ames was short, for I learned that to obtain veterans housing at the University of Chicago I must actually be enrolled. Hence, in September 1946, I entered that intellectually awesome institution as a Ph.D. candidate in sociology. I found myself one of hundreds of veterans filing through registration in our mixed attire of uniforms sans insignia and civilian clothing. Six months more passed before the barracks apartment to which I had been assigned was ready for occupancy. In the meantime Kay, Kit, and I lived in one large room in the basement of a private home on the South Side. Then, on a sunny day in March, a new friend and fellow sociology student, Ralph Turner, joined forces with me as we both moved our meager furnishings into newly remodeled apartments on the corner of Kenwood Street and Sixtieth, on the Midway just opposite the campus.

Chapter 4

CHICAGO: FROM THE MIDWAY
TO UPPER SKID ROW

Hughes, Blumer, Wirth—Fellow Students—"Hillbillies"
in Chicago—Segregation, Northern Style

Chicago in 1946 was in transition from wartime to peacetime. The city had escaped the race riots that had bloodied the streets of Detroit, Harlem, and Los Angeles. Now numerous tensions simmered beneath the calm surface of city life. The "meat strike," triggered by President Harry Truman's refusal to lift price controls at the end of the war, made even hamburger a precious commodity, sometimes to be obtained only by slipping the butcher a little extra money. Returning veterans crowded both the job and housing markets. The workers and their families, white and black, who had poured into the city from the South and Midwest, were still there, and still more were coming, even though jobs were no longer so plentiful. The southside ghetto that St. Clair Drake and Horace Cayton had called "Black Metropolis" was ready to burst at the seams; so was the smaller black area on the West Side, along Randolph and Washington Streets.

The University of Chicago was burgeoning with students subsisting on the GI Bill; how to render an accurate accounting of their attendance was a problem for an institution at which class attendance was not compulsory. We simply went by the veterans affairs office once a week and signed a book to indicate that we were still in school. Even to be accepted at this great university was a boon; to obtain veterans housing was an even greater stroke of luck. I was one of the most fortunate, for I had not only the GI Bill and a low-rent apartment but, during my first quarter of enrollment, had obtained a Julius Rosenwald Fellowship to supplement my income for the next two years. Once again, the "race relations industry" had come to my assistance, as it had when I won the Phelps-Stokes Fellowship at the University of Georgia. The Rosenwald awards were given to scholars who were members of a racial minority or to white southerners who wished to study race relations. The foundation's office was on 57th Street. I was able to walk my application through the little bureaucracy there, actually meeting Edwin R. Embree, whose *Brown America* had contributed to my interest in race relations, and the almost legendary "Mr. Will" Alexander, a famous southern liberal and New Deal administrator.

Thus, comparatively well situated to take care of a wife, a small daughter, and another baby soon to arrive, I was able to embark on my quest for a Ph.D. without being hampered by working part-time, even as a graduate assistant. My fellowship was for research, and research I would do, although of a kind yet unknown to me. The University of Chicago Sociology Department had a strong tradition of empirical research. Robert E. Park had taught his students to treat the city as their laboratory, just as Odum had taught us to regard the southern region as our laboratory. Although Park was gone, his colleagues and students, Ernest Burgess, Everett Hughes, Louis Wirth, and Herbert Blumer, were there and would become my professors.

It was through Burgess that I picked up the trail of my research topic. Every new student was required to enroll in a course that provided an orientation to the department. Each member of the faculty made an appearance to speak about his or her ideas about research, ongoing investigations, and topics that students might pursue. Hughes, Wirth, Blumer, Burgess, Herbert Goldhamer, Philip Hauser, William Foote Whyte, William F. Ogburn, Josephine Williams, and W. Lloyd Warner were among the galaxy of stars who passed before our wondering eyes. Some distributed lists of suggested research topics. In his, Burgess mentioned investigation of the situation of white southern workers concentrated in certain Chicago neighborhoods. The next day I was in his office, eager to find out more about a topic that seemed a natural for me.

Somewhat to my chagrin, I found that Burgess wasn't doing any research on the so-called hillbillies but had heard about them from others. One such source was Samuel Kincheloe, professor in the Chicago Divinity School. He was as much a sociologist as a theologian. The elders of an old Presbyterian church on the West Side had come to him asking for help in locating a southern clergyman who would know how to relate to the many white southerners who had become a major part of their membership. He had found a minister of the Cumberland Presbyterian denomination, then almost defunct, who was willing to move from Tennessee to Chicago. The Reverend Mr. Gardner, a very intelligent, sensitive man, proved to be my entree to the Campbell Park area, which included Oakley Boulevard, known to many people as "Tennessee Street." I attended the church whenever I could, meeting the members and exploring the surrounding community area. The time I could devote to this was limited, however, by the necessity of getting some courses under my belt, an enterprise that was challenging and exciting enough by itself.

My favorite professors were Everett Hughes and Herbert Blumer, but I learned as much or more about race relations from Louis Wirth. He frightened and angered me, but still goaded me into painfully hard thinking. Blumer was strong and positive but was one of the gentlest, most caring teachers I ever knew. What I learned about race relations from him was indirect but of great significance during the rest of my career. He relentlessly attacked the cult of attitude measurement that so dominated both social psychology and ethnic studies at the time. In the research I would soon begin, and later when I returned to the South, I would witness firsthand the complexity of the relationship between attitudes and actions to which Blumer alerted me.

Hughes, a master of teaching as well as of ethnographic research, introduced me to a comparative approach to ethnic relations. In his seminars we examined not only black-white relations in the United States but also the experiences of what would later be called "white ethnics," analyzed so brilliantly in the immigrant studies of Robert E. Park and W.I. Thomas. Studying situations in other lands, I learned that in South Africa the "race problem" referred to relations between whites of English descent and the Boers, or Afrikaners, while black-white relations were called "the native problem." Long before the term apartheid became commonplace and Nelson Mandela and Bishop Desmond Tutu became world famous, what was called the color bar existed in the Union of South Africa, and "kaffirs" (the equivalent of "nigger") were segregated, exploited, and oppressed.

For the test of my ability to read and understand French, Hughes had me write an essay on ethnic relations in Algeria, based on untranslated writings by French colonial anthropologists. What I learned came back to me fifteen years later when Frantz Fanon's *The Wretched of the Earth* became a best-seller among black nationalists in the United States. Most of all, Hughes inculcated in his students the ability to look at intergroup relations from the perspectives of the different parties. He played the role of devil's advocate in order to counterbalance the prejudice against the prejudiced that obscured our understanding of the dynamics of intergroup conflict. I remember the day he challenged us with the question, "Suppose someone did prove to our satisfaction that some races are truly inferior in intelligence to others. What would be the character of a just and democratic racial order then?" We dedicated young liberals were so certain that racial differences in innate ability were a myth—which I still believe—that it was shocking to be asked to consider that we might be wrong.

While there was no doubt as to where either Blumer or Hughes stood on the immorality of racial discrimination, Wirth was an unabashed crusader. He seemed guided by Gunnar Myrdal's notable appendix to *An American Dilemma*, "Facts and Valuations in the Social Sciences." In his acid, almost sarcastic tones he would declare, "The only place to find people without bias is in a cemetery." He argued, as did Myrdal, that objectivity consisted of the social scientist's making explicit his biases instead of pretending that they did not exist.

In his classes in race relations, in his capacity as president of the American Council on Race Relations, and in his many appearances on the University of Chicago Roundtable, a popular radio panel, Wirth manifested his faith that federal laws could change not only actions but also attitudes regarding such practices as segregation in the South, denial of voting rights to blacks, and discrimination in employment. He had long since rejected the dictum of William Graham Sumner that "stateways can't change folkways." He was equally vehement in his rejection of a mental health approach to effecting change, then being promulgated by psychiatrists, child development experts, and frustration-aggression theorists. With a sneer, he would say, "We all know that what this country needs is a good five-cent psychiatrist, but until we get one we'll have to find other ways to change the behavior of bigots!"

Through his lectures and suggested readings, he guided us to view race relations from an activist perspective that seemed very radical to me. It appeared both idealistic and dangerous to a young sociologist nurtured on a philosophy of gradualism, which was itself dangerous in the South. Although critical of them, Wirth also introduced me to more radical theories than his own, found in the writings of Oliver Cromwell Cox and the Marxist historian, Herbert Aptheker. The latter's book *Slave Revolts in the Old South* had a strong impact on my thinking because of its highly effective refutation of the myth of the happy black slave.

The implications of proposals for radical social surgery, whether legal or extralegal, frightened me, although I accepted most of the arguments for immediate action. With images of white supremacists who had surrounded me in the South still vivid, I could not help but envision a bloodbath in my homeland if the attack on de jure segregation was as precipitous as Wirth advocated. We read a *Survey Graphic* special issue with the theme "The High Cost of Prejudice." The high cost referred not only to psychological damage to both bigots and their victims but also to the economic costs of segregation. I was convinced, however, that many white southerners would be willing to pay a high price to preserve what they revered as their way of life. Enlightening them as to the costs was unlikely to change them, I was sure.

Wirth, as well as Hughes, Blumer, and Joseph C. Lohman, a part-time faculty member who would one day be sheriff of Cook County, also taught me much about de facto segregation and discrimination in the North, and I learned more about them from my own research. Segregation in housing was extensive in Chicago, as in other northern cities. The handbook of the National Association of Real Estate Brokers frankly advised realtors to make every effort to preserve the integrity of neighborhoods; in other words, don't even show a black buyer property in a white area. Most Chicago realtors followed this advice, but a few indulged in "block busting," deliberately introducing the first black family to a neighborhood in the hopes of starting a wave of panic selling by white homeowners. The Chicago ecologists called this the segregation-invasion-succession cycle. It was happening frequently; often violence against the first black family preceded the panic flight of whites. Racial restrictive covenants would be declared unenforceable by the U.S. Supreme Court in 1947, in *Shelley v. Kraemer*. In 1917 the Court had ruled, in the first civil rights case won by the National Association for the Advancement of Colored People, that a governmental agency such as a city could not require segregation in housing based on race. Now a later Court ruled that the judicial arm of government could not enforce a private agreement requiring the same practice. Forty years later, Judge Robert Bork would find himself under attack for questioning the constitutional wisdom of this decision.

Neither the covenants nor the decisions actually affected what went on in the housing market appreciably. As I did research in neighborhoods where most of the property was covenanted, I learned that when white homeowners began to invoke the covenants, it was a sure sign that the area would soon enter the invasion phase of the cycle. It was the fear that a neighborhood would turn predominantly black that caused it to do so. Several cases brought in Chicago before the *Shelley* ruling were thrown out of court because, by the time they came to trial, the plaintiffs had themselves sold to black buyers and did not come into court "with clean hands" to sue others who had done the same thing, only sooner.

Public housing was still segregated in 1946. The Chicago Housing Authority had followed a policy of not assigning black tenants to de facto white projects, and the white-occupied units were usually located in white areas. Under pressure from the Chicago Commission on Race Relations and black and liberal organizations, they changed their policy. There were several near-riots as white householders from the surrounding areas violently assaulted the buildings into which blacks were moving, threatening the lives of the new tenants. These near-riots, during which the police sometimes kept an area cordoned off from public traffic for several days, were not widely know, for all the Chicago newspapers except the *Tribune* imposed a voluntary blackout on the news. They feared, as did the city authorities, that reporting the protest movements might attract segregationist supporters from all over the city to the scene.

Students living in private housing near the university, in the Hyde Park section, were also encountering resistance to the invasion of blacks. Black students found it almost impossible to rent apartments; interracial parties in white flats were sometimes broken up by the police after complaints from neighbors or landlords. Restaurants in the vicinity were failing to comply with the Chicago civil rights ordinance by refusing service to blacks. Some of the earliest campaigns of the Congress for Racial Equality (later known as CORE), founded in Chicago, attacked these restaurants. When blacks would insist on being served, citing the law, the restaurateur was apt to serve them food salted so heavily as to be inedible.

Horace Cayton, coauthor of *Black Metropolis*, told one of Joe Lohman's seminars about an episode in one of these restaurants. He, the author Richard Wright, and another black man entered an eating establishment and asked for service. They were not refused but were seated at a table next to the kitchen door. They waited to be served as one loaded tray after another passed by their table. Finally, a waitress placed a tall stack of dirty dishes on the edge of the table.

Cayton then conveyed to us the suspense that prevailed among the three men as Wright's fingers started moving ever so slowly toward the offending chinaware. Many years later, I had coffee with Cayton during a sociology convention and reminded him that I remembered the story. Before I could finish repeating it, he interrupted impatiently to ask, "And what did I tell you Dick did? What did he do?" The ending was, of course, that the stack of dishes crashed to the floor, and the three men stalked out of the restaurant, unserved and unrepentant.

These events were taking place outside the walls of the Social Science Building and did not affect me personally. More significant, especially for the first year of my graduate study at Chicago, was my association with other students in what was an exciting, even historic cohort. It included, among others, Ralph Turner, Erving Goffman, Gregory Stone, Otis Dudley Duncan, Lloyd Ohlin, Fred Davis, Bernard Meltzer, Bernard Farber, Warren Peterson, Ed Rose, Jim Short, and Howard Becker. Morris Janowitz, Al Reiss, and Tom Shibutani were ahead of me in their programs but were also friends. There were only a few black students, but they were the first with whom I had ever sat in lectures and suffered through examinations. I remember five of them well.

One, Bob Johnson, I wish I had gotten to know better. He was the son of the distinguished scholar Charles S. Johnson and a combat veteran of General B.O. Davis, Jr.'s Black Eagles. Less than a decade after we left Chicago, he died without having realized his potential as a sociologist. In the cohort just ahead of mine was Tilman Cothran, who would become well known as a sociologist, an administrator at Atlanta University, and an editor of *Phylon*. He struck me as very dignified and reserved, almost to the point of appearing unfriendly, but I soon learned that he could be a friend even to a Cracker. I felt privileged when he agreed to tutor a small group of us for a theory examination he had taken a year or two before. Although our subsequent meetings have been sporadic, Tilman and I have maintained a friendly relationship for many years through our activities in the American Sociological Association. Equally impressive to me was one of my contemporaries, G. Franklin Edwards. We developed a friendship that I still treasure, even though we see each other infrequently. I liked and admired these men; I thought of them as equals and stood in a bit of awe of Tilman.

One black student I met in a seminar remains nameless because I did not like him. Almost from our first meeting, I felt that he was "tomming" me for some unknown reason. He was overly friendly on very short acquaintance and his undue familiarity seemed false and obsequious. I was not convinced that we had enough in common to justify it. Perhaps I misjudged him, but the experience of disliking him without feeling guilty represented yet another step in the development of my attitudes—the recognition that to dislike *some* blacks is not evidence of prejudice but of discrimination in the best sense of the word. I was beginning to perceive blacks as individuals.

The closest relationship I formed was with William H. ("Bill") Hale. He was a graduate of Langston University in Oklahoma and eventually would return there as president. He and I were at the same point in our studies; he had come to Chicago with an M.A. in sociology from Wisconsin. His dissertation research was a study of Negro lawyers in Chicago—he found that half of the blacks with law degrees were working for the U.S. Post Office, not as lawyers. Through his fieldwork, he established valuable contacts in the black community, some of which he shared with me as aids to my own research.

I think I began to feel at ease with Bill Hale when he shared what we both felt was a wonderful joke, either on me or on one of his lawyer contacts. He had given me the name of a very successful black lawyer who knew a great deal about residential segregation in Chicago. A few days after I had called him and obtained an appointment for an interview, Bill greeted me with a big grin. "That attorney I told you about called after you telephoned him. He said he wasn't sure whether you were a brother or not!" This was the first time I realized that with my Georgia accent I could "pass" for black on the telephone. That Bill would tell me this and laugh with me about it made me feel that I indeed had a friend. Some time later, another test of our relationship confirmed this. Kay and I invited Bill to have dinner with us in our cramped barracks apartment one night. This was an insignificant event for her but another first for me. As we sat eating at our little table, Kit, our four-year-old daughter, with no warning at all, looked at Bill and said, "You're brown, aren't you?" He looked right back and said with a trace of a smile, "Yes, I am." After we had put her to bed he said to us, "You know, that was beautiful. She didn't mean a thing cruel by her question." Kay was pregnant at the time. The next day, Kit informed us that she hoped the baby would be brown, which gave Bill a kick when I told him.

During the next two years, we shared many experiences with each other. One of Bill's stories I have never forgotten, and it helped me develop genuine empathy with blacks in their encounters with segregation. Mrs. Hale and their young daughter were not in Chicago; she had a job as a schoolteacher in Florida and was staying there to contribute to the family's income. At Christmas time, Bill took the train from Chicago to meet her in Atlanta. When he boarded the train, he found a seat in an unsegregated car without hindrance. During the night, as the train traveled farther south, the conductor and other trainmen stopped by his chair and asked, "Wouldn't you be more comfortable in Car Number 1?" My friend knew very well what they meant—Car 1 was "Reserved for Colored." "Finally, the conductor became explicit: "We'll be getting into Tennessee soon, and I don't know that may happen after we cross the line. I recommend that you move to Car 1." Breaking out in a cold sweat, Bill persisted, "No thank you, I'll just stay here." He said that he made one hurried trip to the bathroom and then stayed glued to his seat for the rest of the journey. He told me,

"I'm not particularly militant and I was scared stiff, but I decided this was just one time I wasn't going to move."

The law was on Bill's side by this time, for in *Morgan v. West Virginia* (1946) the Supreme Court had ruled that segregation in interstate transportation was unconstitutional. Railroads and bus companies were not observing the new law unless challenged, and not always then. Harry Walker, a black sociologist who had finished his Ph.D. a year or two earlier and was working with Louis Wirth in the American Council on Race Relations, told me of an instance in which he outwitted such evasion. He wanted to reserve a berth in a Pullman for a trip south. When he went to the ticket window in Chicago, the ticket agent told him no berth was available but Lower 13, the compartment traditionally reserved for black passengers. A day or two later, Harry called the ticket office, asked for a reservation, and told the agent he would send his colored chauffeur to pick up the ticket. When he presented himself at the window, a different agent was on duty, and he had no trouble purchasing the ticket.

In a talk to a seminar—the same one in which Horace Cayton had appeared—E. Franklin Frazier told of a different reaction to the persistence of Jim Crow despite the *Morgan* ruling. He related, "The last time I was on a train I went into the dining car for dinner. They seated me at the end of the car and the headwaiter pulled a little green curtain in front of my table so the white passengers wouldn't have to look at me. I just tore the damn thing down!"

Even as I continued to be exposed to exciting new perspectives and a variety of new friends in my classes, I spent more and more time conducting interviews and observing life in "Tennessee Valley," the "hillbilly" area on the Near West Side. For two years I tramped the streets, running down leads to houses or apartments in which white southern migrants lived. On Sunday and some Wednesday nights, I attended churches where they worshipped. On other days, I drank cheap beer with the men in "hillbilly taverns," regarded by many northern residents of the area as a scourge. I interviewed the personnel managers of plants and attended union meetings. The focus of my research was the experience of these working-class white southerners who found themselves labeled, stereotyped, sometimes discriminated against, and widely disliked and looked down on despite the fact that they were white and of old American stock. I got to know Italian-Americans, members of the group that had been predominant in this area before the southerners moved in and that still regarded it as their turf. Blacks were slowly beginning to invade the streets south of Madison Avenue, adding to the complexity and volatility of the ethnic mix. Hence I had an opportunity to witness kinds of intergroup relations that I had never seen in the South.

For readers who might have known Chicago in the 1940s, the area in which I did my research stretched from Madison Street south to Harrison Street and from Ashland west to Kedzie. This square mile contained nearly 40,000 residents, nearly all of them white and working class. This was not the notorious vice district of the Near West Side, but I once heard a waitress in a Madison Street bar describe it as "upper skid row." Today much of it consists of parking lots, and the expressway along Congress Street pierces it from east to west. The people who live there now are black or Puerto Rican.

In 1946 this part of the Near West Side stood as a monument to the succession of different ethnic groups in the city. First there had been English and Welsh immigrants and a few Scots. Then came the Irish, and some of their descendants remained. As in so many northern cities, the Italians succeeded the Irish, and in the 1940s they still gave the area its predominant cultural tone. Beginning in 1939, a stream of white southerners, mostly from western Tennessee, not the mountains, came to take jobs in the many small factories. Like the previous newcomers, they were characterized by a derogatory nickname and were stereotyped. The term "hillbilly" joined the earlier slurs "mick" and "wop." The stereotype portrayed the southerners as a mixture of Snuffy Smith and Jeeter Lester: rural, hard-drinking, given to knife fighting, accustomed to living in filthy hovels, and unaccustomed to wearing shoes. If they went to church, it was assumed that they worshipped in one of the storefront, "holy roller" churches that were evident in the area. They were thought to be more likely found in "hillbilly taverns," however, drinking cheap beer, listening to country music, and fighting each other as well as nonsoutherners who wandered into their territory.

Of course, some of these traits were found among some of the migrants, but like many stereotypes, this was a cruel caricature. The hillbillies—I will use the term as a member of the in-group—were well aware of the stereotype and resented it deeply. They sometimes called themselves hillbillies, but flared up at anyone who said the word with any but a southern accent. They felt that they were a minority group in Chicago and that even blacks were better off, particularly in encounters with the law. Some made such extreme statements as, "We used to fight the niggers every time we got a chance before the war. But you can't do that now—there's too many of them." And, "You don't want to do nothing to a nigger and then come up before a judge. He'll throw the book at you."

My major goal was to discover how these small-town southerners who had followed the lure of jobs adjusted to living in a northern metropolis where they themselves were often compared to blacks. A second focus was on how they actually got along with blacks in the North and how they affected race relations in the areas where they lived. There were many suggestions in the press and the sociological literature of that time that their presence was certain to increase racial tension and perhaps lead to violence. One journalist wrote of Detroit, after the race riot of 1943, "Southern whites have come here in vast numbers, bringing with them their Jim Crow notions of the Negro." In their study of that riot, *Race Riot*, Norman Humphrey and Alfred McClung Lee stated, "The effort to make Detroit conform to Kentucky 'hillbilly' and Georgia 'red neck' notions of white domination is reflected in frequent white comments in buses and streetcars and bars, such as: 'It wouldn't have happened down home. We know how to keep niggers in their place'."

I was eager to find out whether or not the hillbillies were remaking the North in the image of the South. What I found indicated that the kind of talk Humphrey and Lee quoted was just that—talk about what would have happened down home, but not action to make the northern city like home. That was regarded as a hopeless task, and the motto of the hillbillies was "When in Rome, do as the Romans do." Sometimes they expressed this view in exactly these words, at other times with cruder statements: "I don't like the way the niggers do up here, but I put up with it." I go ahead and put up with it—there ain't nothing you can do about it." "We have to do what these people up here do, even if we don't like it."

"Doing what these people up here do" did not, of course, mean living in an integrated society. Northern white people had their own ways of keeping blacks "in their place." Like the hillbillies, I learned a great deal about the mechanisms of de facto segregation and discrimination. First, I knew that this working-class area, where blacks were frequently seen and the threat of residential invasion was immediate, was vastly different from large areas of Chicago and the suburbs where a black face was rarely seen. Even in the little part of Kenwood where our apartment was located, I realized that my family and I had far less contact with blacks than we had had in the South. They were becoming strange persons to my daughter as she grew older; this explains her "discovery" that not all people had white skin when she met Bill Hale.

The churches that the hillbillies attended were evidence of the continuing truth, North and South, that "eleven o'clock on Sunday morning is the most segregated hour in the United States." I found only one church, attended by very few white southerners since it was a Congregational church, that had some black members. The pastor, who was deeply dedicated to building a stable interracial fellowship, recognized the near impossibility of his task. When blacks began to appear in the churches in this inner-city area, the white attendance began to decline, even if the newcomers were received courteously. Doubts arose among the staunchest supporters of the church, many of whom no longer lived nearby, as to how long it could remain predominantly white. The idea of using the assets of the parish to build a new structure closer to where the older members had moved became a matter of debate. Then an offer by some black congregation to buy the building would give the coup de grace to the continued existence of this particular church.

Southern white laborers did not always have to work with blacks in order to have a job. While some plants had a policy of not hiring white southerners—"We instruct the gate guard to tell anybody with a southern accent that we're not hiring today"—others used the same sort of tactic to maintain an all-white labor force. The plant that employed the highest proportion of hillbillies of any in the area had only one black employee, a janitor, despite the fact that most of its contracts were with the War Department and it was thus subject to the federal Fair Employment Practices Order—the prototype of equal employment opportunity laws. The personnel manager told me frankly, "During the war we found out that when we needed more workers we didn't have to advertise and risk having Negroes apply. We'd just put a notice on the bulletin board one week and by the next Monday we'd have more whites from Tennessee than we could use. We recruited through the grapevine."

The place where the exclusion of blacks was most blatantly accomplished was in the taverns, where so many of the men spent much of their leisure time. The device used was not a southern invention, however; it wasn't even needed in the South of the 1940s and 1950s. It was borrowed from the other ethnic taverns, mostly Italian, and was used in many parts of the city. Even then, Illinois did have a civil rights statute requiring that an establishment licensed to serve the public should accept all customers regardless of race. Some blacks were aware of this and would occasionally dare to enter the lily-white precincts of a tavern. Moreover, CORE was beginning to test observance of the law by sending biracial teams to places suspected of violating it. First a black would present himself and ask for admission or service. If he was refused, a short while later a white member of the team, equally strange to the proprietor, would appear. If his business was accepted, the basis for a complaint or a court suit would be laid.

The excuse usually given to turn away blacks was, "This is a club; we only admit members," or, simply, "Do you have a membership card?" The taverns did not wait for the initial challenge to their discriminatory policy. On every back-bar there hung a sign reading Members Only or This Is a Club. Owners hoped that blacks seeing the sign would get the message and back out. If one did linger, the bartender would simply point to the sign.

The bar owners and their customers were well aware of what a thin line of defense this illegal subterfuge constituted. One afternoon I witnessed an attempt by the part-owner of the Silver Dollar, my favorite hillbilly tavern, to shore up the defenses. As several of us stood around the bar drinking, he suddenly reached under the counter, saying as he did, "By the way, one of these days a nigger is going to come in here and say we don't really have members. I had this bunch of membership cards printed up for our regulars. Here, take one. Now if any of you are in here when one comes in, I can ask you to show him *your* card."

The Members Only tactic did not always work, however. On a few occasions, blacks, and in one instance a Chicano, demanded service and protested the refusal until self-appointed bouncers among the white customers physically threw them out. Another incident in the Silver Dollar illustrated the sense of ultimate powerlessness that led the hillbillies to accept violations of the "whites only" principle even in this *sanctum sanctorum* of ethnic sociability and ex-clusiveness. On this afternoon I walked into the tavern to be greeted by the astounding sight of a well-dressed black man drinking at the bar and talking loudly, as if he were a regular. This went on for half an hour longer. After he left, I quietly asked the bartender, "Who was that guy? How come you were serving him?" He said, "He's a city health inspector; I can't mess with him!"

Despite the presence of northern-style evasions of both the law and morality, the white southerners were confronted by one situation after another in which segregation was not the rule. Frequently I saw them bow to the inevitable. They knew that the law was not on their side in the way it had been in the Jim Crow South. They felt that they themselves were outsiders and almost a minority group. They feared the possibility of naked black power and were not sure how many allies they would have in any confrontation. Therefore they adapted.

Next door to the Silver Dollar was a small restaurant with a lunch counter and a few booths. Many times, I saw hillbillies who would bristle if a black sought service in the tavern sit at the counter next to one to eat lunch. There were package stores with stand-up bars along Madison Street. Sometimes a southerner who wanted a quick drink, not an hour or so of sociability, would stop in such a store and enjoy his drink standing next to black customers. It was known that these places did not exclude blacks from either of their services, so they were neutral ground.

The hillbillies could not always avoid working with blacks, even though there were some plants that hired few or none of them. It was not clear that the southerners were even aware that some companies did have discriminatory policies. They were more likely to say, "They like to hire southerners—they know we work hard!" In plants where they did find black workers, they placed having a good job above avoiding interracial contacts and studiously avoided causing trouble. Some even made friends with their black fellow workers.

The one place where blacks could not be avoided was the public schools. Hillbillies who had children had no choice but to send them to unsegregated schools, in some of which black children outnumbered white. This disturbed parents, and there were many complaints about how much their children "had to take off the niggers," either because they were outnumbered or were afraid to get in trouble with the authorities.

In many areas of Chicago the greatest source of racial conflict was the attempt of blacks to move into previously all-white residential areas, yet here on the West Side the hillbillies were living, at least temporarily, in an area in transition. Eventually they, like other white Chicagoans, would flee to some other part of the city with the hope that blacks would not follow, but for the time being, low rent overcame their aversion to residential nonsegregation. The most remarkable adjustment I discovered illustrates both the accommodation to necessity and the complexity of attitudes, with the white southerner clinging to his belief in "the Negro's place" even as it was being contradicted in practice. This story was told by a man from Tennessee with a wife and children:

There's niggers living in the house with us now—we're the only
white family here. The landlady has tried to get us out, but she ain't
gave us no eviction notice and I ain't fixing to move. She wants to
put niggers in our place, but my money is just as good as theirs. But
it ain't so bad. Some of those niggers are better than some of the
white people that used to live here.

Hell, I got out my knife and started to kill the first one that moved
in here, but then I found out that he was a nigger I knew from down
home. He's a good southern nigger and he stays in his place. The
trouble with the niggers up here is they'll run over you. You know,
in the South we make 'em stay in their place.

Not all the hillbillies put their knives away in encounters with blacks.
Although avoiding contact or adjusting to it when it seemed necessary was the
predominant pattern, some white southerners did have violent clashes. They
were not typical hillbillies, however, but rather fitted the extreme stereotypes
held by northerners. Such was an habitual brawler who, after having helped
throw a black out of the Silver Dollar, stood outside for two hours with an open
"pig knife" in his hand, apparently hoping that his antagonist would return. This
man and his family were notorious among the tavern patrons. One of his brothers
was serving a life sentence for murder in Arkansas.

I also heard indirectly of another white southern man who had been one of
several conspirators, the rest nonsoutherners, who bombed a black residence on
Jackson Boulevard. But I never interviewed any hillbillies who boasted of such
activities. None of them had anything to do with the only organization that
attempted to keep the community white, the Illinois Property Owners' League.
In the long run, the white southerners did what most northern whites have done
in the face of invasion by blacks. They moved out.

I completed my research far better informed than I had been about the
extralegal but pervasive nature of northern segregation and discrimination.
Blumer's cautions against reliance on attitude and opinion surveys to predict
action took on added cogency for me. Finally, in Chicago, of all places, I came
to know and love lower-class white southerners even better than I had as a child
at South Macon school.

With the completion of my field work, my energies and anxieties were
concentrated more and more on writing my dissertation and studying for
"preliminary examinations," which were hardly preliminary but more like
British-style honors examinations, covering all the course work I had taken. My
tension was shared by many of my fellow graduate students at this stage.
Fortunately some of my tension was relieved by free psychotherapy consisting
of nondirective counseling in the Center supervised by the famous Carl Rogers.
One of my close neighbors and friends was a clinical psychology student. I did

not strongly feel the need for therapy but thought it would be worthwhile to become better acquainted with Rogers's theories of social psychology. Hence, my friend arranged for me to have several sessions with one of Rogers' best students. The principal gain resulting from these sessions was a greater insight into the dynamics of my rebellion against white southern orthodoxy.

As I reviewed the events of my life, current and past, while the therapist nodded and grunted and "h'm-m-d" encouragement for me to go on, I found myself talking more and more about my relationship with my mother. While the reservoir of hostility I felt toward her did not gush forth in the way it would years later when I was in therapy for severe depression, I did begin to voice my hidden resentment against the demands for excellence she had made on me and the almost puritanical manners and morals she and her circle of friends represented. There was also anger against the white society of Macon in which I felt marginal, always in danger of rejection, because of my lack of a father, our income level, and where we lived. It came to me that perhaps I embraced the cause of black Americans so readily not so much out of love for them as from a desire to strike back at my mother and the white middle-class society in which I had been reared. My studies in sociology and the mind-blowing experiences I had as I began my race relations research in Athens were essential to my conversion, but did not fully explain it. Now it seemed to me that I had been prepared to view blacks in a new way because I was ready to rebel against my own group. I realized how often as I was going through my conversion I would say things to shock my mother. I did not come to accept a psychiatric explanation of my well-considered views on race relations, nor do I now. The personality factor involved in my change of perspective was seen as facilitating it, not causing it. Now I recognized that I still had a long way to go before my love for black people would equal my anger at middle-class white society. It would also be a long time until I could fully accept my own people of the South, with all the fault that we as Crackers shared.

As the completion of my degree seemed assured, I began to think of a job. With both a missionary spirit and a desire to return to my homeland, I concentrated on positions that might be open in the South. This preference was strengthened by a remark Louis Wirth made to me one day as we met in the halls of "1126," the Social Science Building. In his usual dry, unsmiling way he said, "Killian, I hope you will keep that southern accent and go back to the South to teach race relations."

So I did, although I went to the very edge of the region. The most attractive offer I received was from the University of Oklahoma. While the town of Norman was more southwestern than southern in most respects, the university was the scene of two of the most significant battles in the fight against segregation in higher public education. These were the court fights of Ada Lois Sipuel Fisher to be admitted to the law school and that of George W. McLaurin, still ongoing, to end segregation within the university after blacks were admitted.

In August 1949 I moved my little family to a new home, assured that I would be allowed to teach the race relations course instituted many years before by Jerome Dowd, now in his eighties, and pleased that I would have a seat on the 50-yard line at the contest between Jim Crow and blacks who would wait no longer for justice.

5   ON THE WESTERN FRONT

Creeping Desegregation—Learning from Students, White, Black, and Indian—Muzafer Sherif—Disasters and A-Bombs

Although Norman, Oklahoma, was not a Deep South town, neither it nor the university were models of racial democracy. While President George L. Cross was ready to desegregate his institution, he had to cope with resistance from above and below. The Board of Regents was fighting the integration of black students. Ada Lois Fisher, George McLaurin, and a few other blacks had been admitted under a court order, but they were still legally segregated within the university. I soon learned that many of Cross's deans and faculty were not as liberal as he. After I had been appointed, my department head informed me, with a big laugh, "I told the dean that even if you said the wrong things in your race relations course, you'd say them with a Georgia accent." He was to be disappointed in the redeeming power of my accent; before I left, he was spreading the word that I was a troublemaker.

In Oklahoma I became acquainted with yet other forms of racial discrimination. Although I later realized that my father had been born in a similar town in the mountains of north Georgia, I had never heard of a "sundown town" before. I never saw a sign saying, "Nigger, don't let the sun set on you in this town." But no blacks lived in Norman. Carl Rowan, who visited there while doing research for his first book, *South of Freedom*, claimed that the town had an ordinance forbidding them to live in it or to remain there overnight. The restaurants would not serve them, nor could they enter the movie theater. There was no black section of town where they could find any amenities, as there would have been in most small towns in Georgia.

Yet from the day George McLaurin attended his first class at "OU"—Ada Lois Fisher was still being asked to attend a one-room "separate but equal" law school in the basement of the capitol—there were a few blacks on campus, faced with exclusion at almost every turn. Before joining the faculty, I had seen a picture in a national news magazine of McLaurin sitting in an anteroom off a main classroom, listening to lectures, but not "mixing." When I met my first class I found a sign, Reserved for Colored, hung on the back row of seats. Such signs had to be replaced frequently, however, for neither white nor black students paid attention to them unless it was to remove them from the room.

57

Black students did have to eat during the day, and eventually some insisted on living on campus instead of commuting from Oklahoma City. How were they to eat unless they "brown-bagged" and sat on the grass? The Student Union building contained two eating facilities, a snack bar called The Jug and a large cafeteria. After McLaurin and the other pioneers were admitted, The Jug was closed to whites at the noon hour to permit black students to get lunch there, but I do not recall any of them availing themselves of this "privilege". The year I joined the faculty, there was a table in a corner of the cafeteria with a sign stapled to the wall above it, Reserved for Colored. Some black students did eat there, and I quickly learned that whites could join them with impunity, which became my custom. I suspect that my department head had me in mind when he remarked, with obvious distaste, "I hear that some whites are sitting with the Nigras [sic] in the cafeteria."

In this way I became acquainted with black students and learned some interesting facts about race relations in the Sooner state. The NAACP always seemed to be prepared for every move the Board of Regents made in their effort to delay further desegregation as long as possible. One reason they were forewarned, I learned, was that members of the board often discussed business over lunch at an exclusive club in Oklahoma City, unmindful of the black waiters who served them. These "invisible men" picked up bits of information, which they promptly relayed to Roscoe Dunjee, a militant black newspaper editor and the strategist for the NAACP. Largely because of his leadership, Oklahoma, a border state, was the source of some critical cases challenging segregation in higher education.

When the administration was faced with the inevitability of providing housing for black students, their solution was a heartless one. Owned or leased by the university were two abandoned World War II naval training bases. One, called South Campus, was hardly used, except for a few classes that met during the day. At night it was a ghost town. Two black women who demanded housing were given rooms in a fifty-five-man barracks adapted for their use. Their quarters were comfortable but hardly cheery, for the two constituted the total nighttime population of South Campus.

My principal activity in race relations was teaching the undergraduate course. It was popular; nearly every semester I taught a section of fifty or sixty students. At first there were no blacks, but later an occasional one did take the course. Most of the white students were liberal about their behavior, but naive. My greatest challenge was to sensitize them to their unwitting prejudice and unintentional discrimination. One device was sociodrama, in which I had them play the role of blacks. One simple but very effective drama had white students play the roles of a black parent and her child. The parent had to explain to the child why a bus driver made them move to the back of the bus when the child wanted to sit on the front seat.

The device that seemed to make students think most deeply was the required term paper. The papers were not easy to evaluate; they were, by definition, subjective. The students were asked to trace the development of their attitudes toward blacks from earliest childhood, an aim of the present work. Most accepted the challenge and dredged their memories for experiences to which they had reacted. Save for the unpleasant task of assigning grades, reading the papers as each semester drew to a close was both enjoyable and enlightening.

My professor at Chicago, Everett Hughes, once gave a memorable address to the Eastern Sociological Society on "Teaching as Research." During many years of teaching courses in race relations, the meaning of his title was brought home to me; I never ceased to learn from my students. Oklahoma, a southwestern state and Indian territory until 1909, was quite different from the Deep South. I soon learned that the word "easterner" had many of the same connotations as "Yankee" did in Georgia, but also often carried anti-Semitic overtones. The prejudice against Roman Catholics also seemed more pronounced than any I had encountered, except during my early childhood. A story in one term paper confirmed the salience of this religious identity. A young Catholic woman told of an experience on a cruise in the Caribbean. On shipboard she became acquainted with a priest, identifiable by his backward collar. To her surprise, he turned out to be a Protestant, an Anglican from the West Indies. In her paper she expressed her delight at finding a Protestant clergyman to be so delightful. The fact that he was black came out only at the end of her story, as if it were an afterthought.

Another student writer was a middle-aged woman who had grown up in a small town in Nebraska. Her story revealed how subtle and pervasive are the signals in our culture that blacks are different and inferior. She wrote: "In the town where I grew up there was only one black family and they were accepted. They attended our church: of course, they always sat on the back row. I grew up without any prejudice against Negroes. I must admit, though, that when I first went to college and had to hold hands with a colored girl in a physical education class I almost fainted!"

An army air corps veteran, a brilliant student and an outstanding football player, displayed another kind of naiveté. As I read his paper, I realized that he was not prejudiced against blacks but instead had difficulty finding fault with them. It seems he had grown up with only minimal contact with black people. After he entered the air corps, he found himself assigned to a unit in which his primary duty was to play on a football team. His best buddy and barracks-mate was a black airman who was an All-American before being drafted. So the first black my student had come to know well became a hero and a role model for him.

Another veteran, a former bomber pilot, told me his story during a conference in my office. He had grown up in the part of Oklahoma called "Little Dixie" and had acquired typically white southern prejudices. During the war, he had flown in an all-white bomb squadron based in Italy. On a raid over the oil fields at

Ploesti, his aircraft had been badly shot up and had become separated from the squadron. Alone and crippled, he and his crew fully expected to be shot down by Luftwaffe fighters, but then a flight of American fighters picked them up and escorted them to their base. That night, he said, he found out where his rescuers were based and went to thank them. They turned out to be the 332d Fighter Group, an all-black unit. He ended his account by declaring in his Oklahoma drawl, "I got drunk with them and we had a hell of a party. Ever since then, niggers [sic] have been just the same as white people to me!" It was evident I had a little more work to do with him, but only on his rhetoric.

Any pride I derived from the belief that my course might enlighten students was tempered by the recognition that the large majority of those who elected to enroll were already somewhat liberal. This remained obvious throughout my teaching career. Rarely was I challenged by students expressing extremely bigoted opinions. In my introductory sociology courses I encountered students with a broader range of attitudes. As a new assistant professor, I taught four courses each semester, including two introductory sections. On Tuesdays and Thursdays my classes were long enough to allow for a short break, long enough for us to run to the Union for a Coke. After one break, I returned to find that someone had slipped into my briefcase a placard advertising a play entitled *The Traitor*. I never learned whether it was my unorthodox views on race or my generally liberal approach to social problems that evoked this sneaky criticism.

I remained at Oklahoma for only three years, and my teaching load was greatly reduced after the first year because of my involvement in disaster research. Yet even before I left OU, I began to see some gratifying dividends from my race relations course through feedback from former students. One young woman became an airline hostess after graduation. She told me that having taken my course helped her greatly because her job required that she treat black passengers as courteously as she did white ones. Another woman married an air force ROTC graduate, who, after commissioning, went to Tyndall Air Force Base, in Florida, for flight training. She wrote to thank me for helping prepare her for her first encounter with desegregation in the service. She reported that the first time she went to a dance at the Officers' Club, a black lieutenant asked her to dance. She wrote: "If I hadn't learned something from you about how black people feel, I don't think I could have danced with him. If I had refused I could have gotten my husband in trouble."

I studiously avoided telling my students what they should do in particular situations, and I felt that it would be unethical to incite them to engage in protests that might run afoul of the law. There would be little point in teaching, however, if stimulating students to think differently did not lead them to act differently. With no great drama and without publicity, at least one student, Jim, did engage in social action at some risk. Returning from a visit to Oklahoma City, he sat down next to a black man on an intercity bus. The driver ordered him to sit somewhere else, toward the front of the bus. Jim answered, "I don't see why I should. He puts his pants on the same way I do, one leg at a time!" The astonished driver dropped his objection to this challenge to Jim Crow seating. Jim was not an activist; I knew of no organizations to which he belonged except the Roman Catholic church and his fraternity. He spontaneously reacted against following a law that was of questionable legality and a custom that he now perceived as unjust and demeaning.

Another facet of race relations in American society about which a thoughtful observer could learn in Oklahoma was the inconsistency of racial classifications and the color line. I had grown up around blacks, but I knew American Indians only through reading and movies. As a little boy, I had "killed" hundreds of them as I played cowboys and Indians. From my studies in sociology, I knew that Indians were one of our most sorely oppressed minorities. Now I found myself in "Indian country." During Home-coming, the Indian students had their own "pow-wow," complete with council fire and native dress, and elected their own homecoming princess. I found, however, that it was not easy to know which of my students were Indian because most were of such mixed ancestry that they could easily pass as white. Some were "real" Indians regardless of appearance, however, for they were listed on the rolls of their tribes. I remember one in particular, a blonde, blue-eyed Osage who had been an infantry major during World War II. The insight that struck me with greatest force was my recognition that in the United States a person could be "part Indian" but not "part Negro." I came to use this as a pedagogical tactic in my classes. I would ask the students who were "part Indian" to raise their hands. Sometimes as many as three-quarters of a class would do so, for many Oklahomans had Indian ancestry of which they were not only aware but proud. Then I would ask how many were "part Negro." A shocked silence would fall over the class; no hands ever went up. In the light of what we know about "passing" it is likely that a few did have some black ancestors, but it is unlikely that they would know of them. And it was certain that even if they did, they would not acknowledge them publicly.

Not all Indian ancestry was to be acclaimed. There were Indians and then there were Indians, even in a state where a candidate for governor emphasized that he was part Indian. Johnson Murray's father, "Alfalfa Bill" Murray, had helped formulate Oklahoma's Jim Crow constitution imposing segregation on blacks when the former territory became a state in 1907. He had married a woman who was part Indian, and his son, in campaigning for office, boasted of having an Indian grandmother. Had this forebear been a Choctaw, Seminole, or Creek, he might not have emphasized the fact, for these tribes were known to have intermarried extensively with black runaway slaves. The Cherokees, who themselves kept slaves on their plantations in Georgia before Removal, took some blacks as wives or concubines, but the mythology of the Cherokees contended that they were free of black ancestry. Thus they were regarded in the same way as were the western tribes, the Osage, Arapaho, Apache, and Cheyenne. Intermixture with blacks was so extensive among the Seminoles that one band in Oklahoma, known to be mixed, were classified as "Negroes" under the state's constitution and came to be shunned by other bands of the tribe. Yet they never regarded themselves as "Negroes."

Both Indians and whites also recognized class differences within this ethnic minority. It was socially acceptable to be an Indian, but not to be a poor Indian. I was reminded of the saying from some parts of Brazil to the effect that a poor black man is a Negro, but a rich one is a white.

During my three years at the University of Oklahoma I was fortunate enough to meet two outstanding black men. One was a young, little-known journalist who was the first black reporter hired by a major white newspaper, the *Minneapolis Morning Tribune*. Carl Rowan, a World War II navy veteran from Tennessee, had been given leave by his editor to make a trip through the South and write a series of articles on post-war segregation. I was one of the people he interviewed for his article on the University of Oklahoma. His book *South of Freedom* (1952) is an excellent volume, still well worth reading. I was not surprised when Rowan went on to become a nationally known journalist.

The sociologist Mozell Hill never became famous, but he had great influence on my emotional and intellectual development. A Ph.D. from the University of Chicago a few years ahead of me, he was teaching at Atlanta University in 1951. Although we had never met, I knew of him because of an important article he had coauthored on race and class in a south Georgia town. When my friend, Muzafer Sherif, asked me to suggest a black sociologist to participate in a conference on social psychology, I recommended Mozell. Kay and I invited him to have dinner with us after he gave his paper at an afternoon session and then to spend the night in our home prior to his departure for the Oklahoma City airport the next morning.

Being a guest at one of Muzafer's conferences could be a trying experience. He clearly expected to be the star of each session. I think he chose participants primarily on the basis of the congeniality of their work. Woe be unto the speaker who did not live up to his expectations! Sherif had no hesitation about mercilessly attacking his guests during the discussions. Mozell did not know Muzafer; he was the only black scholar at the conference, and his presentation came during the last session of the day. Apparently his stomach was truly "in an uproar" by the time he gave his paper. It was an excellent essay, and he delivered it clearly although with evident nervousness.

By the time we reached my house and sat down to dinner, Mozell was in agony, apparently with acute indigestion. He left the dinner table and asked if he could lie down. Kay was gracious and offered him what home remedies we had, but finally he asked me to drive him to Oklahoma City where he had a friend who was a doctor. I saw Mozell several times in ensuing years and attended some wonderful parties in his home in Atlanta. Each time Kay and I saw him, his account of how she came to his aid grew more laudatory until she sounded like Florence Nightingale.

From Mozell and his wife, I learned aspects of race relations in the South that we whites rarely noticed. For example, going on a shopping expedition with her daughter in downtown Atlanta was an ordeal for Mrs. Hill. She had to plan her route from store to store because there were so few places where a little black girl could use a bathroom. I remembered her story later when black students were sitting-in at Rich's and Ivey's demanding equal treatment in their lunchrooms.

Mozell told me a story that enriched my knowledge of class differences between black people. One night, as he was pulling out of a parking space on a street near his office, a speeding taxicab sideswiped him. The driver was black. Mozell called the police to the scene and called his lawyer, a black woman. It was well that he called her, for when a white police officer arrived, the taxi driver immediately started "tomming," pleading that he was just a poor, hard-working man whose taxi had been struck by this "hincty nigger" from Atlanta University. The Cracker cop's sympathies went immediately to Uncle Tom, but Mozell held his tongue until his lawyer arrived. Subsequently, he was vindicated in traffic court.

It was because of Muzafer Sherif that I met Mozell. Despite my harsh words abut Sherif, he became one of the most significant intellectual influences on me. We arrived in Norman at the same time, I as an unknown sociologist, he as a social psychologist already widely celebrated for his work on the formation of individual and group norms. Our families soon developed a warm relationship, and Muzafer and I became colleagues. It was not easy to be his friend or his colleague, for he demanded a great deal of you in either role. Yet witnessing the brilliance of his mind at work was well worth the adulation he felt was his due. The experiments he conducted in the series of boys' camp studies, of which the "Robber's Cave Study" became best known, broadened my perspective on intergroup relations in a way that concentration on black-white relations could never do. From Muzafer's research, writing, and conversation—the latter never casual—I learned to recognize generic features of intergroup relations that arose whether racial differences were present or not. I agreed with the logic of his concept of the "superordinate goal" that would unite conflicting groups in a common endeavor, demonstrated with small groups in the camp experiments. Yet I never shared his optimism that such goals could be equally efficacious in reducing tensions between large groups such as nations, classes, and ethnic groups.

By the beginning of my second year at Oklahoma, chance and the lure of research funds diverted me from my interest in race relations. I became the director of field research in a disaster research project funded and controlled by the Department of Defense. The purpose of the research was to try to make predictions about the behavior of troops under atomic attack; this was before tactical nuclear weapons had been developed. Our data were to come from studies of the reactions of civilian populations to precipitous disasters such as tornadoes and explosions. The first study was conducted in Texas City, about a year and a half after the explosion of two ships loaded with ammonium nitrate had devastated the town. Toward the end of the contract, I was able to witness an actual atomic blast, as a civilian consultant accompanying the first troop units to be near a firing at Yucca Flats, Nevada.

Even while studying disasters, I was confronted by racial prejudice. In one amusing but embarrassing episode, the prejudice was my own. Late one afternoon in Texas City, my two research assistants dropped me off to do some interviewing in the black district of town. As I got out of the car, I handed my wallet to one of them and said, "Keep this for me while I'm down here." They both guffawed as they pointed out that I had never taken this precaution when working alone in white areas of the city.

When I went to Yucca Flats, the Korean conflict had been going on for many months, and the army, under pressure from the NAACP as well as the need for replacements in white combat units, had adopted a policy of integration at all levels. Among the troops participating in the exercise were two battalions of the 101st Airborne Division. Much to my dismay, I observed that one battalion was all black except for the officers, almost all of whom were white. I learned that the current division commander had disregarded the new policy and had maintained the separate black battalion in his division, almost as if it were the army I had entered in 1942. Yet there was a tremendous amount of unit pride among the paratroopers, cutting across racial lines. To them, any airborne officer or soldier was superior to any "straightleg," regardless of race. Furthermore, they stood together in defiance of civilian prejudices. One night, one of the few black officers went into Las Vegas with some white officers. When a nightclub owner refused to admit him, the whole group left the place, loudly denouncing the owner.

Disaster research precluded concentration on race relations for four years, continuing to do so even after I left Oklahoma. Although two articles from my dissertation were published during this time, I gained more recognition in the profession from my article "The Significance of Multiple Group Membership in Disaster." Furthermore, in 1950 my friend from Chicago days, Ralph Turner, persuaded me to join him in writing a textbook on collective behavior. For six years, this project demanded a great deal of my time.

I continued to teach my course in race relations. During the brief period I was in the Southwest, the pace of legal desegregation quickened but still remained torturously slow. While the U.S. Supreme Court had not yet overthrown the constitutional principle, established in 1896, that separate could be equal, the

Court's definition of equality in educational facilities was narrowing. George McLaurin and the lawyers of the NAACP had broken down the last legal racial barriers at the University of Oklahoma when they persuaded the Court that limitations on social relations between white and black students, as exemplified by separate eating arrangements and housing, were an unconstitutional interference with their education. Associating with each other and discussing their studies was held to be essential to learning.

In the *Heman Sweatt* case, from Texas, the Court had ruled that such intangible factors as the reputation and traditions of the University of Texas Law School made it impossible for a newly built law school for blacks to provide a substantially equal education. It seemed that the Court must soon accept a case in which the constitutional issue of whether segregation based on race was inherently unequal because of the stigma it placed on blacks, as Justice John Harlan had argued in his famous dissent in the case of *Plessy V. Ferguson* in 1896.

As desegregation slowly progressed on the OU campus the contrast with the situation in the town of Norman grew starker. Black students were discouraged from shopping there and were refused service in all the restaurants. A small group of faculty members arranged a meeting with some of the owners we believed might be "softest." We got the usual excuses for not serving blacks: "My white customers wouldn't stand for it;" "I'm not going to be the first;" "I don't have anything personally against them, but—." While I didn't think that he would choose to be a test case, I thought of one black student who was an ROTC cadet. So I asked the owner of the most popular off-campus establishment, one that sold food, beer, and books, if he would refuse service to a black person in uniform. He quickly replied, "Of course not." This was not long after World War II, and now the armed forces were being built up again because of the Korean conflict. Within a few weeks, the businessman was forced to live up to his words. An air force technical training unit was established on the campus, and the first class included several black airmen. Their presence broke the barrier for blacks in Norman.

As gratifying as it was to watch the crumbling of racial barriers in Norman, I chose to return to the Deep South in the fall of 1952. This move was not prompted by my interest in race relations. Once again, chance, plus issues not related to race, took me to a new position, at Florida State University in Tallahassee. Beginning in the second year of my stay at Oklahoma, I had become increasingly dissatisfied with the administration of the Sociology Department. During my final year, the whole university was gripped by tension and even fear. The legislature had imposed a loyalty oath, ultimately declared unconstitutional, on all state employees. Although I did not courageously refuse to sign, I started contributing part of my salary each month to a defense fund for a professor at Oklahoma A and M who was serving as a test case. In the meantime, a very fine geneticist, Richard Blanc, was fired because he had belonged to a communist cell for a few months while a student at Harvard, and his wife had served as a nurse with the Abraham Lincoln Brigade in Spain. The witchhunt extended even to "New Dealers." A friend, Clay Cochran, a liberal economist, was informed that his contract would not be renewed. The only charge the administration brought against him was that he had smoked his pipe in a graduate seminar after a "no smoking in classrooms" edict had been issued.

Now luck intervened to give me a happy way out of what was rapidly becoming an intolerable situation. Meyer Nimkoff offered me a position at Florida State, reminding me that in 1949 he had invited me to Bucknell University, where he was head of the Sociology Department. I had declined the offer, explaining that I was determined to take Louis Wirth's advice to return to the South. "Now," Meyer wrote, "I'm in the South; what can you say?" I was pleased to accept his offer and to tell the administration at Oklahoma not to bother to consider me for tenure, although I would like to have learned whether or not they would have awarded it. I am confident my department head was relieved that I was leaving.

Some of my radical friends at OU—I knew most of the "left wing" on the campus—tried to dissuade me from moving to Florida. They said that the recently elected governor had run on an extreme segregationist platform, which was not true, and that the state president of the NAACP had been murdered by a bomb planted under his bedroom. This, I learned later, was indeed a fact; Harry Moore became a martyr to Florida's blacks before the civil rights movement began. I was sufficiently alarmed that I wrote to my best friend from army days, then practicing law in a small town in central Florida, to ask about the current state of race relations there. He sought to reassure me, but in the language of genteel prejudice. Things weren't so bad, he said. Most whites would have no objection to having someone like Ralph Bunche served in a restaurant or hotel, but they wouldn't want "ordinary" blacks associating with white people wherever they pleased. I was reminded of the saying heard during the 1940s: "If all black women looked like Lena Horne, there wouldn't be any race problem." I am happy to say that my good friend later went into the air force and learned to accept and respect blacks, even "ordinary' ones.

Eager to return to my native region and optimistic that change would come to the Deep South as it had in the Southwest, I headed for Tallahassee, thirty-five miles south of the Georgia border. Surrounded by plantations, some of them still producing shade tobacco, others converted into hunting preserves owned by rich Yankees, the capital of Florida is in the northern part of the state, not in the orange groves or in the Florida of Yankee tourists and Golden Agers. I felt I was really going home and I was; culturally, the farther north you go in Florida, the farther south you are.

BACK TO CRACKERLAND
Chapter 6

*Bigotry Under the Live Oaks—A Dream World—The
Brown Decision—Back to Race Relations*

The nicknames used by people from various states usually have interesting histories and a variety of connotations. Oklahoma is the Sooner State. The mighty University of Oklahoma football team is the Sooners, and their fans rally to the fight song "Boomer Sooner." Yet the original "Sooners" were downright cheaters, unscrupulous landgrabbers who, during the land rush, slipped over the line before the official starting time and staked out choice pieces of land in the territory.

Leaving the land of the Sooners, I set out for the region from which the equally questionable sobriquet Cracker came. My dictionary tells me that in an earlier sense it connoted a "braggart, boaster"; it adds, "same as poor white: contemptuous term." Etymologists speculate that it originated in colonial Georgia as a term of derision applied by city slickers in Augusta to the uncouth but swaggering frontiersmen who came to town cracking their bullwhips as they drove their oxen. By the time I was a boy growing up in Georgia, however, the term was used with pride by Georgians of all classes. The minor league baseball team in Atlanta was called the Crackers. Yet the term had a different connotation just across the southern border, in Florida. When my uncle moved to Sarasota in the 1930s, I learned that the label Florida Cracker carried all the unpleasant overtones of "poor white trash" suggested by the dictionary definition.

Tallahassee, the city that was to be my home for sixteen years, was culturally more a part of the homeland of the Georgia Crackers than of the peninsula of Florida, with its orange groves, beaches, and tourists. Cotton plantations had once dominated the area. It had been the territorial capital when south Florida was still a wilderness populated mainly by Seminole Indians. The city had been the capital of a Confederate state, and a point of local pride was that it had never been captured by the Yankees. There was an annual ceremony held a few miles south at the site of the Battle of Natural Bridge, where a pickup force of old men and college students had turned back a Union patrol marching up from St. Marks, on the coast. People stood for "Dixie," as I had while growing up in Macon. Moving to Tallahassee was in many ways a homecoming for me.

There was a three-month interlude between our departure from Norman and our arrival in Tallahassee, a period during which I was able to observe other facets of the complex of black-white relations. Seriously in need of income for the summer months, I lucked into a position on the field research team of the air force base project being conducted by the Institute for Social Research at the University of North Carolina. Nicholas J. Demerath, Jr., and Gordon Blackwell were the directors. Gordon I knew from my student days at Chapel Hill; Nick Demerath was a postwar addition to the faculty. Little did I know that his teenage son, Nicholas J. ("Jay") Demerath, III, would one day be my department chair at the University of Massachusetts.

My task for the summer was to study airbase-community relations at five sites in the South. The research design was already in place. At each base my research assistant and I administered questionnaires to large samples of the airmen and conducted interviews with officers who dealt with the local community. Then I interviewed their civilian counterparts—mayors, police chiefs, civic leaders, and other putative members of the "power structure." Floyd Hunter's book *Community Power Structure*, was very much in vogue at the time and his ideas had great influence on the design of our research. By a coincidence, Kay was able to rent Floyd's house in Chapel Hill while I was traveling. He was away studying another community. She enjoyed being in the town where she had spent so many happy days as a student.

While race relations was not central to our study, observation of the state of black-white relations on the bases and in the host communities was an inevitable by-product. The first base I visited was deep in Georgia, Moody Air Force Base, at Valdosta, only a few miles north of the Florida line. This was 1952, and the armed services were beginning to put into practice the policy of desegregation imposed from the Pentagon. Segregation laws still reigned without successful challenge in the southern states. The contrast was painfully obvious when city buses passed through the gate; they made several stops on the base as part of their route. On leaving federal property, the driver would stop the vehicle while passengers sorted themselves to conform to the civilian Jim Crow law. I rode the bus to town several times and saw this process repeated. In Valdosta I also saw the stark contrast between the white USO and the so-called club for blacks, located in the "colored section" in a shabby, rundown building.

Next came Craig Air Force Base, outside Selma, Alabama. Selma was a little-known Black Belt town, not yet the symbol of entrenched white supremacy it would become. I heard from the chief of police the sort of sentiment that was the background for the brutality that shocked the nation in 1965. I sat with the chief in his office overlooking the street in front of the police station. After giving the usual platitudes about how good race relations were and how "our niggers are happy," he pointed to a beer tavern across the street. "Here's how we handle 'em," he said. "You see that dive? It's a nigger hangout, and they get in there and drink and gamble and fight. We don't bother 'em as long as they keep it inside, but if it spills out into the street, we arrest 'em. They can cut each other up as much as they want as long as they stay inside."

In Louisiana, at Barksdale Air Force Base, a major Strategic Air Command installation, I heard of an instance of military support for the rights of black servicemen antedating the desegregation policy of the Department of Defense. The nearest real city to Barksdale is Shreveport, but in those days one had to drive through the town of Bossier City to get there. It was small and rural, and there was little reason to stop there except to buy gas, pick up a few groceries, or have a beer in one of the cheap taverns on the main street. At the time of my research, the attitudes and behavior of the local police were still a matter of some concern to people on the base. I was told that during World War II there had been a number of cases of police brutality directed at black soldiers—this was during the days of the U.S. Army Air Corps. Things got so bad that the base commander sought the cooperation of the local authorities, but was rebuffed. He resorted then to the weapon available to military commanders from which civilians have no appeal: He declared all of Bossier City off limits. Military personnel could drive through the town, but were forbidden to stop. The commander soon found the city fathers, responding to pressure from the merchants, approaching him hat in hand.

The story may be apocryphal, although I have no reason to disbelieve it. True or not, it illustrates one of the ironies of American race relations: Racial justice can be advanced more quickly by authoritarian means than by democratic measures. Once a policy of desegregation and nondiscrimination was adopted by the Department of Defense, the armed forces rapidly became one of the most egalitarian sectors of our society in terms of race. This happened not because of a change in the hearts and minds of the troops but because of command decisions and ensuing orders. At the same time, I observed some of the limits to the effectiveness of firm enforcement of a novel policy mandating changes in behavior. By the time my assistant and I started administering questionnaires to random samples of all the units at Barksdale, we came to recognize what sort of outfit was represented as our subjects would file into the theater or mess hall. If the proportion of black airmen was high, we could be sure that we were dealing with troops from air base maintenance squadrons, transportation units, or air police squadrons. The air force did not deliberately assign Blacks to these outfits but aptitude test scores led to their concentration in work that did not require higher skill levels. This was an early illustration of the principle that my friend and fellow sociologist William Julius Wilson would emphasize in his controversial work *The Declining Significance of Race* (1978): Even after racial barriers are removed, inequality can persist as a consequence of past discrimination. It would have been unjust to label the officers who assigned troops to units that turned out not to be racially balanced "racists."

Another place where concentration and even segregation persisted on all five bases we studied—Amarillo AFB in Texas, and Brookley AFB at Mobile, Alabama, were the other two—was in the service clubs. When I was on active duty in the army, these on-base recreation centers were officially segregated, the clubs for blacks being located in areas where black units were quartered. This had been true at Camp Reynolds, Pennsylvania, where I had witnessed a near-riot over "turf." Now there were no racially homogeneous squadrons, no black troop areas, and, officially, no segregated clubs. Yet, on the bases I studied, de facto segregation did exist in the service clubs. Particularly on Deep South bases, white servicemen seemed to frequent them very rarely. The reason was apparent. While the civilian communities offered a wide variety of recreational opportunities for whites, decent facilities catering to blacks were scarce. To many black airmen, the on-base service clubs were far more attractive than anything the towns had to offer, so they utilized them. The more they did so, the less attractive the clubs became to whites, unless they could informally take one over and make it "the white club." There was little, if anything, that base commanders could do to counter this process of self-segregation. A dozen years later, historically all-white universities trying to integrate their student bodies would be confronted with the same phenomenon, and it would be accentuated with the rise of black consciousness during the Black Power movement.

As I completed my field research and returned to academia at Florida State University (FSU), the problem of de facto, self-instigated segregation did not impinge on my life. The halls of ivy were still segregated de jure, at least insofar as the law was interpreted in Florida. So determined were the white rulers that their universities would remain segregated that the *Sipuel* and *Sweatt* cases had no impact on them. When a black man, Virgil Hawkins, applied for admission to the University of Florida Law School in 1949, the Board of Control stubbornly proceeded to set up a small "College of Law" at Florida A and M University, the still-segregated institution for blacks. Hawkins refused to attend it and kept his case alive. Not until 1956 was he allowed to attend the University of Florida. The little college of law survived with a tiny faculty and few students until the Board of Control decided that there was a real need for another state-supported law school, to be located in Tallahassee. Cynically, they established one at Florida State University, and abolished the one they had offered as a "substantially equal" option for Virgil Hawkins. So, while other southern universities—in Oklahoma, Arkansas, North Carolina and Texas—complied with the decisions of the Supreme Court, albeit slowly and reluctantly, the powers that be in Florida acted as if the state were beyond the reach of the federal law.

These machinations to preserve white supremacy as long as possible took place in a beautiful setting. In 1950 Tallahassee was a small city, with a population of only about 30,000. It had almost no industry; the state government and the two universities were the major employers. It was clean and worthy of being called a "garden city." In the winter and early spring camellias, azaleas, and dogwood made it a blaze of color. Many of the streets were lined with huge old live oaks, many of them festooned with Spanish moss. One tree symbolized both the beauty and the bigotry of the historic city; the May oak. A great, spreading patriarch of oaks stood at one end of the many parks that gave Park Street its name. For years each spring the queen of the May—white, of course—was crowned beneath its branches. When I came to know Tallahassee, I learned that there were little white-haired ladies who still prided themselves on having been May queen in their senior year at high school. Mothers dreamed that their infant daughters might someday be at least a member of the court. This lovely, lily-white festival persisted until Leon High School, from whose senior class the court was elected, was forced to admit black students, and the specter of a black May queen cooled the ardor of the old families for their tradition.

As a city with two universities, Tallahassee was very much a middle-class community. The educational level of both whites and blacks was higher than the average for the state as a whole. The median income of whites was higher than that for the state, and that of blacks was only slightly lower than the statewide figure.

In spite of having this population of "high-class colored folks," Tallahassee was still very much a deep-southern town. Its hinterland was positively anachronistic. The nearby towns of Quincy, Havana, Monticello, and Madison were service centers for shade-leaf tobacco plantations. Conditions for blacks in these rural areas were as oppressive as they might have been during the early part of the century.

Life for the black citizens of Tallahassee and for the students at Florida A and M University (FAMU) was better, but Jim Crow remained unchallenged. Segregation was characterized by the same sort of inconsistencies that could be found in most southern cities, however—perhaps more so.

Ecologically the city was not unusual. There were two large black sections, one surrounding FAMU on the south side and the other stretching to the north from the black business district called Frenchtown. The two sections narrowed like funnels toward the middle of town, where they almost met. Near the dividing corridor, many blacks and whites lived close to each other, physically near but socially distant. Moreover, the FSU and FAMU campuses were only about two miles apart. The social distance was maintained not only by custom and white tastes but also by a Board of Control order forbidding any sort of interracial social gatherings. Students from FSU could visit the black campus only if accompanied by their parents. Over the years I learned that many FAMU students, in contrast, did visit the white campus daily in the roles of dormitory maids and building janitors. Occasionally they struck up casual friendships with whites, who discovered that they, too, were university students, sometimes studying the same textbooks.

Yet, white Tallahasseeans regarded "Black Tallahassee" as an integral part of the community and took some pride in this segment. They boasted particularly of the Rattlers—the FAMU football team—and the black marching band that gained national recognition for its fast, high-stepping performances. Jake Gaither, the Rattlers' coach, was something of a local hero because of his team's winning record, the respect in which he was held by other coaches, and his folksy sayings, such as, "I want players who are mobile, agile, and hostile." When the team played a home game in the stadium on the FAMU campus, large numbers of white fans attended. Although in theory they were provided with segregated seating, they actually sat wherever they wanted. If a view of the 50-yard line required sitting next to a black person, so be it.

The same was not true when black fans chose to journey the short distance to Doak S. Campbell stadium to watch the FSU Seminoles play. The few blacks who did were forced to sit in a small section overlooking one end zone. Even on a few occasions when FAMU team members were invited as guests of FSU, they had to sit in this Jim Crow section. There was little reason for black spectators to endure this indignity, for in those years the Rattlers were far superior to the Seminoles as a football team, even though they never played each other.

Something very striking to a newcomer was the prominence of blacks in parades—on Veterans Day, at Christmas, and on Armed Forces Day. No parade would have been complete without the FAMU marching band. On patriotic occasions, the Florida A and M ROTC unit marched—always behind the FSU cadets. I will never forget my amazement at a pre-Christmas parade when a float passed bearing a black Santa Claus; the "white folks' Santa" had gone by several minutes earlier.

Other breaks in the pattern of segregation occurred regularly on the FAMU campus. For many years, the university required students to attend Sunday evening vespers in the chapel. So lovely was the music at these services that white people regularly attended them. There was one annual occasion, however, when the rule of permitting minimal physical distance while maintaining maximum social distance still held. Once a year, members of the Florida legislature—all white—visited FAMU for Legislative Day. They actually ate there, but no black administrators, faculty members, or students sat at the tables with them. Tables were set up on a greensward on the campus, and the white lawmakers enjoyed the best of southern cooking while black faculty members waited on them.

It was probably easier for white southerners living in Tallahassee to believe that race relations were "good" and that "their colored folks" were happy than for their counterparts in many other cities to do so. Preoccupied with adjusting to a new job and a new home, I lived in this dream world for nearly two years before reality forced itself upon me. I played the roles of a white southern professor, husband, and father in a peaceful community where one had to probe beneath the surface for evidence of racial tension. We were lucky to find a house on a little cul-de-sac with only twelve houses. Most of our neighbors worked for FSU or in some department of state government. We visited in one another's homes a great deal, but I don't recall that race relations was a prominent topic for discussion, nor was politics generally. In the fall of 1952 most of us voted for Adlai Stevenson; only my nextdoor neighbor, an air force officer, had an *Eisenhower for President* bumper sticker. Two or three families employed black women to come in one or two days a week to clean house and do washing and ironing. We did not feel the need for a domestic servant and did not feel that we could afford one on my meager salary.

At the university, I carried what was really a heavy teaching load but quite normal for everyone but the department head at that time—four courses each semester. One of my offerings was race relations, but at first the classes were very small. My large classes were the two sections of introductory sociology, which I always taught. These proved to be "feeders" for my upper division courses, and by the fall of 1953 I was facing a large group in my race relations class. Here I was able to challenge the complacency of my students, all white, about the "southern way of life." I struggled to make them aware that change would come to the Deep South as it was already coming to the Southwest. I explained the implications of the *McLaurin* and *Sweatt* decisions, warning that the Supreme Court already had before it a public school case in which the constitutional principle of "separate but equal" might finally be at issue, and I told them of my personal observations in Chicago and Oklahoma. Yet the downfall of segregation, de jure or de facto, seemed a dream or nightmare, depending on one's perspective. The only blacks any of us saw on campus were service workers. I drank coffee at Jim Crow coffee shops adjoining the campus. I became acquainted with the boys of the Kappa Alpha chapter. As had been true when I was an undergraduate brother at the University of Georgia, none of the other fraternities seemed to take seriously their claim to be distinctively southern. Their Secession Ceremony, held each year at the time of the annual Old South Ball, attracted less attention than did the Sigma Chi Derby. In 1952 the Confederate battle flag waved by the KAs was still a romantic symbol of a lost cause, not a banner of defiance and racism.

I did not even take time from my busy schedule to visit the FAMU campus to get acquainted with the black sociologists there. It was in Atlanta, when I attended meetings of the Southern Sociological Society for the first time since 1941, that I first met Charles U. Smith, head of the FAMU Sociology Department. In a few months we would become colleagues and close friends.

Attending a segregated school and living in an all-white neighborhood, my children had almost no contacts with black people. Yet I soon learned that constant vigilance was required to protect them from developing prejudices of which they would not even be aware. One day, as I was driving with the family somewhere in town, Lew, about five years old, pointed to a shabby little house as we passed it and said, "That's a nigger house, isn't it?" Shocked, I asked, "Where did you get that idea?" He replied, "Mr. W. said niggers live in houses like that." It seems that not long before, Lew had ridden somewhere with a playmate and his father. As they drove through part of Frenchtown, the man had pointed to some rundown houses and told the little boys, "Niggers live there." So Lew had established a connection, unfortunately too accurately, between being black and living in poor housing. We had an impromptu lecture on language, race relations, and economics for the benefit of all three of our children.

On a later occasion, Lew, with his endless supply of questions, brought home to me how complex a segregated society is for a child. By now I had become acquainted with the FAMU campus, and one day I drove there on some errand, taking my two small sons with me. As we drove through the campus, they saw students of all shades of skin color. Accustomed to being on the FSU campus, the juxtaposition of so many dark-skinned and light-skinned people was quite a novelty to Lew and Johnny. They started pointing to individuals and asking, "Is he a Negro?" "Is she?" As I answered yes regardless of how light the student might be, Lew finally asked, "Is this how it is? All white people are white, but some Negroes are colored and some are white." Perplexing as it seemed, he accepted my explanation that this was indeed the way it was.

On another occasion, I was reassured that the boys were not developing a high degree of color consciousness. As C.U. Smith and I became better acquainted and began to work together, he would sometimes come to my house. He is quite dark but is also a full six feet, six inches tall. The little boys always greeted him happily when he came to visit. I was delighted when one day, one of them asked me, "When is that great big man going to come see you again?"

After Johnny, the youngest, entered kindergarten, Kay obtained a teaching job, and hired a maid to come in once a week to clean house and do the washing. We had a succession of helpers. Conscious of my research on domestic service back in Athens, I tried to pay them as much as I felt we could afford, and we faithfully paid their social security tax. In dealing with these black women, with most of whom we had excellent relations, I was harshly reminded of how pervasive and subtle discrimination was and of how easy it is to be unaware of the significance of one's own behavior. One of our best maids was the wife of an air force sergeant; during the months she worked for us, she was waiting for a port call for her and the children to join him at his station in Spain. As with all the others, we followed the old southern custom of calling her by her first name. She didn't seem to mind, but one day she said to me, "Sometimes when I'm here at work one of my children may need to call me on the telephone. Is it all right if I tell them to ask for 'Mrs. ———'? They're not used to calling me by my first name!" Red-faced, I assured her that we had no objection at all.

One thing we had to play by ear with different maids was seating in the car when we drove them to and from our house for work. Usually only one of us would be in the car, and we preferred that the black servant sit in the front seat with us, despite the peculiar but hoary southern tradition of having the black passenger sit in the back seat, as if the white driver were a chauffeur. We found, however, that one older woman was quite uncomfortable in violating the etiquette, so we allowed her to sit in the back.

Beneath the tranquil surface of race relations in Tallahassee were forces that would break forth and stir up unpredictable turbulence, but only because of changes originating outside the community. Even as I told my students that the legal battle over segregation might soon be over, I could not really envision how the South would react if the Supreme Court did go beyond their decision in the *Sweatt* case and rule that schools segregated on the basis of race could not be equal. Even less was I able to foresee how it would affect my life. The focus of my professional activities would shift. My relationship with both blacks and whites, in Tallahassee and elsewhere, would change drastically. My family would be subject to strains of which I had never dreamed.

I happened to be meeting a race relations class on Tuesday, May 18, 1954, the day after what came to be called in Mississippi "Black Monday." I remember saying to the class, "Yesterday the Supreme Court of the United States declared segregation in the public schools unconstitutional, overruling the principle of 'separate but equal' that has prevailed since 1896. Yet the sun rose this morning, there were no earthquakes in the South, in fact life seems to be going on as usual." Then I launched into a lecture on how law made by judicial interpretation is implemented, but is also sometimes vitiated by lack of enforcement. Florida was not a party to any of the five cases before the Court on May 17. Furthermore, we could expect a period of waiting and inaction because of the Court's call for a rehearing at which testimony could be presented by all parties as to how they felt this momentous decision should be implemented.

After four years during which all of my research had been in disaster studies, I would soon return to my first interest, race relations and desegregation in particular. Once, in a speech before the Tallahassee Rotary Club, I said, "I have had two major research interests, disasters and desegregation." The proverbial voice from the back of the room boomed out, "What's the difference?" It was chance, once again, that was the catalyst for bringing about one of the changes in my life, beginning just a few days after the *Brown* decision reached the desk of the attorney general of Florida, Richard W. Ervin.

One of my neighbors and close friends was Dr. Robert D. Gates, consultant on special education in the Florida Department of Education. He had not limited himself to the problems of special education. Through diligence, a winning personality, and a certain amount of "nosiness," he had become a confidant and general adviser to Thomas Bailey, the state superintendent of education. One afternoon when we had both returned from our offices, Bob approached me in my front yard and asked, "How would you like to direct a study of how Florida will respond to the desegregation decision?" The magnitude of his proposal left me speechless. He explained that Attorney General Ervin and Superintendent Bailey, both members of the Florida cabinet, had decided that the state should respond positively to the Supreme Court's invitation for states that would eventually be affected by the ruling in *Brown* to submit *amicus curiae* briefs at the rehearings on implementation. Furthermore, Ervin Believed that since the Court had relied so heavily on social science findings in arriving at its first decision, then Florida's brief should also incorporate data gathered by social scientists. Neither of these officials knew me at all, but Bob had already persuaded them that I was qualified to direct whatever research was done. Hardly believing that anything would come of it, I told him that I would accept the assignment if officially asked.

Ervin and Bailey presented their idea to the Florida cabinet at its next meeting and asked for a special grant of $10,000 to conduct social science research. Had it been in the power of the governor to block the whole project he probably would have done so, for Governor Charlie Johns subscribed to the "Deep South says never" position already adopted in Georgia and Alabama. Under the state's cabinet system of government, however, he had only one vote among eight, and the majority voted for Ervin's motion.

Shortly afterward, I found myself thrust into the position of directing my first large research project in race relations, but doing it for a southern state government. Partly because of Bob Gate's irrepressible optimism, his great respect for Tom Bailey, and his persuasiveness, I did not question the morality of my decision to accept the job of consultant to the attorney general for the summer of 1954. Instead, I was both excited and daunted by the magnitude of the task before me, one that had to be completed in three months. The brief had to be submitted in time for the October term of the Supreme Court. My contribution was needed at least a month before the final version of the brief went to the printer. I entered the most intense, demanding three months I was ever to experience.

Chapter 7

WORKING FOR THE
SEGREGATIONIST ESTABLISHMENT

*Designing Research on Desegregation—Dreams and
Reality—Criticisms, Right and Left —
Doubts and Disappointments*

When I accepted the appointment as consultant to Attorney General Ervin, I was idealistic, naive, and brash. I was riding high because the disaster studies had brought me an edifying amount of professional recognition. The budget provided by the Florida cabinet was only $10,000, but the project I was to direct would be on a much larger scale than my disaster research. More important, I would be burdened with unaccustomed political restrictions. The disaster studies, funded by a defense agency, were classified; I had to obtain approval to publish my first article based on them. The desegregation research would be open to full view of the public and the press. I would be working for the government of a state whose laws still required racial segregation, although the constitutionality of these laws was now in serious doubt. Yet the opportunity for both research and public service seemed so great that I did not give serious consideration to the ethical questions involved in working for the segregationist establishment.

I went to work as coordinator of research immediately after my appointment. I was not independent, for an assistant attorney general, who was my liaison with Mr. Ervin, was armed with a great deal of vaguely defined authority. If Ralph Odum and I disagreed, I had to appeal to the "General," but Odum had known him much longer than had I. In addition, the research was an instance of what two political scientists, Michael Lipsky and David Olson, called "commission politics" in their 1977 book with that title. A "research advisory committee" to which I formally reported was chiefly symbolic. It was created to reassure the citizens of Florida that their state government was doing something about the crisis generated by the *Brown* decision, not just standing idly by while the floodwaters of desegregation rolled over the school system. Therefore, creating a certain image was as important as doing properly designed research, as I would soon learn.

When the Florida brief was published, it stated that the Research Advisory Committee "was chosen by the Attorney General to assist him in conducting a survey to determine leadership opinion among Florida citizens regarding problems created by the U.S. Supreme Court's decision of May 17, 1954, abolishing segregation in the public schools." The committee was structured to create an impression of intellectual respectability and political neutrality. Sixteen of the eighteen members were educators, administrators, or faculty at universities, employees of the State Department of Public Instruction, or executives of teacher associations. Both white and black teacher associations were represented, and the presidents of Florida's leading black institutions of higher education, Florida A and M and Bethune-Cookman College, were appointed. Except for myself and three political scientists, none of the members had any training or experience in social science research.

This was not important, for the role of the committee was to approve the plans I submitted as coordinator of research and present a reassuring image to the public in doing so. Committee meetings were open, and the press gave them annoyingly intensive coverage. As a consequence the sessions had to be staged carefully. Proposals as to how the research would be done had to be presented in a way that would evoke only token debate, for the reporters would have pounced on any signs of real dissension. Even then, there was a constant battle with them. For example, they wanted me to release questionnaires to them before they were mailed to subjects all over the state. Their publication would have hopelessly contaminated our results.

In actuality, the research was designed not by the committee but by me and the assistant I employed. She was a mature graduate student in psychology, well trained in statistical analysis. That the research would be a study of leadership opinion was my idea. When I took on the job, I was determined that I would not direct a survey of attitudes and opinions among the general public. The result was too predictable, and there was nothing in the Supreme Court's questions to indicate that public opposition would be considered. Ironically, I derived the idea of a leadership survey from an article by Kenneth B. Clark, the key witness for the NAACP in the school cases. Writing in the *Journal of Social Issues* in 1953, he had concluded that studies of school desegregation in cities and counties outside the South showed that its accomplishment with a minimum of social disturbance depended on the stance taken by authorities and leaders with prestige. Firm statements of policy, firm enforcement even in the face of initial resistance, and continued strong enforcement action were necessary in order to prevent hostile public attitudes from being translated into action. I persuaded the attorney general that the most significant findings we could offer would be an assessment of the attitudes and opinions of people in positions of leadership, power, and prestige. These, I argued, would be more important than the attitudes of larger numbers of citizens not occupying such positions. He and Odum accepted my proposal, and we carefully packaged it for presentation to the committee.

At this early stage I had a satisfying vision of what the research might be like. My lovely dream arose in part from my inexperience and naiveté, but partially from a need to justify doing research that had a high probability of supporting the gradualist position I knew Mr. Ervin espoused. Yet I dreamed, "Who knows what we may find?—perhaps the attitudes of leaders will be more moderate than those of the general public." My vision also encompassed our methods. In keeping with the best survey techniques, we would use samples, and our instruments would be pretested carefully.

I soon came up against the harsh realities of the client's influence over sponsored research. In a series of confrontations in the privacy of my office, Ralph Odum let me know that we had to get into the field soon; there would be no time for pretests. Nor would there be any samples; what would impress the citizens of Florida most would be to obtain responses from great numbers of them. All my cautions about prospects for low returns from mailed questionnaires and how tenuous any claims for representativeness would be made no impression on him.

Consequently, my assistant and I had to construct questionnaires that we felt had face validity; in layman's language, they seemed to make sense. Our research became a brainstorming operation. Open-ended questions were out; there would not be time or staff available to read and analyze them. During the summer of 1954, we mailed out nearly 8000 questionnaires. Amazingly, slightly over half were returned, despite the fact that we had no follow-up mailing. We queried a wide variety of groups, including school officials, PTA officers, county judges and officials, and peace officers. The respondents were assured of anonymity.

The questionnaires were designed to elicit information on two broad questions. First, we tried to estimate the subject's own feelings about the decision and what action should be taken pursuant to it. Second, we sought to elicit estimates of the degree of resistance desegregation would encounter in the subject's community, the forms it might take, and the ability of the police to maintain order.

Frustrated in my desire to do a sample survey, I came up with an idea for a backup study in which I felt I could place more confidence. Odum really didn't care how this was done as long as we had the extensive coverage of the mailed questionnaires with which to impress the public.

The secondary study was an intensive one done in ten counties representative of different areas of the state, urban and rural, northwest to southeast. Interviewers, black and white, were recruited from school principals and supervisors in these counties. They were brought to Tallahassee for a day of training and then sent out to conduct interviews, but not in their own counties. They were given thirteen questions, covering the same topics addressed in the mail questionnaires, to be asked of public officials and civic leaders. Even in this phase of the research, reality intruded to impose constraints. In five counties, blacks who knew the state well said that the climate was too dangerous for any black interviewer to work on such a sensitive subject. White interviewers had to be used for both racial groups in these countries.

To analyze the long answers to the questions asked in these interviews, I was able to utilize a fine biracial team of scholars, including four from the faculty of Florida A and M University. My friend and colleague C.U. Smith not only worked on this team, but came to be a valuable unofficial consultant to me.

Whatever its merits, my work for the state establishment had two unanticipated consequences involving C.U., or "Chuck" as I now knew him. First, it laid the foundation for a personal and professional bond between two southern sociologists that would grow stronger and endure in spite of the barriers of race. Second, it gave my friend an entree into the state capitol and political circles that would expand until he became an important figure not only in his own institution, but throughout the whole state. In future years he and I would work as a team in both sociological research and social action to promote desegregation.

One of Chuck's saving graces is a wonderful sense of humor, particularly where matters of race are involved. As a result of his work on my team, he had occasion to attend several biracial gatherings in which what to do about the crisis was discussed. Often biracial committees were nominated to follow up, and he always seemed to be selected to represent blacks. He joked, "You see, it's my height. These white folks want a black to be on the committee but they don't know any. So they look around and say, 'Who's that big, tall one?' So I get chosen."

Under tremendous pressure of time and unwelcome political constraints, the research was completed soon enough for me to write up the results, submit them to the Research Advisory Committee for pro forma approval, and turn them over to the attorney general and his legal staff for incorporation in the brief then being drafted. My contribution constituted Appendix A. I had no control over what went into the main body of the brief, including the use of my findings. Some of the harshest criticism I received after publication was based on statements about differences in levels of school achievement, health, and morals between whites and blacks that I had never seen. They were derived from analyses done by staff members from the Department of Education.

My own findings and conclusions, stated separately, were not surprising to me, for they accorded generally with other studies of readiness and resistance to desegregation done during the mid-1950s. The majority of the white subjects disagreed with the decision, but a large majority of the black leaders acclaimed it as right and just. Yet only about 30 percent of the white leaders indicated that they would refuse to cooperate with any move to end segregation or would actively oppose it. The majority seemed ready to go along with whatever the courts or school officials decided, like it or not. This did not mean that the whites thought things would go smoothly.

courts or school officials decided, like it or not. This did not mean that the whites thought things would go smoothly.

The most ominous finding was that police officers, city and county, were the group most opposed to desegregation. More important, they, more than any other group, expected violence to occur if desegregation were attempted, and at the same time expressed great doubt as to their ability to cope with serious disorders. This finding bothered me more than any other in the study, for its publication might prove to be the basis for a self-fulfilling prophecy. Fortunately, the violence over school desegregation that almost half the officers anticipated did not occur, so their prediction that they could not cope with it was never tested.

The most interesting result to me was the disclosure of the great gap between the hopes of blacks and the expectations and attitudes of whites. Only a minority of either group of leaders advocated immediate, complete desegregation, but blacks advocated a gradual change over a short period of time. Whites wanted a very gradual, indefinite period of transition, with a great deal of education preceding the first admittance of black children to white schools. The personal interviews conducted in ten counties showed that the majority of the black leaders believed that desegregation could and should begin within the next three years. Blacks had far more faith in the goodwill and respect for the law on the part of whites than the white answers justified. Three-fourths of them believed that most white people agreed with the decision; 77 percent of the whites believed the opposite. A majority of whites even believed that most blacks disagreed with the decision and did not want integrated schools. Whites predicted violence if desegregation were inaugurated soon; blacks did not. Less than half the white leaders believed that the police could (would?) control violence if it occurred; 90 percent of the blacks believed they would and would maintain order.

One finding, strongly supported by both the mail results and the intensive personal interviews, had clear policy implications. I concluded that regional, county, and community variations in responses were sufficient to suggest that in some communities desegregation could be undertaken very soon if local leaders so decided, even though in other counties resistance and disorders might be expected. As I still believe was true throughout the South, had school boards sought ways to comply with the *Brown* decision instead of ignoring it or seeking means of evasion, the course of school desegregation might have been very different. What happened was that a united front of resistance and delay was presented, suggesting a "solid South" that my research did not show to exist. Consequently, the initiative was forced on black plaintiffs and the NAACP. They and the federal courts chose which communities would start first and what sort of plans they would follow.

Not surprisingly, the Florida brief urged the Court to permit a period of adjustment to desegregation rather than issue a "forthwith" decree. As I wrote not long after the brief became public, "There is no doubt that, in terms of his

Critics of Florida's brief interpreted it to mean exactly that. In 1976 Richard Kluger wrote in *Simple Justice*, "The South's skill at erecting legal barriers to slow the desegregation process was foreshadowed by Florida's suggested 'plan' to implement the Court's decision. Under it, even the most ungainly camel in Islam would have had an easier time passing through the eye of a needle than a black child getting into a white school in Florida."

The brief and my own contributions were attacked by some sociologists in 1955. A resolution to censure me was introduced at the annual meeting of the Eastern Sociological Society. The motion was defeated, but when I heard of the effort I was deeply concerned and hurt. A few months later, I presented a paper, "The Social Scientist's Role in the Preparation of the Florida Desegregation Brief," at the joint meetings of the Society for the Study of Social Problems and the American Sociological Association. Some of my critics confronted me on this occasion, and I was able to answer them. Although some remained unforgiving, others were mollified by my explanation that I did not write the objectionable parts of the brief that had so infuriated them. I was particularly gratified that another good friend from Chicago days, G. Franklin Edwards, now of Howard University, accepted my explanation after being initially critical.

While the work was in progress during the summer of 1954, it was not any criticism that I might receive from fellow sociologists that concerned me most. Instead, I found myself part of a task force publicly defined in Florida as liberal, moderate and even integrationist. Compared to many other southern politicians and government officials, Mr. Ervin had taken the *Brown* decision calmly and professionally. The attorney general of neighboring Georgia had violently denounced both the Supreme Court and its decision, declaring, "I will not help the Supreme Court choose the weapon with which to stab Georgia in the back!" The posture characterized by *Saturday Evening Post* writer John Barlow Martin as "the Deep South says never" prevailed in most of the southern capitals. The middle ground was already beginning to disappear between those who wanted desegregation imposed as rapidly and forcefully as possible and the diehard segregationists.

I realized how courageous Ervin's stand was when I accompanied him to a conference of attorneys from the northern counties of Florida. In a gentle, dignified manner he explained his position. Whether we liked it or not, he told his audience, the *Brown* decision was the law of the land and the southern states not directly involved in the case were fortunate that they had been offered a chance to influence the manner in which the decree would be implemented. Ervin was determined that Florida avail itself of that opportunity. When the floor was opened for questions, the attorney general was bombarded with queries, often delivered in hostile tones. Over and over he was asked, "Is this *stare decisis*?"—another way of asking, "Is the decision going to stand, or can we persuade the Court to reverse itself?" The questioners implied, "Why are you surrendering instead of doing all you can to make the justices reconsider this communist-inspired ruling?"

This sort of attack went on all summer in some news media outlets, in other meetings, and in letters mailed to the attorney general's office. Even some of Ervin's own staff strongly disagreed with him.

Because the research I was conducting was "big news" in Florida that summer, my name appeared in newspapers all over the state. In addition, I sometimes replaced Ervin when he could not accept speaking engagements with civic clubs, PTA groups, and meetings of teachers. I tried to explain in an objective manner how the Court seemed to have arrived at its decision, and I tried to make some predictions as to how school desegregation might take place. This approach infuriated people who regarded anything but last-ditch resistance as treason to the South. I also shocked some listeners when I tried to disabuse them of the belief that blacks did not want desegregation. I told them that the fiction that "our colored folks are happy with the way things are" had always been a costly exercise in self-deception.

I realized how intense the hostility to me might become when one night I received a long-distance call from a man who had been a close friend during my high school days. He was now a postal worker in a very conservative town in central Florida. Somewhat inebriated, he had gone to the trouble of finding my home telephone number and calling to denounce me for taking part in this infamous plot to betray the state of Florida. He wanted to know what had happened to change me so much from the boy he knew in Macon.

Such criticism had a net positive effect on my work. It kept me from brooding about criticism I might receive from militant advocates of immediacy. The viciousness of the attacks from the hard-line segregationists made me feel that Ervin must be doing something right in adopting his moderate stance. We were communicating unpleasant truths that, we believed, might create some cracks in the wall of resistance and preclude disruption of public education in the state.

The pace I maintained took its toll physically as well as psychologically. After working far into the night, I would find myself unable to wind down and go to sleep. Yet, after a few hours' rest, I would again be going full speed. It did not help that my father-in-law died of a heart attack in mid-summer. My schedule would not even permit me to go to his funeral in North Carolina. Kay and the children left to stay with my mother-in-law for the rest of the summer. By the latter part of August, I was beginning to feel the effects of having driven myself so hard. I went to my family doctor; he found that my blood pressure had jumped forty points since April, when I had undergone an annual checkup. I wasn't surprised, but I was frightened. This was for me the first intimation of my own mortality. I was only thirty-five years old and had always been in near-perfect health. Now I was frightened, but I was still trapped by a deadline.

As bad as I felt physically, I was still on an emotional high at the end of the summer. I remember telling Ralph Odum over lunch one day, "If I were to die tomorrow I would die happy because I feel I have done something really worthwhile this summer." I had come to share Ervin's vision. He had steered the government of Florida into a path of cooperation with the U.S. Supreme Court, responding to its unwelcome decree with respect rather than defiance. By doing so, he hoped to generate an atmosphere of moderation that, given some time for adjustment by the Court, would lead to slow but peaceful change instead of violent resistance. The peace we dreamed of did prevail in the coming years. The changes came far more slowly than I anticipated or could justify, however. On May 25, 1955, the Supreme Court, just as Ervin had hoped it would, handed down its gradualist decree allowing implementation of the new principle "with all deliberate speed."

The academic year of 1954–1955 was exhilarating for me. Not only was I still speaking to local groups about the research, but the attorney general invited me to accompany his legal team to Washington to the hearings before the Supreme Court. There I enjoyed the rare privilege of watching the historic Warren Court in action. Thurgood Marshall of the NAACP, the solicitor general of the United States Ervin Griswold, Attorney General Ervin, and attorneys general from Kansas, Delaware, Virginia, North Carolina, South Carolina, and Mississippi presented oral arguments.

My nagging concerns about having participated in preparing a "gradualist" case were alleviated somewhat when Griswold advocated a period of gradual adjustment. I also overheard Thurgood Marshall say to a group of lawyers in the cloakroom, "Whatever the Court decides, we will be faced with years of litigation. We'll have to fight school segregation county by county and district by district."

The Supreme Court's gradualist decree gave Florida and other states time for adjustment, for which they had pleaded. I hoped that Richard Ervin and Tom Bailey would go home and provide strong leadership in moving the state school system toward desegregation, even if only with deliberate speed. They issued some high-toned pronouncements about the need for local school officials to respect the law and start making plans for moving toward a unitary school system. These pleas fell on deaf ears, however, and the two politicians did not push the issue; after all, they were elected officials.

County school boards and school officials breathed a sigh of relief. Even if they became defendants in desegregation suits, the Supreme Court had decided that the pace of change would be left initially to federal district judges, who would decide how fast "speedy" was. Hence, except in Dade County, where just one school was desegregated, local officials sat back as if to say, "As long as we do not have a suit to fight, why do anything?" In Tallahassee and Leon County, my home, white leaders in the shadow of the state capitol declined to take nay action on local black leaders' request that they at least set up a biracial committee to discuss school desegregation.

The worst blow to my naive hopes came less than a year after the 1955 decision. Both Ervin and Bailey ran for re-election. Bailey had no significant opposition. Ervin, however, was opposed in the primary by a segregationist demagogue from a tobacco-raising county marked by grossly inferior black schools, cruel exploitation of black fieldhands, and a significant amount of Ku Klux Klan activity. This candidate took an extreme position of massive resistance to desegregation, advocating a law requiring that any public school in Florida faced with Court-ordered desegregation be closed. To my chagrin, Ervin responded by espousing an alternative local-option law that would allow any county faced with desegregation to decide through a referendum whether to comply with the law or close its schools. Ervin was neither the first nor the last honorable and intelligent white southern politician who felt forced to take a compromise position to keep an extremist waving the Confederate battle flag from gaining power. He succeeded in this goal, but his escutcheon as a champion of southern moderation was now tarnished. One of my saddest memories is of a bitter letter that I wrote during his campaign and the tragic plea for understanding with which he replied. He saw himself as a man assailed from all sides who was now being deserted by his best friends. Once he was reelected, he did nothing to promote his local-option plan, but he also took no steps to promote desegregation.

Instead, by virtue of his office as chief advocate for the state, he found himself once again fighting a delaying action. When the *Brown* decision was handed down, the Supreme Court still had before it an appeal from a ruling by the Florida Supreme Court refusing to admit Virgil Hawkins to the University of Florida Law School. The U.S. Court returned the case to the Florida court for rehearings in the light of the *Brown* decision. Ervin, strongly urged by Odum, I suspect, decided to follow the same strategy he had in preparing the *amicus curiae* brief. He would have another study done to identify problems that might arise in desegregating the state's system of higher education. Perhaps if this had not come before my disillusionment over the electoral campaign, I would not have been as incredibly gullible as I was. Odum called to ask me if I would direct yet another study. By this time, we had come to be good friends, although we often disagreed. I told him that I would if I could do it in my own way. I was confident that a properly conducted sample survey with good, pre-tested instruments would show that a population of university students and faculty was far more ready for change than had been the population of white leaders we had studied. I actually started planning how to draw a sample, not a difficult task given a population with known parameters and official rosters. I even hired a few interviewers to start pretesting schedules. This activity lasted only about two weeks. Then I was asked to meet with yet another advisory committee to discuss the research design. When the discussion started, Odum took charge and to my dismay announced that we would follow the same strategy used before—no sample but a massive mailing of questionnaires that would impress the public. After a few minutes of heated discussion, I announced that I would have nothing to do with the project. The kind of study Odum wanted was subsequently carried out by the staff of the Board of Regents of the university system, assisted by part-time student help. This was the end of my association with the attorney general's office. In spite of my disappointment, Richard Ervin and I remain good friends, and I continue to respect him for what he had tried to accomplish during the summer I worked with him. Later he proved the genuineness of his liberal impulses during several terms as a justice of the Florida Supreme Court and eventually as chief justice.

What did we accomplish? Had I allowed myself to be used and my sociological skills prostituted in support of a cause with which I certainly did not agree? Would desegregation have proceeded at a surer, faster pace had the Supreme Court issued a "forthwith" decree, as the NAACP asked it to do? Did what Attorney General Ervin and his staff said in Florida's brief even influence the Court's decision?

I will never know the answer to these questions, but they will always haunt me. The tentative answers that I come up with when I think about them bother me even more. Are they still only rationalizations for a betrayal of my own liberal principles?

All I have read about the decision of the Warren Court in the school cases makes me believe that it really did not make much difference what Florida pleaded or whether we even appeared. This conclusion is in accord with my generally pessimistic outlook on the practical significance of most of the sociological enterprise, particularly with respect to public policy. I did not, of course, possess this outlook when I idealistically embarked on Ervin's crusade in 1954.

Now I draw an analogy between this experience and the one I had doing disaster research. In the latter instance, the U.S. Army was the ultimate consumer and potential user of our conclusions concerning human reactions to nuclear attack. The feedback I received from army officers who reviewed our studies took two forms. One can be summarized as, "I agree with these conclusions but what else is new? I already knew what they say." The other was, "I disagree with these conclusions. The studies are worthless." I feel that the old joke still applies: "Social Science is to a politician as a lamppost to a drunk; it is to provide support, not light."

Suppose, however, that my pessimism is unjustified and that that summer's work did have some impact on history? My hopes that the moderate, law-and-order approach adopted by Richard Ervin would lead to a progressive, active gradualism were soon dashed, but Florida did come through the whole civil rights era with less violence and psychologically searing human conflict than did other southern states. This was partly because Florida's elected officials proved to be adept at fighting a delaying action through the use of legal stratagems rather than through brutal defiance.

In the conclusion to the brief Ervin wrote:

> There are two ways in which the *Brown* decision may be viewed by history. First, it may be considered as a seismic shock which struck without warning and engulfed a large part of the nation in a tidal wave of hate and enflamed emotions and carried away a public school system which took half a century and billions of dollars to build, or
>
> Second, it may be looked upon as a high goal which this Court has fixed for men of good will to strive to attain and which they may attain in due course if rational consideration is given to human frailty and faith is maintained in the slow but sure upward movement of democracy.

While working for him, I came to believe strongly that Richard Ervin was a man of goodwill who sincerely hoped for a peaceful transition—a belief I still retain. On this basis, I can live with my decision to help him in his endeavor. A terrible question still remains: Who helped the civil rights movement the most, people of goodwill such as Ervin, or those such as Bull Connors and the bombers of Birmingham? Perhaps I would have been truer to my own principles had my efforts been devoted to precipitating confrontations with such extremists rather than cooperating with a peacemaker.

Chapter 8

RESEARCH AND ACTION: BROWN TO THE SIT-INS

Southern Regional Council—Tallahassee Bus Boycott
Studying Black Leadership—The Storm Gathers

Except for the flurry of activity during and just after my work for Attorney General Ervin, my first four years at Florida State University constituted a peaceful time of transition from the years at Oklahoma. I actually enjoyed teaching twelve hours a week. Ralph Turner and I had already started work on our textbook *Collective Behavior*, and I was still involved in disaster research as a member of the Committee on Disaster Studies of the National Research Council.

Given the publicity I received throughout the state while doing research for the brief, it was inevitable that after the summer of 1954, my attention would become focused on race relations. Opportunities to address audiences within and outside the university multiplied. The dean of the School of Education at the University of Florida invited me to contribute an article on school desegregation to *Phi Delta Kappan*, the journal of the educational honorary by that name. I was particularly pleased at this, for near the end of her long career of public school teaching, my mother was honored by election to the fraternity. The only picture I have of her in a long evening gown was taken the night of her initiation, one of the proudest moments of her life. Just a few months after I had refused to continue working with the Attorney General's Office because of Ralph Odum's insistence on dictating the methods I would use, I received an invitation from Gainesville. I would serve as one of the speakers on the University of Florida's Annual Religious Emphasis Week. This was an exciting prospect for several reasons. First, I always enjoyed the give and take of discussion with students, especially if the subjects were controversial. Although the scene in Florida remained peaceful, the campus of the University of Alabama had already been the stage for demonstrations and legal evasions resulting in the withdrawal of Arthurine Lucy, the first black student to attempt to enter a Deep South state university. The eyes of students throughout the nation had been riveted on this episode, long before George Wallace became the symbol of resistance to desegregation. Finally, I was thrilled by the prospect of meeting one of the other speakers, Will

Herberg, whose *Protestant, Catholic and Jew* was one of the latest contributions to the literature on assimilation in the United States.

Participation in Religious Emphasis Week was exciting but not always enjoyable. The schedule was grueling each day, beginning with appearances in several classes during the day, speaking at dinner at a fraternity house or dormitory, and then leading another discussion somewhere else during the evening. At one of these late-night sessions it became apparent to me that I was being deliberately baited by two students. One, a calm, dignified law student, asked cogent but very prosegregation questions about the new legal structure. The other, peculiar looking and very dogmatic, asked "questions" that amounted to declarations that the whole desegregation movement was communist inspired. His assertions were familiar ones, and I felt very competent to answer them, but he finally provoked me to anger. I turned the tables on him and started quizzing him about how much he actually knew about communism, which turned out to be very little. I succeeded in destroying his credibility in the eyes of most of the other students, but I didn't feel good about the way in which I did it.

The next morning, as I left my room in the student center, I overheard a conversation going on in the corridor. The president of the student body, who just happened to be the son of one of Ervin's assistants who had opposed his participation in the *Brown* hearings, was haranguing the director of the Religious Emphasis Week program. He described in detail the events of the previous evening, charging that my treatment of the dogmatic red-baiter had been unmerciful and inexcusable. He told the director that I had been "fired" by the attorney general and demanded that I be told to leave the campus immediately. It was evident to me that the calmer, more scholarly young man, a fellow law student of the SGA president, had been sent to the session to report on what I said. I wondered if there was a conspiracy to discredit me, but I was not asked to leave and I completed my schedule of talks.

One dividend from my research on the brief was the expansion of the fledgling Institute for Social Research at Florida State University. The institute had been started during my first year in Tallahassee when Basil Zimmer, who went on to a distinguished career at Brown University, obtained a castoff IBM machine from the registrar's office and began using it to process sociological data. Robert McGinnis, who later moved to Wisconsin and then to Cornell, took over when Zimmer left. Some of the money I had at my disposal while doing research for the brief went to rent a larger counter-sorter; on it, McGinnis tabulated all the data collected in the questionnaires. During the summer, Bob was able to get enough departments interested in using the computer for their contract research to let him keep the machine on a permanent basis. Later, Charles M. Grigg, who became a close friend and coauthor, developed the institute into a large facility with its own staff, but this was the actual beginning of it.

My next research project involved the institute, which even under Zimmer's direction had begun doing small opinion surveys in Tallahassee. Students in methods of research courses were used to doing the interviewing. In 1955 another colleague, Jack Haer, and I put several questions regarding desegregation on the schedule of one of these surveys. We drew a sample of 536 white respondents in Tallahassee. Our questions concerned their attitudes toward the school desegregation decision and what they thought "we" should do in response to it. Choices ranged from "start trying to comply because it was a good decision" to "never let black children in the white schools even if we must go against the law." Our findings were in accord with what other research on readiness and resistance to desegregation revealed. A small minority thought it was a good decision, a slightly larger minority would resist desegregation by any means necessary, and another small minority would comply with the law even though they didn't like it. Over half the sample took a position similar to the one that public officials in Florida had already taken: It was a bad decision, and we should do all that was legally possible to avoid compliance.

Not just the results but even doing the research aroused some angry reactions in Tallahassee. In the interviews, we asked some questions designed to test Gunnar Myrdal's hypothesis that Americans held simultaneously contradictory attitudes concerning the general values protected by the Constitution, such as freedom of speech, and their application in specific cases. The questions were carefully separated, and we did find that many subjects contradicted themselves. Some, however, were perceptive enough to see what we were doing and became furious, berating the interviewers for trying to trick them! Since we did not conceal our sponsorship of the project, I received some angry telephone calls, including one from a local judge drawn in the sample. He lectured me on the fact that, our assurances of anonymity and confidentiality notwithstanding, he could not possibly reveal to us his attitudes on such sensitive questions.

Since the sessions on race relations at the ASA meetings received unusually extensive press coverage that year, the paper that Haer and I gave was the subject of a brief Associated Press story. This led to the first hate mail I had ever received, some of it from segregationists as far away as New York. What seemed to infuriate them was our characterization of those who accepted the decision as "good" as being better educated, higher in occupational status, and having higher regard for individual constitutional rights than those who would violently resist the law. Most of the letters were anonymous, of course. One was signed, however, and the author let me know that I was either a Yankee who did not understand the South and the Negro, or I was a traitor to my region. He informed me that some of his family had been killed by blacks during the Nat Turner rebellion! I wrote him a long letter expressing my deep sympathy for the loss of his loved ones, but telling him that my own great-grandfather, a Confederate soldier, had suffered grievously while in a Yankee prisoner of war camp. I concluded by saying that happily I had been able to recover sufficiently from my grief to wear the uniform of the United States Army during World War II. I didn't hear from him again, but I had fun composing the letter.

As the political scenario in the South, particularly in Florida, began to develop, I was inspired to write essays reflecting the disillusionment I had begun to feel soon after the "with all deliberate speed decision" of the Supreme Court. In the spring of 1956 I wrote a short piece for the little publication of the Southern Regional Council, *New South*, entitled "The Subtle Hypocrisy of Delay." It was an attack on the do-nothing gradualism I saw even people such as Richard Ervin and the man who had just become Florida's governor, LeRoy Collins, adopting. I learned after the article appeared that it did come to Collins's attention. James Prothro, a political scientist at FSU and a white southern liberal like myself, was a personal acquaintance of the governor. Jim told me that one day he recommended to Collins that he should read my article. Collins's response was, "This Killian is pretty radical, isn't he?" Prothro replied, "Some people think he is, but I still think you should consider what he has to say!" I did not realize that my notoriety as an integrationist was beginning to spread along with my favorable reputation among sociologists, white and black. It was the latter that led to an invitation to speak on a lecture-forum series at Atlanta University. The topic of my lecture was "Consensus in a Changing South." My first theme was that there was no consensus in the sense of there being a Solid South adamantly opposed to desegregation. Instead, there was a changing South in which many white people were becoming Republicans, often after having been Dixiecrats in 1948; many young people were becoming more ready to accept change in race relations; and black citizens, never happy with segregation, were emboldened to express that dissatisfaction openly. But, I added, this was not leading to a democratic debate in which, according to popular mythology, a new consensus would be reached in the public. What we were seeing was the bitter clash of a social movement and a countermovement, "The Resistance." The opposing sides in a divided public were not being freely heard, for the countermovement was defining agreement with the new interpretation of the Constitution as not only "unsouthern", but also "un-American." The *Brown* decision was being denounced as communistic. The members of the Supreme Court were seen as dangerous liberals willing to take the arguments of "communists" such as Gunnar Myrdal and E. Franklin Frazier seriously. White Citizens Councils were already spreading from their point of origin in Mississippi. Good friends could not discuss the topic of desegregation without risking name-calling that might put an end to their relationship.

My two major themes reflected both the research I had been doing since May 1954 and the changes in the political and intellectual climate I observed from day to day. It would not be long before I would personally feel the force of the segregationist countermovement.

It was not only the invitation to speak at Atlanta University that took me to Atlanta, and particularly to that part of the city in which middle-class blacks lived. After returning to Florida, I renewed my association with the Southern Regional Council, which had its office not far from the university and often used university facilities for meetings and to house guests. The organization had set up a consulting service just after the May 17 decision, and I became one of the first consultants. There had always been a warm spot in my heart for the Southern Regional Council. It was formed in 1944 at the instigation of Howard W. Odum, and the first executive director was Guy Johnson, both my former professors at Chapel Hill. The organization brought together white liberals and black moderates, all of them southerners who wanted the region to change and who felt that they, as natives, should take the lead through education, research, and interracial cooperation. Over the years, the council has been condemned as quixotic, subversive, and cowardly. The very fact that it was an openly biracial organization and that it pressed for equal treatment of all southern citizens aroused the ire of segregationists even before the crises of the 1950s. But that it did not openly attack segregation before 1954 brought criticism from fellow white liberals, such as those who were active in the ill-fated Southern Conference on Human Welfare, and from blacks who believed the legalistic strategy of the NAACP was the only moral stance to take. Its strategy was without doubt a gradualist one, and it took a great deal of faith even on the part of those of us who were loyal to it to believe that it could accomplish much.

Since it was not a membership organization, its personnel consisted of a small staff, a Board of Directors, and a diffuse following of subscribers to its publication, *New South*. Hence the first "meeting" I attended was a briefing for consultants in which we met with the executive and the Board of Directors. Harold Fleming, who had succeeded George S. Mitchell, and who went on to a long career in race relations research and action, was the executive. The president of the Southern Regional Council was James McBride Dabbs, retired professor of English at Coker College in South Carolina and owner, by inheritance, of Rip Rap Plantation, where his ancestors had owned slaves. As a forthright advocate of racial democracy, extending even to integration, he had borne the hostility of erstwhile friends and neighbors in the small South Carolina town near Rip Rap. His whole manner conveyed a powerful impression of graciousness undergirded by courage. As soon as I could after meeting him, I read his book *The Southern Heritage*. In it he conveyed both his love for the South and southerners, white and black, and his conviction that the old ways in race relations were wrong and must change. In the eyes of many white southerners he was a "nigger lover," as were all of us gathered in Atlanta that day. He did love blacks, but, unlike many white liberals I have known, his love for them as human beings was not coupled with hatred for those whites who denounced him. He still saw their humanity, no matter how flawed it seemed. He was one of those southerners who loved the

South, despite its grievous faults, "as a mother loves a sick child," in the words of Ralph McGill, another great white southern liberal.

Dabbs was only one of the inspiring people I met during our meeting. Guy Wells, a fellow Georgian, had been president of Georgia State College for Women, but had lost his position because he incurred the wrath of the segregationists in the state government. Yet he could still joke about them. A story for which he was famous among his friends involved a visit to Georgia by a foreign journalist who was touring the United States. When he visited Wells, he said, "There are three things you are supposed to have in Georgia which I've never seen—a peanut, a mule, and a Ku Klux Klansman." Wells replied, "I'll take you over to Augusta and introduce you to Roy Harris, and you'll have seen all three!" Harris was editor of a viciously racist newspaper called *The Statesman* and was one of the Talmadges' most ardent supporters.

It was also at this meeting that I first met Kenneth Clark, the black psychologist whose work I had known and admired even before his research on the effects of segregation on black children was cited by the Supreme Court in the *Brown* decision. Once again, I was reminded of how narrow my white view of the world was. When we chatted during a coffee break, I couldn't think of anything to talk about but race relations, but Kenneth asked me about my children, how many I had and where they were in school. I would be with Ken many other times in the future; this was the only time I ever thought of him primarily as a black man. I realized that for all the liberalism of which I was so proud, I still had to rid myself of a lot of impedimenta from my southern upbringing.

This was only one of many visits to the Southern Regional Council and Atlanta University. What stands out most about these visits is not the business that justified them but the personal experiences with black people, some of whom became good friends. Mozell Hill I already knew from our experience together during his visit to the University of Oklahoma. I visited him in his office on the campus and was in his home more than once. It was there that I first had the experience of being one of a small minority of whites at a black party.

Through Mozell, I became acquainted with other Atlanta University faculty members, whose friendship I would enjoy for many years to come. One was Whitney Young, then dean of the School of Social Work. He would go on to become executive director of the National Urban League. While he held that post, Charles Grigg and I prevailed on him to write a foreword to our book *Racial Crisis in America*, published in 1964. Another new friend was Hylan Lewis, who would later author a classic study of a southern black community, *The Blackways of Kent*. In 1968, after I had moved north, he invited me to visit New York to give a lecture at Brooklyn College, where he taught until retirement, and to meet with the staff of MARC, the Metropolitan Applied Research Center, directed jointly by Hylan and Kenneth Clark.

It was from Mozell that I caught a glimpse of what would one day become a significant theme in black-white relations. One morning we were in Hylan's office, just chatting about current events, when the subject of Gamal Abdel Nasser came up. The Egyptian strongman was at the height of his glory, having recently dethroned King Farouk and founded the United Arab Republic. As we all agreed on the danger that Nasser posed to peace in the Middle East and condemned his totalitarian methods, Mozell interrupted to say, "But you know, as much as I dislike what he's doing, I must confess that I feel some satisfaction that here is a powerful world leader who is an African!" I would remember this comment in the 1970s when I saw American blacks siding with Palestinians as a Third World, nonwhite people opposing the Israelis.

My first adventure in actually violating Jim Crow laws occurred on one of my visits to Atlanta to attend an SRC conference. It was a large meeting attended, not only by SRC staff and consultants, but also by a number of NAACP officials from the Southeast. One of the Atlantans had a big reception at his house the night before the meeting began. Once again I would be one of a minority of whites in the crowd.

I arrived at the party late because I had come from Washington, where I had been working for the Committee on Disaster Studies. When I boarded the plane at National Airport, I was delighted to find that Harry Walker, my black friend from Chicago days, now teaching at Howard University, was bound for the same meeting. We obtained seats together and had a wonderful time catching up on old times while enjoying our in-flight meal. When we arrived at the Atlanta airport, Harry abruptly separated himself from me, saying, "I'll meet you at the baggage counter." I headed for the front entrance, past the white-haired "Uncle Tom" who for years opened the door of the airport restaurant for the white customers who were the only ones allowed to eat there, wondering whether I would see Harry again until we got to the meeting. Sure enough, though, he met me at the baggage counter, but he said, "We have a problem—the cab's not here!" As I looked out at thirty or forty taxis lined up in the parking area, I had no idea what he meant. He explained that an Atlanta city ordinance prohibited whites and blacks from riding in the same cab and that since there were so few black airline passengers, only one "black taxi" served the airport—"the cab" to blacks who knew Atlanta. He had ascertained that "the cab" was not there and that it might be an hour before it returned from a run into Atlanta. He was as anxious as I was to get to the reception, for we both knew we were late. Then he said, "I've got an idea. We'll tell a white cab driver that I am your chauffeur and that you have left your car in the city and need to get to it. Maybe he'll take us both." Pulse racing, I went along with his scheme and told our story to a white "cabbie." Not only did he agree to take us; a white passenger who had just arrived from Memphis asked if he could share the cab with us. We all loaded our baggage in the trunk and got in the vehicle, but the driver had to check with the dispatcher before leaving. We drew up in front of that petty official, who immediately went into a paroxysm of segregationist rage. He screamed, "You can't ride 'em mixed like that; you can't do it unless one of them is a prisoner!" The driver, perhaps anticipating a big tip, calmly stated his destination and drove away. It didn't take long for me to realize that he never had believed our story and was more interested in the fare than in obeying Atlanta's anachronistic law. The high point of the adventure came when Harry and I walked into the party, and he announced, "You're not going to believe this. Lewis and I rode from the airport in a white cab!"

There was another level of my participation in the work of the Southern Regional Council. In the early 1950s the organization sponsored the formation of state and local affiliates called "human relations councils." These were membership organizations, supposed to engage in action on the local and state levels. Two senior members of the faculty at Florida State University, Raymond Bellamy of the Department of Sociology and Paul Finner, recently retired from the Psychology Department, called a meeting of a few like-minded white liberals to start a Tallahassee council. In his younger days, Bellamy, a graduate of Clark University, had fought many battles against southern bigotry, religious and political. In his latter years, he was not afraid to tackle racial issues.

At first there were so few of us that we met in members' houses, but soon we began to garner more allies, white and black. We changed our meeting venue to the Methodist Student Center near the FSU campus. Most of our little band were faculty members from the two universities, and sometimes their spouses accompanied them. A very small minority of our white members were "town," not "gown," a distinction that was highly significant in Tallahassee at that time. They were among a small band of liberal Democrats in Tallahassee, but now found that most of their liberal friends would not join them in questioning the "southern way of life." Being for the United Nations and world peace was one thing, but advocating integration was too much.

Our black members also included some "townies," all of them ministers. The one I remember best was the young pastor of a black Presbyterian congregation, J. Metz Rollins. He was one of our most active members until he was forced to leave Tallahassee in 1957, largely because of pressure from white Presbyterians. He was regarded by many white citizens and fellow churchmen as a "radical outside agitator." He was actually a gentle but courageous "moderate," particularly when compared with some of the angry black leaders who were at that time still invisible to the white community. He was eager to work with white liberals to try to bring about gradual but steady change within the framework of the new legal principle set forth by the Supreme Court. He wanted to build bridges, not create confrontations. Had he not been such a man he would not have spent, or perhaps wasted, so much time with the Tallahassee Council on Human Relations.

Why "wasted"? Did we not all of us invest time and energy in the council's work, and suffer slander and threats for doing so? Just as I had doubts about the possible effects of my research for the attorney general, I often wondered whether our good works helped anybody but us. More than once, I confided in Kay my feeling that the council was nothing more than a mutual admiration society in which powerless white liberals and black moderates got together, each feeling, "Aren't we brave, righteous people for meeting like this and talking about ending segregation?" For talk was most of what we did; I think each of us knew, deep down, that we had no real clout. We were optimistic and idealistic and naive, particularly at the beginning. We dreamed of enlisting the support of decent citizens who did have some power in the city, such as some of the erstwhile allies of our white "townies." It took only a few approaches to such people to teach us that we would either be brutally rebuffed and told that we should stop our attempts at "race mixing," or that, even if what we were doing was right, the person could not possibly risk being openly associated with us. Sadly, we had neither the numbers nor the temperament to precipitate confrontations, legal or moral. If we did make any positive contribution to social change in those times, it was primarily because of the reaction, or overreaction, of our enemies.

Yet, for a few months, our meetings were as non-controversial as they were ineffective, for Tallahassee remained quiet for a year after Brown II, the gradualist decree of the Supreme Court that Attorney General Ervin had acclaimed as giving time for adjustment. Nothing was being done to move "with all deliberate speed" toward school desegregation. My race relations classes at the university did become much more popular and more exciting, for the end of segregation now loomed as a possibility to the students. Most of them could not imagine what the South would be like without it.

While Tallahassee and most of Florida remained quiet, some other parts of the South did not. In December 1955 the Montgomery bus boycott showed the nation that blacks were not going to wait forever for whites to obey the law of the land. Then, on a warm sunny day in May 1956, the civil rights movement came to Tallahassee. We in the council were caught by surprise as much as was anyone else in the city. On a hot Saturday afternoon two young ladies from Florida A and M refused to move from their seats in the white section of a city bus. The two seats they occupied were the only ones left when they entered the bus, and a white woman sitting next to them made no objection. When the driver ordered them to move to the rear and stand up, they refused but offered to leave the vehicle if he would refund their fares. Instead of doing so, the driver stopped, called the police, and had the two coeds arrested.

The two women were released to a Florida A and M official and were allowed to return to the private home near the campus where they lived. The charges were later dropped. During the afternoon, however, news of the arrest spread rapidly in the city, and that night a cross was burned in front of the coeds' residence. This event was the major topic of discussion by the students on Sunday. By Monday morning, student government leaders had called a mass meeting in a campus auditorium to discuss what to do about the events of the preceding forty-eight hours. A decision was made: Students would refrain from riding the city buses for the remainder of the school term. They rushed forth to put their boycott into effect immediately, stopping buses that passed through the campus and asking black passengers to get off. The Tallahassee bus protest had begun.

Many students of the civil rights movement have dismissed this boycott as simply an imitation of the Montgomery protest. When it was fully organized, it was led by the Reverend C.K. Steele, a friend of Martin Luther King, Jr., and one of the founders and vice-presidents of the Southern Christian Leadership Conference (SCLC). As C.U. Smith and I have emphasized in our writings since that time, beginning with "The Tallahassee Bus Protest," published in 1958 by the Anti-Defamation League of B'Nai B'rith, important differences give the events in Tallahassee a significance of their own. As Smith has pointed out, the mass meeting of the FAMU students might well be designated as the beginning of student protest in the 1950s and 1960s, rather than the sit-ins of 1959 or the Berkeley student uprising of 1964. In fact, he has charged that the neglect of the activism of black students prior to the student protest movements after 1964 constitutes an instance of "benign racism and scholarly irresponsibility." The Montgomery protest was initiated by black citizens under the leadership of E.D. Nixon and, later, Martin Luther King, Jr. The Tallahassee protest was initiated by black students. Their actions stimulated the Tallahassee Ministerial Alliance, comprising black ministers, including C.K. Steele and my friend Metz Rollins, to call a mass meeting of black citizens. Out of this meeting grew a new organization, the Inter-Civic Council, with Steele as president, which took over the boycott and carried it on for nearly two years. There was another difference, which came to have theoretical importance for sociological analysts of social movements. Some twenty-five years after the events of the mid-1950s, some students of the civil rights movement made a great deal of the "discovery" that in Montgomery, Rosa Parks was not an ordinary woman who refused to move to the back of the bus simply because she was tired but had taken such action on earlier occasions, being evicted from the bus but not arrested. Moveover, she had been a very active member of the state and local chapters of the NAACP. Whether "spontaneous" acts could play a significant part in the emergence of collective action became a point of theoretical controversy in sociology, generating arguments that would seem important only to a sociologist. Smith and I became involved, for what we knew of the Tallahassee protest did not jibe with the new theory of collective action being propounded with such vigor, particularly by Aldon D. Morris, author of *The Origins of the Civil Rights Movement: Black Communities Organizing for Change*.

I decided to write an article challenging the new propositions, which were beginning to take on the status of dogma with some sociologists. Smith and I spent hours reviewing our own work and our recollections of the events we had witnessed and studied years before. Had our observations been as inaccurate as the new theory suggested? Of two things we remained convinced. One was that whatever Rosa Parks had intended, the two coeds in Tallahassee were not attempting to create an incident that would lead to a local version of the Montgomery protest. There is no reason to believe that their knowledge that blacks in Alabama were protesting segregated seating may not have emboldened them, but they had no previous history of activism, and they did offer to leave the bus if their fares were returned. After their release and their return to campus, they went back to the business of studying for exams and returned to their homes in other parts of Florida as soon as the term ended. Twenty-five years after the events of that May day in 1956, one of the women returned to FAMU for a celebration of the beginning of the protest, still denying that she and her companion had intended to be heroines or martyrs.

Smith and I also remained firm in our conviction that before the students galvanized the black citizenry into action, there had been no significant organizational activity to promote desegregation in Tallahassee. The local NAACP chapter was small and weak. An organization called the Tallahassee Civic League resembled a black chamber of commerce, while Smith and I knew from our membership in it how innocuous the Council on Human Relations was. The Inter-Civic Council was indeed a new, militant organization, even though it encompassed most of the leadership of the older NAACP chapter, some members of the Civic League, and some ministers from the Ministerial Alliance.

That the bus protest was neither planned in advance nor sponsored by any organization, within or beyond the city limits of Tallahassee, was important to us as citizens and as sociologists at the time it began and twenty-five years later. When the white citizenry of Tallahassee awoke to the fact that the racial peace that their city had enjoyed had been shattered, the predominant reaction was one of indignation. The City Commission dug in to resist the demands of the boycotters. They tried to defuse the protest movement by appealing to influential blacks whom they had known over the years, asking them to come up with some "reasonable" proposals to which they might respond. They refused to recognize the Inter-Civic Council as representing blacks and denounced the protest as having been planned and "stirred up" by outside agitators. A conspiracy theory was widely accepted by whites in the city; it was this theory that Smith and I attempted to discredit in our first analysis of the protest.

One reason for the notion that outside agitators had plotted to initiate "trouble" in quiet, peaceful Tallahassee was that new names began to appear in the paper, names of black people of whom most Whites had never heard. Dr. George W. Gore, president of FAMU, and "Jake" Gaither, the highly successful coach of the Rattlers football team, were well known; but who were C.K. Steele, Metz Rollins, K.S. Dupont, Dan Speed, and other black men whose names had rarely appeared in the *Tallahassee Democrat*? Steele and Rollins were relative "newcomers," having been in the city only a year or two, but others at the top of the structure of the Inter-Civic Council were old residents. It appeared that there was indeed a new group of black leaders. This impression led me to undertake what turned out to be one of my most successful research efforts.

I decided that I would try to discover whether there was indeed a "new black leadership class" in Tallahassee and, if so, what its composition was and how it was regarded by whites. The research was a two-man project. With Smith's aid, I developed a list of twenty-one blacks who might be considered leaders in the black community. I selected a panel of twenty-one white leaders who were known to have had dealings with the black community either in connection with the bus protest or with other, less controversial matters. I interviewed all forty-two subjects myself, eliciting their definitions of black leadership in Tallahassee. It was exciting research. The subjects ranged from staunch segregationists, including all the members of the City Commission, to militant blacks who contrasted sharply with some of the black moderates. At the same time I was doing my interviews, Smith did a sample survey in the black community examining the attitudes of blacks toward the leadership of the bus boycott.

Together we presented a paper entitled "Negro Protest Leaders in a Southern Community" at the 1959 meetings of the Southern Sociological Society. Our research findings were later published in *Social Forces*. We concluded that there was indeed both a new leadership group and a new leadership style. We called the new leaders "protest leaders," contrasting them with "accommodating leaders," who had been able to deal somewhat effectively with white leaders as long as they did not challenge segregation. The protest leaders were not necessarily "new" in terms of residence in the city, as their white critics alleged, but displayed a new form of militant leadership that, we observed, was becoming more prevalent among blacks throughout the nation.

Our article was well received in the sociological community and, as I learned later, was used by many political scientists. What has always amused me is that, except for the uncompensated time that Smith and I devoted to the research as part of our professorial duties, our total resources consisted of a grant of $240, which I received from the Society for the Psychological Study of Social Issues. If this was "grantsmanship," it was certainly on a minuscule scale. My part in the research would later have consequences for my personal life that I could not anticipate, for my interviews, even those with adamant segregationists, were pleasant and went smoothly. At a later date, I would become the subject of a new conspiracy theory.

In spite of my intense interest in the bus boycott as both a social movement and a step toward desegregation, I was still only a spectator. Neither I nor any of my family had ever ridden a city bus. When we could afford to employ a black domestic, we always gave her transportation to and from work in our car. Yet simply to express the mildest sort of approval of the protest would arouse the anger of many white Tallahasseeans, for polarization was accelerating, and the community would never be the same. Those white people who supported desegregation, sympathizing with the anger and impatience of blacks, had to bite their tongues or enter into angry arguments with friends, acquaintances, and sometimes strangers. Some of the students at FSU were becoming more active and were violating the university rules against fraternizing with FAMU students. In 1957 one of them was arrested for sitting with two black students on a city bus and refusing to move when ordered to do so by the driver. Another student was expelled, ostensibly because he had brought two black students to an International Club Christmas party on the FSU campus but actually because he had become active in the Inter-Civic Council mass meetings. These meetings were kept under police surveillance, and any whites who attended were reported to their employers. About the same time, several acts of violence were directed at the property of C.K. Steele and other leaders of the protest. The Ku Klux Klan became visible in the county. One night they held a meeting in a vacant lot on a highway, close enough to my home that I could listen to the speeches on their public address system.

Yet this was a time of excitement rather than stress for me. My teaching became even more enjoyable as the popularity of my race relations course grew and the questions raised by the students became more challenging. After Florida's appeal in the *Hawkins* case was lost, a few black students were enrolled in the university, and some of them took my race relations course. Between 1956 and 1960, some good things happened. The first edition of *Collective Behavior*, which Turner and I had been working on for five years, appeared in 1956. I was promoted to full professor and, when the Faculty Senate at FSU was reorganized, I was among the first senators elected at large from the College of Arts and Sciences. One of the most edifying things was that Doak S. Campbell, the very conservative president of our university, retired and was replaced by a liberal Georgian who was dean of students at the University of Chicago, Robert M. Strozier. I had met Bob while I was a graduate student and knew very well that many white Floridians would be in for a shock if they thought they were getting a "good, safe" Georgia boy to preside over the state's second-largest university. While some of the FSU faculty rejoiced at his appointment, as I did, others had grave misgivings. These were confirmed for them when, at the first meeting of the old Faculty Senate over which he presided, he concluded by saying, "Can't we change the meeting time of this body? It runs over into the cocktail hour!" His predecessor, a staunch southern Baptist, not only allowed no liquor to be served at any faculty social function but listened gravely to any reports conveyed to him about faculty members who drank in public. It was evident that the social as well as the intellectual atmosphere at the university was about to change.

There was one fight I did enjoy before the old president retired, even though I lost it. During my first five years at FSU, some of the "hard" scientists from physics and chemistry had introduced motions in the Faculty Senate that proposed raising admission standards by the use of some sort of standardized admission tests. At that time, any graduate of a Florida high school could be admitted to the university—if he or she were white. Some white students who were barely literate matriculated. Whenever such a motion was introduced, some members of the senate, particularly those from the School of Education, would seem on the verge of weeping as they protested such an undemocratic proposal. Every freshman should be able to try to make it for at least one semester; anyway, you couldn't rely on these tests. The motion would always be voted down, to the obvious satisfaction of the president and his coterie of administrators.

After the *Brown* decision came down and the prospect of desegregation of Florida universities as a result of the *Hawkins* case loomed large, the Board of Regents advised the university presidents that it would be wise for them to set some admissions standards that would screen out unqualified high school graduates. A faculty committee appointed by President Campbell came into a senate meeting with a motion to require all applicants to take a test known as the Florida Twelfth Grade Test and make a set score on it in order to be accepted as students at Florida State University. When the motion was presented and seconded, it appeared that there would be almost no discussion. A few questions were asked, but there was no debate. Finally, I rose to move that action be postponed until the senate could study the matter further. I reminded the senate that this was a proposal that had been voted down several times before and constituted a drastic departure from the traditional stance of the faculty. I took advantage of the opportunity to note that the objections so strongly advanced in previous years to admission tests were strangely absent today. The president and the vice-president turned beet red at my audacity in even so timorously questioning the wisdom of complying with the Regents' wishes. Still, no debate was stimulated, and as I anticipated, my motion failed, with only a minority of my fellow faculty members supporting it.

During these years, my friendship with Chuck Smith grew warmer as we continued our collaboration as fellow sociologists. Now, however, I began to know him as a person, not just as a black and a sociologist. Small incidents contributed to my feelings of closeness to him. One night, several months after work was finished on the appendix to the brief, we met with a FAMU faculty member who wanted to use the data we had gathered and that were now in my custody. There was no objection to his using them, but it soon became evident that he disapproved of our participation in the research and was highly suspicious of our findings. We met at Smith's house, and he furnished the bourbon. After a few drinks, I found myself allied with Chuck in a rather violent argument with his guest. Our racial identities were forgotten for the evening, in the heat of an intellectual debate fueled by the bourbon.

There were occasions when Chuck came to my house to discuss our work. Tensions were high enough in Tallahassee that there was some danger to blacks and their hosts if they seemed to be visiting socially in a white neighborhood, so he always came after dark. We were more interested in getting our research done than in creating an incident.

Smith was under far greater pressure than I was at this time, although I was still going through cycles of overwork, anxiety, and psychosomatic distress *cum* Librium. One night when he appeared at my door, Chuck looked tired and worried, even haggard. I said, "What's the matter, Chuck, are you sick?" He hesitated for a few moments and then replied, "Lewis, have you ever taken sleeping pills?" I laughed as I replied, "Of course I have—sometimes I need them." He came back, "No kidding? My doctor wants to give me some, and I've been afraid to take them. You make me feel safe in taking them." For the next hour, we forgot our racial and ethnic roles and talked person-to-person about our feelings.

During the previous summer, he had been the only black member of a short course on gerontology at the University of Connecticut. Now he described to me how heavily he felt the burden of being the only black person, how he could not get rid of the feeling that he was representing the entire black race and could not relax for a minute lest he let them down. Once again, the curtain that shielded me from knowing the world in which the blacks I had known all my life really lived had been drawn aside for a moment.

Early in 1958 the lightning of the embattled segregationists' wrath struck near enough to give me alarm. Almost entirely by chance, it missed both Smith and me, although as active members of the Council on Human Relations we should have been hit. A few months after the bus boycott began, the Florida legislature had created a special committee to investigate subversive activities in the state, meaning, of course, the promotion of racial integration. "Integrationist" was now a bad word, encompassing the contents of two pejoratives, "nigger lover" and "communist."

In February 1958 the committee met in Tallahassee for public hearings. They subpoenaed as an expert witness J.B. Matthews, a former follower of Gerald L.K. Smith and more recently an investigator for Senator Joseph McCarthy. He entertained the legislators with an edifying but spurious "revelation" of how all the organizations promoting desegregation, including the defunct Southern Conference on Human Welfare, the Southern Regional Council, and, of course, the NAACP, were communist fronts. Then the committee's counsel called for questioning several FAMU faculty members who had been very vocal members of the Inter-Civic Council. Among those they intended to call was a "Dr. Smith," but there were several Smiths on the FAMU faculty and they put the wrong name on the subpoena! They never found C.U. Smith.

The counsel tried to get at the Tallahassee Council on Human Relations by calling its treasurer, but none of the other officers, of whom I was one. Doing this was ridiculous, for we had no budget and no dues; we operated by "passing the hat" at meetings and by getting occasional contributions from a few of our wealthier members. The tactic also proved counterproductive, for the treasurer whose testimony was being coerced was Jim Shaw, a highly respected businessman and an old resident of the city. Instead of cringing before this inquisition, he insisted on giving a statement of his own. He informed the legislators that he had nothing to hide and would have told them anything they wanted to know without being insulted by a subpoena. So eloquent was his declaration that he emerged a martyr and was staunchly defended by an editorial in the conservative *Tallahassee Democrat*, which, at the same time denounced the committee for "witchhunting." Thus a touch of legitimacy was given to the efforts of "moderate" advocates of integration.

I was subpoenaed twice during this period, but not by the legislative committee. The first time led to my only appearance as an expert witness in a court case. A black Anglican clergyman from Jamaica, traveling through Florida by bus with his very light-skinned wife, was ejected from the bus by the driver for insisting on sitting with her. He brought suit against the bus company, and the case ended up in the federal district court in Tallahassee. The judge, Dozier DeVane, was just as conservative as, although much more intelligent than, the man who would one day be nominated to succeed him, Harold W. Carswell. The clergyman's lawyer asked me to give expert testimony on the differences in color classifications and racial customs between Jamaica and Florida. No sooner had I been asked the first question than the attorney for the bus company objected, claiming that my testimony would be irrelevant. The lawyer who had called me tried to explain to the judge why he felt that what I would say was relevant. Judge DeVane heard him and then dismissed me from the stand peremptorily, saying, "I think we can all stipulate that, whatever they do in Jamaica, here in Florida folks don't want Nigras [sic] and whites sitting next to each other on the buses. Witness is excused!"

My next subpoena came from an American Civil Liberties Union lawyer from Miami, Toby Simon, who was representing the state NAACP in its resistance to turning over its membership rolls to the legislative investigating committee. The state president, the Reverend Theodore Gibson, was a former student of my father-in-law at St. Augustine's College who had gone on to become an Episcopal priest and a courageous crusader for black rights. Toby asked me to prepare a statement explaining in sociological terms the possible effects on the NAACP of having to disclose the names of its members. Stung by my first experience as an expert witness, I had grave misgivings about going into court as a sociologist another time. As the newspaper coverage of the forthcoming court hearing intensified, I experienced a failure of nerve. I asked Bob Strozier if it might embarrass him as president if I testified. He said it might very well but that if I were subpoenaed, of course I would have to testify. When I told Toby that I would testify only under this condition, he told me to forget about it and ignore the order when it was delivered. Gibson and the NAACP eventually won their case on appeal to a higher federal court, and I still console myself that my testimony, had I been allowed to give it, would have been immaterial.

There were signs that the struggle against prejudice and racial injustice was gaining some ground. There was more interest in the Tallahassee Council, particularly after the Shaw incident, and we had a regular meeting place. It was the new Unitarian Fellowship, near the campus. The main drawback to it was that it was like a goldfish bowl, with glass doors on three sides. We would all glance nervously out the doors whenever a car drove by, wondering what might come through the glass, or whether the police were about to intrude on our meeting.

More students at Florida State were expressing dissatisfaction with segregation in Tallahassee and at their university. Small, surreptitious meetings of both faculty and students from the two universities began to take place; I was a participant in some. Secretly, a CORE chapter was being organized at FAMU, and some FSU students were members. Any increase in my own activity centered primarily around my church, however.

A lifelong Episcopalian, I attended St. John's, the only white parish in Tallahassee when my family and I moved there. We were not very happy with the parish, for as a university faculty family and as liberals, Kay and I felt out of place in this conservative, "downtown" church. We jumped at the opportunity to move when a young, dynamic priest came to Ruge Hall, the Episcopal Student Center on the edge of the campus, and started holding regular services. Harcourt Waller, a renegade Georgian like myself, became my spiritual adviser, an ally, and one of my best friends.

Harcourt could trace his ancestry back to some of the leading families of colonial Georgia. He was a graduate of Princeton and Virginia Theological Seminary and a combat veteran of the U.S. Marine Corps, wounded in one of the island landings in the Pacific. A towering figure of a man with a booming voice, he would overpower strangers with his friendly, confident introduction, "Hi! I'm Harcourt Waller," which seemed to say, "Of course you want to know me." His theology went beyond the optimistic social gospel, which I had long embraced as a liberal, to preach practicing Christian love even with no prospect of earthly success as a reformer. He reminded me that Jesus said, "My kingdom is not of this world." In one of his best sermons he interpreted the Sermon on the Mount not as an attainable guide to human perfection but as a set of ideals to which

Christians should strive, even though, like Sisyphus, they could never reach them. He suggested that Jesus' words, "Be ye therefore perfect" must have been said almost with a sneer, for the message of the Gospels was that not even Peter, the first of the disciples, could be perfect.

Soon after this arrival, Harcourt started a drive to build a real congregation of Episcopal students and faculty rather than conduct what he contemptuously called "The ministry of Ping-Pong." He had to fight the rector and vestry of St. John's because, while they were all for a student center, they did not want competition on Sunday morning. Harcourt was able to persuade the bishop and the diocesan committee to permit us to have a chapel, supported by the diocese, to which people connected with the university could belong. He also obtained the release of funds from a trust to build a new structure, which was consecrated as The Chapel of the Resurrection.

The chapel and the adjoining student center soon became the center of revived Episcopalian activity on campus in which even the downtown church people took pride. They might not have been so enthusiastic if they had known how Harcourt was constantly challenging his flock to live their Christianity. He did not tell them exactly what they should do, but no one could feel comfortable or complacent after one of his sermons or one of the many discussion groups that went on at the center.

With a great deal of financial support from townspeople we launched another religious enterprise. An old house next door to Ruge Hall was purchased and transformed into a religious community in which ten deeply committed Episcopal young men could live at low cost. They pledged themselves to take part in regular study and discussion of religious topics under the guidance of an assistant chaplain added for this special mission.

In the fall of 1958 Canterbury House was host for several days to a famous visitor who was speaking on the campus to a variety of audiences. He was the Reverend C. Kilmer Myers, who had gained national fame for his work with street gangs in New York City, described in his book *Light the Dark Streets*. He challenged his audiences even more sharply than Harcourt did, particularly on the matter of racial discrimination. He angered some of his listeners, but lit a fire in the young men at Canterbury House. Not long after his visit, one of them would be arrested for civil rights activity, and some people would begin to call our little congregation The Chapel of the *Insurrection*. The era of good relations with the Episcopal community outside the campus would come to an end.

With all these signs of growing opposition to the segregationist status quo, I experienced an unwarranted sense of exhilaration. This was heightened by my continued activity as a consultant to the Southern Regional council, including trips to other parts of the South to meet with local councils on human relations. The most memorable of these jaunts was to Raleigh, North Carolina, in February 1960. It was a few days after the historic sit-in in Greensboro, a form of protest that was spreading rapidly in North Carolina. Raleigh, with two black universities, St. Augustine's and Shaw, was a likely prospect. Harold Fleming, executive of the Southern Regional Council, asked me and another consultant, John Hope II, to go there and see if we could persuade the mayor and the store managers at least to reach some compromise with the students, such as the "vertical integration plan" proposed semifacetiously by Harry Golden, that is, removing the seats at the lunch counters so that blacks and white could be served together without sitting down.

John and I had been on consulting trips before but had never stayed in the same hotel: he always said he was staying with friends. When we arrived in Raleigh, I asked him where we might stay. He replied, "You can stay in a hotel, but of course I can't stay with you. I'm going to stay at Augustine's." This was the first time I realized that John was not white. Had I been better acquainted with black history, I would have known that he was named after his grandfather, one of the early presidents of Atlanta University. I immediately informed him that my wife had grown up in the president's house at "St. Aug's" and that I would love to stay there also. We not only stayed in a dormitory on the campus, but I had the pleasure of attending a party in Kay's childhood home. This was the last time either Kay or I would see the old house, for the next time we visited the campus it had been torn down to make way for a new library.

John and I talked to the mayor and the store managers, but returned to our home bases without knowing how much good we had done. When I returned to Tallahassee, I was still undaunted by the lack of a positive rather than just a courteous response in Raleigh. There had already been two sit-ins in our city, but they had caused no great excitement because the store managers had simply closed the lunch counters and after a short wait, the demonstrators had left. They were following a strategy prescribed by CORE that required maximum negotiations before precipitating a confrontation. I took it upon myself to call on the manager of Woolworth's to urge that he try to avoid the kind of scene that had brought national notoriety to Greensboro. His answer was negative, but it had some logic in it: "I'll consider desegregating my lunch counter when you people at the university do more about desegregating it." He also indicated that his orders from his national headquarters were to conform to local customs.

Later that same week, I had another trip, this time to Jacksonville to meet with their Council on Human Relations and speak on race relations to a faculty group at Jacksonville University. On Saturday morning, unusually bright and warm for a March day, I drove back, accompanied by a neighbor who had been visiting in Jacksonville. As we approached Tallahassee, we heard on the radio news that students from both Florida A and M and Florida State had been arrested on charges of disturbing the peace after a sit-in at Woolworth's. At the moment, an angry crowd of black students had gathered near the police station, confronted by police officers and a small group of White Citizen Council members.

Avoiding the downtown area, I hurried home. I could have been there only a few minutes when the phone rang and Harcourt informed me that Bob Armstrong, one of the Canterbury House students, was in jail. He asked me to go with him to bail Bob out. Joined by two other faculty members from the Chapel of the Resurrection, we proceeded to the bail bondsman's shop. When Harcourt told him what we were there for, he blustered, "If I didn't have to by law, I wouldn't even take your business. I could look out my window here and see them white and nigger students mixing with each other and stirring up trouble." Then my chaplain disarmed him with his typical skill. The bondsman's daughter and her husband attended the chapel fairly frequently, so Harcourt said, "We won't debate your views, but I do want to ask how your daughter is. I haven't seen her for a couple of Sundays." The man calmed down and took our $50, required to purchase a $500 bail bond.

Harcourt again turned on his powerful presence when we took the bond over to the police station. About a dozen of Tallahassee's police officers stood in a circle in the middle of the station, glaring at us because they knew why we had come there. With a big smile on his face, Harcourt approached each one with his hand outstretched and his usual greeting, "Hello, I'm the Reverend Harcourt Waller. Glad to meet you." Not one of the officers refused to shake our hands, even though their expressions remained grim.

Despite my activities in research, writing, speaking, and working for the Tallahassee Council and the Southern Regional Council, I had still been primarily an observer of the civil rights movement as it evolved. I had felt the chill of rejection by former acquaintances who knew of my views on integration, but I had never been threatened in any serious way. Kay and I had gotten some dirty looks at football games when we refused to stand up for "Dixie," now widely viewed as a symbol of resistance to desegregation and the Supreme Court. From that afternoon on, however, I was more than a spectator, although the extent of my activity was greatly magnified.

That very night, there was a faculty dance that Kay and I had planned to attend. It was at the American Legion Hall, for now that Bob Strozier was president, dances were held at places off campus where liquor could be consumed openly. We went to the dance; of course, the major topic of conversation was the events of the day. As we were standing in the buffet line midway in the party, an Episcopalian faculty member who was an active member of St. John's approached me obviously well oiled, and announced loudly, "I want you to know that I don't like what you and Harcourt Waller are doing out there at the Chapel of the Resurrection and I am writing the Bishop to tell him so." As if that were not enough, a dean and his wife whom we thought were friends of ours applauded his statement, as did a few other bystanders. As calmly as I could, I said to my tormentor, "You have a perfect right to write to the bishop. Go ahead." He muttered, "You're damn right I do," and staggered away, although I had the sense that he would rather have started a fight with me.

This was only the first of many hostile encounters that Kay and I would experience in the coming months, and it was one of the mildest, since it was neither anonymous nor official. With the sit-ins and the ensuing events, the storm had finally broken over Tallahassee, and we were near the center of it. What appears in retrospect as my euphoria would be replaced by doubts and fears during days of struggle and difficult decisions.

9 TIME OF TROUBLES, TIME OF TRIAL

Witch Hunt—Facing the Enemy—Governor Collins—Death of a Friend—Desegregation of the Army Reserve

Tensions ran higher in Tallahassee on that Saturday in March than at any other time during the entire civil rights movement. Following the arrests at Woolworth's, about a hundred students from FAMU marched to the center of town and demonstrated outside McCrory's. Undaunted by the arrest of seventeen of their number, they marched on toward Woolworth's. En route they encountered a band of club-wielding members of the White Citizens Council. After a dangerous standoff, with members of the Tallahassee police force standing by and doing nothing, the black students retreated to their campus. Later in the afternoon, however, there was another march toward the center of town, but now the marchers numbered in the hundreds. Not far from the campus, they were met by the police. An order to disperse was followed almost immediately by a barrage of teargas. Not only were many black students arrested during the ensuing mêlée, but three members of the staff of the *Florida Flambeau*, the FSU student newspaper, were hauled off to jail. Two of them were young women. The jailer found it both amusing and just to throw them in the same cell with a number of male inmates and then turn off the lights. The prisoners responded by singing freedom songs, as happened so many other times during the movement.

I knew some of the white students involved in these events. Bob Armstrong was a faithful member of the Chapel of the Resurrection. There is no doubt that his motives for joining the sit-in were predominantly religious. So also were those of Oscar Brock, whom I didn't know so well. He was the son of a YMCA secretary from south Florida. His father rushed to Tallahassee to post his bond and secure an attorney. He was unsuccessful in the latter quest; he could not find a lawyer in the capital who would defend his son! Reluctantly, he accepted the aid of the American Civil Liberties Union, which defended all the white demonstrators.

Jefferson Poland was another matter. He was the son of a poor widow who could not possibly have afforded to send him to college, even to a state university. Jeff had a brilliant high school record, however, and was provided room and board in a cooperative "scholarship house" sponsored by a religious foundation established by a wealthy faculty member. He was a rebel against middle-class white society. It appeared to me that, as in my own case, this contributed strongly to his identification with the cause of blacks. He was the only one of the white arrestees who ever served a sentence in jail, refusing offers to pay his fine. He seemed to continue to court martyrdom even after his participation in the civil rights movement ended. Moving to San Francisco, Jeff gained nationwide notoriety during the late 1960s as president of the Sexual Freedom League. Dubbing himself "the Reverend J. Fuck Poland," he was arrested for such antics as a nude wade-in and preaching in public parks clad only in shoes and a clerical collar. Immediately after he was arrested in Tallahassee, the sponsor of the scholarship house evicted him and we took him into Canterbury House. He left shortly thereafter because he clashed with other residents over their religious beliefs and devotion.

Virginia Delevan, editor of the *Flambeau*, had been a student in my race relations course. She was never charged with any misdemeanor and was released to a grim-faced dean of women after the ordeal of being locked in the dark cell. When her paper next went to press, she attempted to expose the brutality of the local police through first-person accounts written by herself and her fellow student journalists. Whatever faculty member supervised the paper censored these stories. Defiantly, Virginia refused to remake the entire front page but let the paper come out with white spaces manifesting the amount of material excised.

The "respectable" white citizens of Tallahassee were angry, but not too greatly surprised, at the militance of the FAMU students. They could not help but be aware that black students throughout the South, with the backing of their elders, were defying Jim Crow. That white students from Florida State University would join them was infuriating; they were not expected to engage in disorders any more political than a "panty raid" or a fraternity initiation. Many people were convinced that there must be faculty members behind this subversive student behavior, and the search for a villain was on. I managed to make myself the quarry for the witch-hunt.

On the Monday evening following the sit-ins, the Tallahassee Council on Human Relations held its regular monthly meeting. I can't even remember what our program was to be but, as president, I opened the meeting. Seeking to hearten members of this quite uninfluential group, I made the statement, "The Southern Regional Council has played an important *mediating* role in the events of the past few weeks." I referred, of course, to attempts to get store owners to compromise with demonstrators made by consultants, including John Hope and myself. Unbeknownst to me, a state senator from a nearby county had a spy, an FSU student, planted in the audience. Apparently, he quoted me as saying, "The Southern Regional Council has played an important role in the events of the past few weeks"—no "mediating" qualifier included.

I went blithely on my way for the rest of the week, unaware of what was going on "downtown". On Friday afternoon, however, I was called to the office of the dean of faculties. There an old friend, Dean Milton Carothers, informed me as gently as he could that the executive committee of the Tallahassee Chamber of Commerce had passed a resolution demanding that I be dismissed from the faculty and that the entire Leon County legislative delegation was scheduled to call on President Strozier in support of the resolution. Bob was out of town and could not see me until the next week, so despite Milton's assurances that I should not worry, I went home in a state of high anxiety at this unexpected development. It did not help my nervous state when, late Saturday night, as Kay and I were about to go to bed, the telephone rang and my friend and fellow army reservist, Jimmy Gwynn, said he needed to talk to me right away. I told him to come on to the house. Jimmy was the Leon County judge. He had served in the post at an earlier time but had been defeated in a run for reelection. He took the defeat very hard, I was told, and developed something of a drinking problem. Apparently his friends in the local Democratic party had staged a rehabilitation project by seeing to it that he had no opponent when he ran again for the bench. He and his wife, Annie, were both from old families in the area, and I probably would not have known them had I not become his executive officer in the 160th Military Police Battalion of the U.S. Army Reserve. Despite differences in our backgrounds and ideologies, we had developed a sincere friendship and mutual respect. Jimmy and Annie arrived in evening clothes; they had just come from a dance at the country club. He told me, "Lewis, I'm worried about you. All anybody is talking about at the club tonight is how they're going to get you for being behind all these sit-ins." He went on, apparently reflecting something from his own political experience, "It isn't worth losing your job to help these Nigras; they won't appreciate it and they'll let you down when you need them. I know!"

From our conversation that night and information picked up from other sources in the next few days, I learned how complex had become the web of rumor about me. Not only was it believed that the Tallahassee council and the Southern Regional Council were the prime instigators of subversion in the South and that I was their local agent; in addition, some members of the white power structure remembered that I had interviewed them in my leadership study following the bus protest. My research was now being characterized as one step in a long conspiracy to stir up trouble in the black community!

The following week, Bob Strozier met with the delegation of outraged citizens and let them know that Killian would not be fired peremptorily, if at all. Then he invited me to come to his office to meet with Wilson Carraway, local banker and president of the Florida Senate, who had headed the delegation. Knowing whom I was to meet, I went in well armed. When I entered his office, Bob said, "Senator Carraway, this is Professor Killian." I replied as quickly as possible, "I know Senator Carraway. I have been a depositor in his bank for the past eight years." My tactic succeeded; the Senator spluttered a few almost conciliatory words and the conversation was quite bland. This did not mean that he would not continue his campaign against me, but from now on it would go on more surreptitiously.

Another event took place behind the scenes during these tumultuous days. It was fortunate that it remained hidden from public knowledge. One morning, Harcourt Waller called me from his office and said that Carl Braden was in town and was coming to talk to him. Harcourt wanted a third party to be present and asked me to join him for the interview. Knowing who Carl was, I understood my chaplain's concern. I had read the book by Carl and his wife, Anne, describing their attempt to desegregate a white neighborhood in Louisville, Kentucky, and the ensuing persecution of them by the local authorities. I knew also that he was now working for the Southern Conference Educational Fund, the remnant of the ill-fated Southern Conference on Human Welfare. However much I respected the Bradens' humanitarian motives, I had reservations about some of their tactics. When Carl came into the Ruge Hall office, he told us that he had just come from Auburn, Alabama, where he had been trying to facilitate protests against segregation. In his conversation he made repeated references to "the enemy" who, he was sure, we were also confronting. Finally, Harcourt interrupted to ask, "Just what do you mean by 'the enemy'"? Carl replied, "The segregationists, of course." My friend came back quickly, "We are not thinking in terms of our being integrationists and those who disagree with us as being enemies. Many of those who oppose our views are good friends and fellow church members. We are thinking in terms of Christian love, not warfare."

I never knew exactly what Braden hoped to accomplish by his visit to the Chapel of the "Insurrection," but our discussion terminated soon after Harcourt's statement. That night, however, he attended a meeting of Tallahassee CORE and announced that SCEF would be willing to contribute $5000 to the local organization. Probably to his surprise, his offer was not snapped up; instead, a debate ensued. Some members of CORE wanted to accept the money, but others argued that accepting money from an outside organization, particularly one that had been a prime target of "red-hunters," such as the House Un-American Activities Committee, would only provide more ammunition for the Tallahassee witch-hunters. Braden's offer was refused, but that was not the end of the matter.

I did not know about all this until the next morning when a young FSU student came into my office and said he had a serious matter to discuss with me. He said that he had been one of those opposing accepting the SCEF money the night before and that he was so upset about Braden's being in town that he had just written a letter to the radio commentator, Fulton Lewis, Jr., telling him about his activities. Now he wondered if he should have mailed the letter. Well he might have, for it was incongruous that a white student supporting CORE's demonstrations should be a regular listener of such a right-wing radio journalist.

Aghast, I told him that it was indeed a mistake to enable Lewis to fulminate against alleged communist influences in the local desegregation movement. When I found that he had just mailed the letter that morning, I took him to the central post office immediately and asked if he could retrieve his letter. After filling out the necessary form, he was allowed to have it back, and what could have been an ugly development was forestalled.

Like politics, a single-issue controversy such as that over desegregation creates strange bedfellows. The popular view of the sit-in movement in Tallahassee envisioned a conspiracy of like-minded black and white students, egged on by teachers and preachers, united by some sort of unsouthern and un-American ideology reflecting the U.S. Supreme Court's "communistic" decision in the *Brown* case. In fact, the students were a diverse group, divided in motivation as well as in preference for tactics. One of my graduate students, Robert M. White, was an associate member of CORE. He was in full agreement with their goals but, as a husband and father, felt constrained from joining in any direct action that might jeopardize his status as a Ph.D. candidate. CORE accepted such members and included them in its councils. Bob observed the diversity of the students, particularly the white ones, who became involved with the organization. The Episcopalian students, like Bob Armstrong, emphasized their religious commitment but found themselves in disagreement with a group of Unitarian students, whose ideas of religion were quite different. Jefferson Poland was moved by yet other internal forces, and none of these whites had the kind of commitment that the black students did.

This blazing-hot issue also split friendships and alliances. The small group of "white liberals" in downtown Tallahassee found that some of their old allies in the United World Federalists now almost ostracized them because of their integrationist views. One of Harcourt's most faithful followers, a woman with deep roots in the South, who had worked at the university for many years, announced that she would not attend the chapel on any Sunday that she found blacks present. The man who had upbraided me at the faculty dance just after the sit-ins was a fellow Episcopalian who had attended several faculty discussion groups at Ruge Hall. In addition, his son was a classmate and close friend of Lew, my older son. The father continued to be openly hostile to me until I left Tallahassee and let it be known that he thought the town would be much better off if both Waller and Killian left.

Governor LeRoy Collins, a "local boy" recently reelected, much to the delight of most Tallahasseeans, would soon feel the brunt of the divisive power of this issue. Never before identified as a liberal Democrat, and certainly not as an integrationist, he would endure having men ride by the mansion at night shouting "nigger lover" because he adopted a moderate and moral stance on the issue of segregation.

Once again, an informal, non-professional network would bring me into close contact with the establishment. One of Governor Collins's aides, John Perry, was a neighbor of Charles Grigg. While he had to be circumspect in what he said, it was evident that John shared many of our liberal sentiments on the matter of race. He knew of our professional interest in the subject as well as our personal views.

On a Sunday morning shortly after the sit-ins, I received a telephone call while at the Reserve Armory with my military police unit. Charlie Grigg informed me that Governor Collins had asked that the two of us meet with him at the mansion that afternoon. It seems that Perry had persuaded his boss that we had some views on the sit-ins and the arrests to which he should listen. When we arrived, we found the governor surrounded by John and three other aides. After we expressed our views, it became evident that these advisers represented a spectrum of political positions, from John Perry's liberal one to a staunch segregationist, law-and-order stance. The governor was prepared to hear us all out.

LeRoy Collins had won reelection in spite of a vigorous and vicious campaign by a very right-wing opponent, Sumpter Lowry. Identifying himself as "General Lowry" because he had been a brigadier general in the Florida National Guard, this newcomer to politics promised to do anything necessary to keep blacks out of the public schools. He featured his little blonde daughter in television spots, vowing that she would never have to sit in the classroom with black boys if he were elected governor. Collins had responded with a "moderate segregationist" message, assuring the voters that he could keep the schools segregated by legal means, but that he would never see the schools of Florida closed. Blacks in Tallahassee also remembered that during the bus protest, he had denounced the boycott as "short-sighted and unreasonable" and had, at one point, used his emergency powers to suspend bus service in the city because of the climate of racial tension. Recently, after the attempt of black students to march downtown, the Governor had ordered the state police to restrict Florida A and M students to their campus overnight.

Nevertheless, he was gravely concerned over the escalating tension and hatred between white and black Floridians and the bad publicity the state was receiving in the press throughout the nation. Grigg and I felt, and told the governor, that his recent statements and actions conveyed to black citizens the impression that he was solidly behind the city government and the police force of Tallahassee. He appeared to have denied any moral basis to the actions of the demonstrators and to have treated the whole issue as one of "law and order"— at a time when the laws involved were appearing more and more at odds with a changing national morality.

Collins listened patiently to all the points of view presented by us and his advisers. He asked searching questions, which implied to us a genuine desire to understand the feelings of the students and their supporters. Toward the end of the session, he indicated that he was thinking of making some sort of public statement on the issue and that he hoped that demonstrations would at least be suspended until he could do so. Perhaps without warrant, Charlie and I took this rather tentative declaration as a promise that if the demonstrations were suspended, he would make a constructive statement. We proceeded to ask Professor Richard Haley, a faculty member at FAMU and adviser to CORE, to meet with us. On Tuesday night, we met with him at Harcourt Waller's house and urged him to persuade CORE to suspend demonstrations and give the governor a chance to speak. He did so, although not without difficulty, and there were no demonstrations in Tallahassee the next weekend. Both CORE members and Grigg and I waited nervously for the next move from the governor's office, wondering if we had been betrayed. Then, without any advance notice, Collins went on radio from Jacksonville on March 20 and made a speech that proved to be the foundation of his future reputation as a southern liberal but that also earned the opprobrium of many of his erstwhile supporters. Conceding that a store owner had the legal right to deny service to blacks at one counter while accepting their money in other departments, he declared, "But I still don't think he can square that right with moral, simple justice." He also asserted that "we can never stop Americans from struggling to be free."

There is no doubt in my mind that this courageous speech reflected a genuine conversion in LeRoy Collins's beliefs about race relations. This conviction is sustained by my contacts with him in the ensuing years and by the brave deeds that resulted in destroying his political career. Charles Grigg and I felt proud that we had played some part in this conversion, even though we learned later that Collins attached minor importance to our meeting. Apparently he had already been secretly moving in that direction in spite of his public stance.

Following the events of what remains one of the most memorable weeks of my life, there were no more sit-in demonstrations in Tallahassee. CORE decided to change to a different strategy, the majority of their leaders feeling that more demonstrations might undermine the gain that the governor's speech represented. Furthermore, some demonstrators were still in jail awaiting trial, and further demonstrations might affect them adversely.

The segregationist who had launched the witch-hunt with me as the primary target did not become idle, however, nor did the gossip about my activities cease. Friends would report scurrilous criticism to me as if they were doing me a favor, something I have never understood. I was certain that more than one member of the police department had my red and white Ford station wagon earmarked. I have never driven so carefully as I did during that period, for I knew the city judge would love to have me before him on any charge. Already, a student who worked as a computer assistant in the Institute for Social Research had been the victim of his ire. When the young man appeared before the judge for a traffic violation, "his honor" asked whether he was employed nd where he worked. When the institute was mentioned, the judge exclaimed, "Oh, that's where they punch cards and put them through a machine to prove that niggers are equal to whites!" and proceeded to impose the maximum fine.

If I had not already known that I was a marked man, the "hate calls" in the middle of the night would have convinced me. Shortly after Grigg and I had met with Governor Collins, I was awakened from a deep sleep by the ring of the telephone. Half asleep I answered, only to hear a voice say, "Is this Dr. Killian? This is LeRoy Collins." Caught totally unaware, I quickly replied, "Yes sir." The caller went on, "I've got a bunch of nigger gals here at the mansion and I want you to come down here and help me screw them!" The calls persisted every half hour or so, with new obscenities and the assurance that the caller intended to keep me awake all night. Finally, I had enough sense to leave the telephone off the hook. This was the first, but not the last, experience Kay and I would have with midnight callers. It was particularly frightening to her to receive such calls when I was out of town.

I did not need to provide any new ammunition to the witch-hunters. Some of my associates in the Council on Human Relations and at the Chapel of the Resurrection did so without my concurrence. I missed the next meeting of the council because my reserve unit had a drill that night. Another FSU faculty member, Jackson Ice, presided and did a lot of talking. A philosopher, he offered a theoretical justification for civil disobedience and concluded, "If you always obey the law and the law is no good, you get nowhere." His remarks were picked up by yet another politician and made the occasion for one more attack on FSU professors. Next, a group of my friends in the council, all faculty members, composed a letter to the City Commission urging them to appoint a biracial committee to try to bring about peaceful change in Tallahassee. My name was appended as an officer, although I had never seen the document. Within a few days, the letter was circulating downtown with a heading asking, *Do you know what Commie Professors are trying to do to your town*?

The annual Religious Emphasis Week at FSU was scheduled for this momentous week, and one of the main speakers was Joseph Sittler, famous for his writings on situational ethics. As the lay leader of the small faculty group who were members of the Chapel of the Resurrection, I arranged for Sittler to speak at a special service scheduled for one afternoon at 5:00 o'clock. We invited Father David Brooks, rector of the black Episcopal church near the FAMU campus, to celebrate communion at the service, and we urged him to invite members of his congregation to join us. As if this were not radical enough for a city tense with racial hostility, some other laymen took it upon themselves to schedule a covered-dish supper to follow the service. This, too, I first heard of indirectly. Millard Caldwell, a former governor and still a behind-the-scenes political power, mentioned in a radio speech that now white and black faculty members from the two universities were planning to eat together! The next day, I received a telephone call from a faculty friend who was a communicant of St. John's, the downtown church, but still supportive of the chapel. He diplomatically conveyed to me the message that while Bob Strozier, also a member at St. John's would not use his authority as president to try to stop us from having the dinner, it would make life much easier for him if we called it off.

I had high regard for Bob as a man of principle and as a president who was trying to bring about changes of which I strongly approved. I knew that he had already gone to bat for me and felt sure that he was also having to defend Jackson Ice. With heavy heart and deep misgivings, I decided that I would accede to his wish, even though it would constitute retreating in the face of bigotry. My friends in the black parish would be offended, and the members of the chapel who had decided to issue the invitation would be disappointed in me. Harcourt was out of town for the week, so the decision was entirely mine. We had the service: David Brooks was the celebrant, Sittler spoke brilliantly, and a few black Episcopalians worshipped with us, but I took little joy from the event.

My hunch that Strozier was besieged with demands to repress his faculty and fire the worst of us was right. Although I had defused Senator Carraway's wrath during our meeting in Bob's office, he and his allies had not relented from their campaign to get rid of me. On April 16, after things seemed to be quieting down, I ran into Bob in the center of town. He told me that he had to meet with the Board of Control the next week to discuss me and Jackson Ice and that Fred Kent, a member from Jacksonville, had told him, "We have Killian cold." Strangely confident, I replied that we did not need to worry for we already knew what they "had on me," and it could not be grounds for firing me without bringing forth an AAUP investigation of the university. That was the last time I saw Bob. He seemed to agree with me; I didn't interpret his statement as a warning. I never learned what happened at the board meeting, for we never had a chance to talk again. Four days later, he boarded a plane for Chicago where he was to address the prestigious City Club and, rumor had it, be considered for the presidency of the University of Chicago. En route, he suffered a fatal heart attack. While there were, no doubt, some Floridians who secretly rejoiced at his demise, attacks on the university were replaced by a great show of mourning.

My grief was real and profound, for Bob had been both a hero and a warm friend to me. I took some consolation from the fact that I had tried to make things a bit less difficult for him by canceling the dinner at the chapel. No one will ever know, of course, how much the stress of defending faculty members from attacks contributed to what was truly an untimely death—he was only in his early fifties. Ann, his youngest child, was a junior high school classmate of Lew's. His wife, Margaret, was a gracious hostess and a highly intelligent woman. She returned to Chicago and resumed her career on the staff of the School of Social Service

Administration. My whole family felt that we had lost not one but three good friends when the Strozier family's association with FSU was so tragically ended.

These weeks and the many months of tension that followed them were exciting but filled with emotional ups and downs. There were times when I reveled in the reputation I seemed to have acquired among the faculty and in the black community as a fighting crusader for desegregation. I felt honored when the Tallahassee Civic League presented me with an award for my contributions to race relations, although I would have felt greater pride had the award been given by the more militant Inter-Civic Council. Yet all the time I felt that neither my reputation as a courageous crusader for civil rights nor my notoriety as an arch conspirator was deserved. Both developed as unanticipated consequences of rather insignificant, timorous steps on the path of militancy. I still conceived my primary role as being that of an educator. As an activist, I tried to be a mediator and a negotiator; more often than I liked, I felt that I was a compromiser. But these were times when no middle ground was recognized, particularly by those who were resisting any change in the old order. As Eugene Fortson, of Americus, Georgia, and Birmingham's Charles Morgan learned at great cost, even much respected civic leaders could be drummed out of town for advocating that whites and blacks sit down together to discuss their differences and problems. The biracial committee, a device that many white southern moderates, including me, were proposing, came to be a symbol of readiness to surrender to black agitators. It was ironic that one of the major steps Governor Collins called for soon after his courageous speech was the creation of a state biracial committee and similar committees in every city. In the eyes of many Floridians, this marked him, too, as a traitor to "the southern way of life." During those years of the early 1960s, I was conscious of being a marked man in Tallahassee. Reports continued to come back to me of things said behind my back by enemies and even erstwhile casual friends. A close friend who worked for the juvenile court and thus had frequent contacts with the police confirmed my hunch that my car was closely watched as I drove about the city. One of the saddest revelations of how I was being discussed "downtown" came one day when I gave a ride to O'Neal Levy, a man who was something of a town character because he was spastic. He was usually treated as if he was mentally retarded, although I suspect that he could have been educated to a higher level of functioning than he displayed. O'Neal hitchhiked everywhere he went, so it was not out of the ordinary for me to give him a lift. I was not even sure that he knew who I was, but on this day I found that he did. First he asked me, "Are you at FSU?" After I said that I was, he went on, "You're not an integrationist, are you?" I gave him a vague answer, which evidently did not remove his misgivings, for then he pleaded with me. "Don't be an integrationist!" Poor O'Neal did not realize that some of the very same businessmen and politicians he heard condemning me made fun of him behind his back.

Two of my favorite undergraduate students at the time of the sit-ins were William Yancey and his fiancé, Jennie Woods, both very liberal but not activists at all. Bill, well known to sociologists in future years for his research and writings on ethnicity, was the scion of an old, highly respected, and quite conservative Tallahassee family. One night a segregationist member of the City Commission "entertained" them at his vacation residence on the coast. It turned out that the main item on his program for the evening was to grill them about me and my activities in an attempt to obtain evidence that I was indeed behind all the student activism that was disrupting the community. They did not have to lie to foil his scheme, but they endured an extremely unpleasant interrogation for several hours.

One of the hardest blows came from an acquaintance in the black community who was an admirer. The antecedent of his attack on me involved the local newspaper, the *Tallahassee Democrat*. The editor, Malcolm Johnson, was a friend of mine, even though we strongly disagreed about the civil rights movement. He clung to the theory that "our" local blacks were being stirred up by outside agitators. He usually gave good coverage to any speeches I made, locally or at national meetings. The story he printed about a talk to the United Church Women of Tallahassee was a disaster, however. In my address I used the term "the Negro Revolution." What appeared in print was "the n i g g e r Revolution. Before the paper could issue a correction, I received a bitter letter from my black acquaintance, expressing his disappointment that I had abandoned the position he had so much admired. The next day, I ran into Malcolm at a barbershop we both patronized. Before I could challenge him, he apologized and offered an explanation for the error. When the carefully read and edited copy reached the linotype operator, that individual decided to do some more editing. Angered by what I said in my speech, he substituted the insulting epithet, emphasized by unorthodox spacing, for my word. After setting the day's edition in type, he walked off the job and left town. Obviously the proofreading on the *Democrat* was not as good as the copyreading. The correction that was finally published was buried on a back page, of course. I do not know how much this misrepresentation hurt me in the black community, but it did not change the opinion held by many whites that I was a "nigger lover." One of the problems I encountered in my military role provided evidence of this.

After my relief from active duty in 1946, I retained my commission in the U.S. Army Reserve. Not until 1959 did my reserve activities consist of anything more than attending meetings "for points only." At these, the officers took turns entertaining, or boring, one another with rather pointless lectures, often consisting of reminiscences of World War II experiences. In 1959, however, a "ready reserve" unit with pay and a compulsory two-week training period in the summer was authorized for Tallahassee—the Headquarters and Headquarters Company of the 160th Military Police Battalion. Many reservists who wanted to be "weekend warriors" flocked to the unit, although few of us were military policemen. Jimmy Gwynn, the county judge, had been a combat MP during World War II, and he became the battalion commander, with me as his executive officer. Not surprisingly, we attracted reservists with civilian police experience, including several from the local police force. Despite the ambivalence they must have felt about me, I believe that I was a popular and highly respected officer. Nevertheless, when I donned my green uniform and reported to the armory for drills, I was very conscious of entering a world very different from the halls of ivy.

Once, despite their knowledge of my liberal views and activities, some of my fellow officers asked if they could propose me for membership in the Elks Lodge. Almost as if offering a dare, I told them to go ahead. I was almost as embarrassed as they were when they had to come back and tell me that some of their brother Elks would blackball me if my name came up for a vote. This came as no surprise to me.

Although I was popular in the unit, my notoriety did come to have a negative impact on my military activities, one that I did not anticipate. Although the active army had been slowly coming into line with the policy of desegregation instituted by President Truman, implementation came painfully late in the reserve forces, particularly in the South. Even black soldiers who had gone through basic training with whites and then served in integrated units found on their return to inactive status that they would be assigned to all-black reserve units. They could not join the National Guard in any capacity.

I succeeded Colonel Gwynn as battalion commander in 1961. About this time, the Department of Defense began putting real pressure on the reserve forces to desegregate their units. Hoping and anticipating that the 160th would have black soldiers assigned to it, I started trying to prepare my troops for the change. We had training periods during which I lectured to them about the history of blacks in the U.S. Army, going all the way back to the Revolution; the harmful effects of white-imposed segregation on the morale of black units; the waste of manpower it entailed; and the reasons for the change in policy. I will always remember one Officers' Call when Major Ernest Webb, whom I had always pictured as a very conservative native of north Florida, said, "We'll have no trouble. We're southern gentlemen, and we'll treat black soldiers with humanity!"

His prediction was true—up to a point. Our first black soldier was a quiet, well-spoken Florida A and M student who had been trained in the Signal Corps. He was the answer to the vacancy we had in the small communications section of our headquarters, for he knew our signal equipment as no one else in the unit did. While there was no display of camaraderie between him and the white members of the headquarters company, he was accepted as a valuable member of the unit.

Then came the annual Armed Forces Day parade. Eager for public recognition to enhance our recruiting efforts, we jumped at the chance to march with our colors down Monroe Street, ahead of the navy, marine corps, air force, and coast guard reserve contingents, as well as the ROTC brigades of the two universities. Already this year a controversy had arisen over the order of march. Traditionally, the army ROTC units from FAMU had marched in the rear; spectators would wait to see them because of their outstanding band. Now a new professor of military science, a regular army lieutenant colonel with a distinguished career, informed the citizens' committee in charge that his cadets would no longer bring up the rear. Military tradition had long dictated that the army, as the senior service, always marched ahead of the other services. Therefore, the army cadets from the black university were entitled to march with the other army units in the vanguard, even though there would be whites marching behind them. He was so adamant that the committee acceded to his demand rather than have a public furor over his refusal to participate. Furthermore, other army advisers in the area supported his position.

My problem was a different one. Much to my dismay, the first sergeant, a man I greatly respected, came to me as we were making plans for the parade and informed me that some of our most loyal enlisted men were very much concerned about having our even-so-slightly desegregated unit march down the main street with a black member in evidence. He said that some men, including our very good mess sergeant, were talking of going inactive, and he revealed part of the background of their concern. Ours was the only desegregated reserve unit in Tallahassee; we were the pioneers. Members of other organizations were taunting men from the 160th, saying that they had a "nigger-loving colonel" and implying that we really did not have to comply with the policy. Sergeant Moore had heard this himself from a marine corps reserve officer with whom he worked in a state office. I allowed myself to be intimidated by the threats. In those days, before joining the reserve or National Guard was a way to escape being drafted and going to Vietnam, we had great difficulty in recruiting; and all the units were consistently under-strength. I came up with what seemed a satisfactory ruse to solve my problem. On the Saturday afternoon after the parade, we were scheduled to have an open house at the armory so that the public could see our arms and equipment. Hence, I called our black signalman to my office and told him, "I'm going to excuse you from reporting for the parade Saturday morning; instead, I want you to set up our signal equipment and stay here all afternoon for the open house." As he saluted and left my office I felt sick, for I knew what I was doing, and I strongly suspected that he did too. It was another one of those decisions I will always regret, although I don't know what the consequences would have been had I decided to let him march with us. Over the next two years, other black soldiers came into the 160th, and our sister unit, a tank battalion, also became desegregated. The newcomers were accepted as a matter of course but with no warmth. In 1963 there was another significant change, however. The remaining all-black reserve units were dissolved, and the members reassigned. Several reservists from Tallahassee had been driving ninety miles to Panama City for their drills. Among them was a very fine sergeant, Carey McQueen, who had been the senior noncom in his unit. When Sergeant McQueen and some other members of his old unit joined, the men of our headquarters company knew that desegregation was firmly established and not simply in the lower ranks filled by draftees just returning from short hitches in the army. Now we had a black veteran with stripes on his sleeve. While the unity that existed during drills did not generally extend beyond the command "Dismiss," one of our veteran Tallahassee police officers did start encouraging McQueen to apply for one of the new vacancies for black patrolmen on the force. Eventually, Carey did get the job and entered on a long career in law enforcement and corrections.

An unexpected test of the degree of integration of the unit came during the last two weeks of active duty for training that I attended with the 160th. Instead of going to Ft. Leavenworth, Kansas, for on-the-job training at the U.S. Disciplinary Barracks, as we had for two years, we took to the field at Ft. Campbell, Kentucky. For a week we were in bivouac in the maneuver area at that vast post.

This period of training was different in another important way. We had attached a large number of reserve soldiers who belonged to no unit but were required to have two weeks of active duty for training. Some of them fitted into our outfit all right, but others did not. One was a strangely acting white man from Mississippi, who soon manifested signs of being a vicious bigot. Unknown to me, his racist remarks began to create tension in the company. On the other hand, we had attached a black soldier whom other blacks would label a "bad nigger." He held a generalized hostility toward whites and was reckless in his display of it.

As has ever been so in the army, our good noncoms defused what was becoming an explosive situation. One night, a patrol was sent into the darkness of the maneuver area to reconnoiter for a night exercise we were to conduct. Unfortunately, it included the two hot-bloods, and within a short time they were about to come to blows. Sergeant McQueen was in the detachment, as was white Sergeant "Buck" Hood, a tough infantry veteran. McQueen took the black soldier and Hood the white, and each duo disappeared into the darkness. When they returned, both troublemakers had cooled off, and they remained so for the rest of the training period. The two sergeants had informed them in firm and even menacing tones that the 160th was a unit in which whites and blacks got along together and that if outsiders created a racial incident, they would do so at great peril to themselves. Years later, in reminiscing about the incident, McQueen told me that the situation was worse than I had known. When he got "his man" alone, he discovered that he had a pistol and was prepared to shoot the white soldier. So the sergeant had to disarm him before giving him a lecture on race relations.

Thirty years after the formation of the 160th, I attended a reunion in Tallahassee. The "veterans" of the unit present included not only McQueen, now a lieutenant in the federal prison system, and former Sergeant Hood, but also women, white and black, who had become members long after I departed. The headquarters company was now about half white and half black, and women soldiers were very much in evidence. As slow as it had been in coming, I felt proud that I had guided the outfit during the first stages of desegregation. After many years of preparation for a call to active duty, which it seemed would never come, the 160th served for over six months in the Middle East during Operation Desert Storm.

For all the doubts and troubles that those days of the early 1960s brought me, they also engendered hope and a feeling of progress. Black students entered Florida State University and the University High School that my children attended. I saw Johnny, my younger son, become a good friend of black teammates in football and baseball. Segregation still prevailed off campus in Tallahassee, but more and more faculty and students were challenging it in different ways. On one occasion, James Geschwender, then a young assistant professor in sociology, put his imagination to work. Count Basie and his band were in town to play a concert at the FSU student center. Yet black students could not eat at the cafés just across the street from the campus. Jim persuaded the famous bandleader to go with him to ask for service at The Mecca, one of the most popular coffee shops. They were refused, as anticipated, but the photographs and news stories about the challenge made Jim's point very effectively. Later, one coffee shop was actually forced out of business by a student picket line.

Governor LeRoy Collins, serving the last two years of his term and ineligible for reelection, had set his foot firmly on the path of promoting desegregation, even if painfully slowly. He had appointed a state biracial committee with a small paid staff. For such small steps, he had been nationally acclaimed as a "southern liberal" and was invited to be the chairman pro tem at the Democratic National Convention at which John F. Kennedy would be nominated. After Kennedy's election, there was speculation that Collins would receive a cabinet appointment at the end of his term as governor, but he was never so rewarded.

The Southern Sociological Society, formed in 1935, was finding some hotels that would allow its white and black members to eat together at a banquet. It had been a long, difficult, and divisive struggle. During the last half of the 1950s some black members wanted the society to engage in confrontational tactics, even if it meant canceling some annual meetings after they were under way. Other members, white and black, wanted to move more slowly. They prevailed. The first year the society met under completely desegregated conditions, 1959, it was forced to go to Gatlinburg, Tennessee, a summer resort area that had few patrons in early April. Slowly, some other hotels in the region began to relax their rigid barriers.

Although the Kennedy administration was often a reluctant ally of the civil rights movement, the national atmosphere was markedly different from what it had been under President Eisenhower's conservative influence. More important, such events as the Freedom Rides, the 1963 March on Washington, and the violence of the southern resistance elevated the status of scholars like myself who had some reputation as "experts" in intergroup relations. With race relations firmly established as the major domestic problem of the decade, the "race relations industry" burgeoned. New opportunities abounded for those of us who were already laborers in the field.

Chapter 10

PROSPERING IN THE RACE RELATIONS INDUSTRY

Becoming a Grantsman—Journey to Olympus—On the Circuit for Integration—Whitney Young—The Industry Goes Federal

I first encountered the term "race relations industry" during my sabbatical leave in London in 1975-1976 while studying race relations under a Guggenheim Fellowship. In England the word *industry* is often used to indicate a body of professionals that has grown up to deal with some social problem. A right-wing columnist for the *London Daily Telegraph* often wrote critically of the "race relations industry," but it was a black community relations officer I interviewed who made me aware of the term's applicability to me. He told me, "I'm part of the race relations industry, and so are you—we both make our living off the race problem."

It occurred to me then that the $500 Phelps-Stokes Fellowship I had received in 1940 as a graduate student doing research in race relations had constituted my first "salary" as a worker in the industry. The Julius Rosenwald Fellowship for graduate study at Chicago had tied me even more closely to this area of research.

In 1953 the sarcastic London Journalist had written that in England "shares of all the big race relations consortia had moved up on the ethical stock exchange." In the United States the race relations industry certainly burgeoned after the 1954 school desegregation decision. I was one social scientist who profited from the increased investment in race relations, for from 1957 until 1965 I engaged in a great deal of sponsored research. I became a "grantsman," albeit on rather a small scale. The experience of obtaining the grants and the real story of how the research was done still overshadow in my mind the research findings and the publications which resulted.

My first grant, obtained from the Society for the Psychological Study of Social Issues in 1957, was ridiculously small—less than $300. I could have done the research without it, but having sponsorship gave me a sense of obligation that kept me from putting the task aside in the face of other demands on my time. This resulted in the study of black leadership that C.U. Smith and I published.

Following Governor Collins's call for cities throughout Florida to establish biracial committees, Charles Grigg and I decided that these new bodies would be good subjects for research. Somehow we learned that the Field Foundation, located in New York but funded by the Marshall Field family of Chicago, was awarding grants for research that had implications for application. Leslie Dunbar, whom I had known when he was executive for the Southern Regional Council, was now with Field.

Charlie and I devised a very imaginative experimental research design to compare two cities, one with a biracial committee and one without one. Apparently, it seemed reasonable to someone on the foundation staff, for I was invited to meet with the Board of Directors to discuss our application. All my expenses for travel to New York would be paid, and a room was reserved for me at the Waldorf, just across the street from the Field Foundation office.

My reunion with Les Dunbar proved to be just that—a pleasant visit, with some discussion of changes in the South since he had left. We discussed very few details of the research design and the grant application. The crucial event was to be my meeting with the board that evening during their dinner at the apartment of Mrs. Marshall Field, Jr., on Park Avenue. To me, this would be a journey to Olympus.

When I passed building security and stepped off the elevator into the foyer of Mrs. Field's apartment, I entered a world that I had seen only in movies. My dinner companions included Adlai Stevenson, chairman of the board; Otto Klineberg, whose research on the intelligence of whites and blacks had been so important in my education; and Ralph Bunche, at the peak of his career as a member of the United Nations staff. I was enjoying dinner with celebrities who were also some of the "big mules" of the race relations industry.

Another guest was a man whose fame, or notoriety, was familiar to me, Myles Horton, of Highlander Folk School. He was applying for a grant to help support his work, which had played a crucial role in the practical education of civil rights leaders, including Martin Luther King, Jr. I found him delightfully humorous even when he was recounting incidents in which he had been cruelly persecuted by the Tennessee police. He said he was not sure whether or not it represented progress when his enemies started calling him a "communist" instead of just a "nigger lover"!

The main thing I remember about the conversation was the stream of jokes told by Stevenson, one of the wittiest politicians in U.S. history. After dinner, we got down to business, but again I was asked little about the proposed research. Apparently, the board members simply wanted to find out what sort of people Myles and I were. They were particularly interested in my experience in teaching race relations to white southern students and encouraged me to speculate about what I had accomplished by requiring each one to write an autobiographical account of the development of his or her attitudes toward blacks.

I left Park Avenue not knowing whether we would receive our grant or not, but soon after my return to Tallahassee Grigg and I were notified that we had been awarded $25,000. My only regret about my journey to Olympus was that Kay had not been with me but was, as usual, at home taking care of the children.

As it turned out, very few communities appointed biracial committees, and Charlie and I were lucky to find even one city where we could gain entré. A special assistant on Governor Collins's staff had been working with a committee in Daytona Beach and introduced us to the chairman, a local undertaker, and the members. They had no objection to our attending their meetings and studying their work, but it was necessary to have the approval of the mayor and the City Commission. This was particularly important since we wanted to do survey research in both the white and black sectors of the community, and we proposed to employ both black and white interviewers. For their own protection they would require clearance by the police. Once again, I was thrust into the political arena, challenged to sell research to elected officials.

The mayor proved easy to work with, and we established a pleasant relationship. Another of my stereotypes was destroyed in the process. He operated a personal finance or small loan company. I learned from him that a so-called loan shark could be a very decent person, who actually provided a much-needed service for people who could not get conventional loans. Perhaps the fact that many of his clients were black accounted for his relatively liberal position on race relations.

The City Commission was a different proposition. So frightened were they of the issue of race relations that they violated the Florida "sunshine law" by having a secret meeting with me before our proposal was submitted for action at a public meeting. Two members gave me a very hard time. One was a Republican, representing many wealthy, conservative constituents. He was not only conservative in his views on race but also held a deep mistrust of social scientists. He stated that he felt the sort of research we wanted to do would not only be meaningless but also might stir up trouble in the community. As soon as he stated his position, he was joined by another member, a crude, conservative Democrat who had once been convicted of election fraud and had to have his civil rights restored in order to run for office again. Without explanation, he exclaimed. "I wouldn't touch this with a ten-foot pole!"

The other members, fortunately a majority, were not hostile but asked reasonable questions about exactly what it was we wanted to do. I did not know what the outcome would be when I left the illegal secret meeting, but it turned out to be favorable. When the commission held its official public meeting, I presented our request and the commission approved it with almost no discussion. Once under way, our research went well. In interviews with members of the biracial committee and while recruiting interviewers for our survey, I became acquainted with faculty and students at historic Bethune-Cookman College. One of our interviewers was the son of Mary McLeod Bethune. As I visited the campus, I was amazed to discover how the spirit of this great black woman haunted the campus, almost as if she were still its president. On every hand there were memorials to her; it seemed to me that nearly every classroom held a picture of her.

Even before all the results of our research were in, Grigg and I went after a larger grant. We went to New York to lay a proposal for a $100,000 grant before the Rockefeller Foundation. Success! We received the grant and went after our next research target, Jacksonville. It had not appointed a biracial committee, but negotiations were beginning between two leadership groups, one white and one black.

Jacksonville's approach stemmed from the initiative of two people in the Chamber of Commerce; it was a project of the business community, not of politicians. While the president of the chamber was on vacation in Scotland, he read in British newspapers of racial disorders in his home city. His reaction was one that many white southern business leaders eventually shared: "What is this kind of publicity going to do to business?" On his return, he conferred with a very shrewd and experienced staff member named E. Howard Hill. Howard, a recovered alcoholic, had in his tragic career been successful as a businessman, a public relations expert, and a lawyer, but now was working in a low-profile job. The two men came up with a plan to stimulate the formation of negotiating teams in the two communities, with Hill to be the liaison. The Chamber of Commerce board went along. When we came in with our sumptuous grant, we were able to work out a nice symbiotic relationship. We rented and furnished an office in downtown Jacksonville that would serve as a neutral ground for conferences between white and black leaders. At the same time, it would serve as our research headquarters while we observed the interaction between the leaders and carried out surveys in the city. For two years we kept a graduate research assistant in that office full-time, first William Stacey and then Henry Stewart. Both have had fruitful careers in sociology since those early days of their training.

Our subjects in Jacksonville were significantly different from the members of the biracial committee in Daytona Beach. They were not politically appointed, and they held no formal positions. Many of the whites were very powerful men who came in and out of the negotiating process in response to threatened crises. The blacks, while hardly radical, were nevertheless people who were creating the crises by their demands. One was the president of the Youth Council of the Jacksonville NAACP; whenever blacks demonstrated, he would be in the van. The young executive of the Jacksonville Urban League was active in a different way, but in spirit he was no less militant. He labored to solicit the financial support of the business community. He monitored the day-to-day needs of black citizens, and he sought to direct the efforts of the social welfare bureaucracy toward them. He also undertook to see that gains won by demonstrators were not lost. He once remarked, "I'm about to develop an ulcer eating hamburgers at integrated lunch counters!"

These two research projects resulted in a number of articles and a book; their success astounded Charlie and me. One article I can only regard as a "sleeper." In one of our attitude surveys in Jacksonville we include the Srole anomia scale; at the same time, we did a similar survey with a sample in Monticello, a small tobacco town not far from Tallahassee. The results, published in the article "Urbanism, Race and Anomia" in the *American Journal of Sociology*, received a lot of attention from sociologists because of our finding that blacks in the rural community had higher anomia scores than did those in Jacksonville, contrary to previous theories about the effects of urbanization on anomia. The recognition was gratifying, but I have often felt that this little project may have been a prime example of the questionable validity of much sociological research. First, despite its popularity I had serious doubts about exactly what the anomia scale represented. Second, as I spent most of my time in Tallahassee designing research and constructing instruments to be administered by interviewers I would never see, I wondered, as I do about most survey research, "How closely did the people in the field actually adhere to the sample design?" "Did they conduct the interviews the way I meant them to?" "Did they actually do all the interviews?" I remembered the chagrin of a famous sociologist I had known early in my career who discovered by accident that one of his field people in a large survey had faked all her interviews. He had to drop these protocols and complete the research with a flawed sample. The study was still published as a book and was highly acclaimed by other sociologists.

Despite the overwhelming popularity of survey research based on large samples, I have never been able to feel comfortable with data I did not collect myself, in the field. Obviously this bias has placed severe limitations on the kind of research I would do and rendered me a "soft sociologist" in a discipline in which large samples and quantification often seem to be defined as the only certain basis of knowledge.

As we began to get well into the Jacksonville research, Grigg and I saw the makings of a book summarizing what we felt we had learned so far. It started out almost as a "cut and paste" job. We planned to incorporate two already published articles and sections of several research reports we had done. The task of putting it all together fell to me. I was the chief writer in our team; Charlie was the statistician. He used to joke, "Lewis writes the conclusions and then I produce the statistics to support them!" As I started putting the material together, I found myself writing more and more original text with a theme that became the title of our book: *Racial Crisis in America*. The first chapter was entitled "Race Relations: An Era of Struggle" and the last turned out to have the ominous heading "The Specter of Conflict." The trend these two brackets enclosed reflected the pessimism I had felt more and more since the hope-filled days following the

Brown decision. Perhaps it was because of this pessimism, out of tune with the still-sanguine ideas of most of my fellow sociologists, that the book received so much attention. Some personal connections also helped. The first review was a lengthy article in the *New York Times Magazine*, written by one of their leading southern correspondents, Claude Sitton. He would later become editor of the *Raleigh News and Observer*, the paper that had become a symbol of southern liberalism under the editorship of Jonathan Daniels. The book came to Sitton's attention because of John A. Griffin, a friend on President Robert Strozier's staff at Florida State University.

John had been an invaluable editorial consultant while Grigg and I were writing the book. Shortly before it was published, he had a memorable party at his farm outside Tallahassee. He had assembled a group of eminent journalists to cut a tape for an educational radio program, to be entitled "Is There a New South?" John favored Charlie and me with an invitation to mix informally with a gathering that include Sitton; John Popham of the *Chattanooga Times*; Harry Ashmore, famous for his leadership in Little Rock; Harold Fleming, now with the Taconic Foundation; Bill Emerson, of *Newsweek*; and Ralph McGill, editor of the *Atlanta Constitution* and one of the most famous white southern liberals. Harold Martin tells of this party in his biography of McGill, including the fact that Ralph slipped away early because of discomfort, which proved to be the harbinger of a fatal heart condition.

Claude Sitton was lavish in his praise of our work. He found the pessimistic position we took convincing and recommended the book as a timely and much-needed warning that the course of racial integration was not going to be as steady and free of conflict as many observers believed. Harry Ashmore, who reviewed *Racial Crisis* in the *Washington Post*, was very critical, however. He found our pessimism unwarranted and alarmist; he implied that we were a couple of "nervous Nellies" who had just discovered that all progress involves some conflict.

What was so pessimistic about our conclusions? The sentiment was really mine more than Grigg's. I do not believe he ever shared it fully, even after the violent racial clashes of the late 1960s lent support to my predictions. After witnessing and studying the ameliorative efforts at conflict resolution of the Southern Regional Council, Governor Collins, and biracial committees, I had become a conflict theorist against all my liberal inclinations. I could not forget the statement made by one mayor in reply to a regionwide survey we conducted to find how widespread biracial committees had become. He wrote: "We are not appointing a biracial committee because we are already negotiating with black leaders. If they have no power, putting them on a committee won't give them any more. If they do have it, you don't need the committee."

In my research in Daytona I had concluded that the main function of biracial committees was what I called a "buffer function." If blacks created a crisis by challenging traditional practices, one way to defuse the crisis was by appointing a biracial committee and assuring the black leaders that their demands could be discussed. A primary condition, however, was that they stop pressing their demands through demonstrations. Thus the biracial committee was more likely to block or limit change than to produce progress.

This conclusion had a corollary with broader implications. I had been enthralled by the philosophy and practice of nonviolent resistance to evil preached by Martin Luther King, Jr. His call to "love your enemies into submission" seemed to epitomize a Christian strategy for social change. Yet, as I studied community strife in race relations, firsthand or through the press, I had a growing conviction that King's philosophy was not working as he hoped and perhaps believed. It appeared instead that it was the threat of creating disorder and thus hurting business that really moved white southern leaders to contemplate changes to meet the demands of blacks. Power was the principal asset in this game, and the ability to disrupt a community and give it a bad press through demonstrations, no matter how nonviolent, was a form of power possessed by militant blacks. Those diehard white resisters who met nonviolence with violence were unwitting allies of the blacks in such conflict. White moderates who sought to cool the conflict by entering into negotiations and making minor concessions and avoiding larger, graver issues were their most effective opponents. One of the things learned by many white leaders, such as those in Jacksonville, was the value of restraining white counterdemonstrators who could make headline news out of a parade or demonstration that might otherwise go unnoticed on the national scene. Hence, I concluded that what we were witnessing in the South was indeed conflict, even when it was muted, nonviolent, and triggered by actions allegedly inspired only by Christian love and a desire for justice.

Finally, our survey research in Daytona Beach led to a change in my thinking about integration as the paramount issue in the racial crisis of which we wrote. In our survey instrument, we had an open-ended question asking people to say what they thought were the greatest needs of the community and to rank those needs in importance. Both Grigg and I were truly surprised to find that while integration of the schools, public facilities, theaters, and the beach were mentioned by many black subjects, these were not what they saw as the greatest needs. The things they ranked highest were economic and material: more industry, higher wages, more jobs, better schools whether integrated or not, better roads in their neighborhoods, better housing, even "better Negro facilities." This strengthened my incipient belief that in the last analysis the problem of race relations in the United States was one of economic inequality, not of color prejudice or "racism." I began to understand the profound truth embodied in the question, first raised by Dick Gregory but taken up by King, "What good does it do a black to be able to sit at a lunch counter if he doesn't have the money to buy a hamburger?" While not relenting at all in my opposition to segregation, I began to see that the issue was primarily symbolic and of minor importance compared to the greater problem of class. It would be many years before I found much company in this position among blacks and white liberals, including many sociologists.

Our presentation of this part of our findings stimulated criticism in a review of our book by Tom Pettigrew, a friend and a social scientist philosophically dedicated to the notion that integration was a value with which there must be no compromise. He questioned the validity of our findings and suggested that we probably had not used black interviewers with black subjects and hence could not have expected them to come out strongly for integration. We were insulted by the naiveté that he, from the empyreal heights of Harvard University, imputed to us. In ensuing years I would disagree with Tom many times on such topics as Black Power, school busing, and affirmative action. Yet, I feel that despite our theoretical differences, we were able to remain friends and even allies in the struggle for racial democracy.

I also began to realize something even more important about integration as an overriding goal for blacks in the United States. As it was being preached, it constituted what Milton Gordon showed to be assimilation through "Anglo-conformity" in his book *Assimilation in American Life*, also published in 1964. We white liberals were arguing that blacks could and would become like middle-class white Americans if only the barrier of segregation were removed, as Gunnar Myrdal had proposed in *An American Dilemma*. There was a trace of bitterness in the words I wrote about the complexity of integration as a goal:

> The Negro is still faced with his ancient problem, the problem of being a black man in America, a white man's world. Here there is a rarely noticed identity between the premises of both white segregationists and white integrationists. The segregationist recognizes that it is a white man's world and frankly proposes to bar the Negro's entrance into it. The integrationist invites the Negro to enter it but assumes that it will remain the same white man's world. . . . At the present time, integration as a solution to the race problem demands that the Negro foreswear his identity as a Negro.

I had no idea that events would soon prove the validity of the last observation as the Black Power movement erupted to overshadow the assimilationist civil rights movement. In their book *Black Power*, Stokely Carmichael and Charles V. Hamilton quoted this passage from *Racial Crisis in America* with approbation in their analysis of the profound effects of white power—not just of segregation—on the black person's psyche.

Thus, while our little book received mixed reviews, it gained us ample publicity and consequent opportunities to be even more active in the field of race relations during the tense, uncertain years of the early 1960s. Charles Grigg and I, along with C.U. Smith, learned to play "the consultant game." In spite of the growing cynicism and despair expressed in my writings, I kept playing the role of a missionary preaching integration to white audiences.

The Southern Regional Council continued to call on me occasionally as one of its stable of consultants available to communities wanting advice on desegregation and tensions related to it. I particularly remember one session with a group in Columbia, South Carolina. It was the first time I can recall encountering the misconception held even by some white liberals that the NAACP constituted an "extremist" group equivalent to the Ku Klux Klan, at the other end of the spectrum. Apparently, these people were quite unaware of the Black Muslims and did not know that the Student Nonviolent Coordinating Committee (SNCC) arose in part out of what many young black activists regarded as the overcautious conservatism of the NAACP and the SCLC.

Grigg and I were also invited to serve as members of a consulting service provided by the National Association of City Managers. Sometimes we would team up with C.U. Smith and put on a three-man performance for conventions of city managers. Whether our "show" caused them to change their policies or not, we certainly entertained them. Charlie and I would speak as sober, concerned white sociologists giving them the benefit of the research we had done on problems of desegregation. Smith, very tall, handsome, and a humorous as well as dynamic speaker, talked from the perspective of a black man, saying, in effect, "Look, fellows, what we're asking for isn't really so much." One of his most effective illustrations was that of the black garbage collector who for years had ridden on the back of the truck, assisting a white driver. His punch line was, "Can you really blame this man for wanting to be able at last to ride in the cab?"

At first, we would have Grigg or me do the initial speech, with Smith taking the middle spot. Soon we realized that C.U. was so effective and entertaining that whatever followed was anti-climactic. After that we insisted that he be the final speaker. One of the most interesting consulting jobs was one I did alone. I was sent to Tampa by the city managers' association to advise the biracial committee the city had finally set up. This committee had gone so far as to employ a staff member to work full-time on anticipating and, if possible, reducing racial tensions in the city. The committee hired a young black businessman who headed a small but successful airconditioning firm. He was a college graduate and had been an army officer during the Korean conflict. After I was on the ground in Tampa, I deduced that he had asked the committee to hire me not so much to give advice but, as an outside expert, to urge on them some of his ideas.

Knowing this made me feel better about some remarks made by a black member of the committee named Perry Harvey, who was also a member of Governor Collins's statewide biracial committee. Harvey, a huge, powerful man, was the business manager of a longshoreman's union. I talked to him privately in his office, prior to meeting with the committee. The reception he gave me was a painful reminder that I was indeed working in the race relations industry. His first remark was, "I don't know why we're paying you $75 a day to come down here and tell us stuff I could tell the committee myself." Throughout our discussion, he would drop hints about the better uses he could find for the money the committee was paying me.

The real goal of my visit proved to be to encourage the committee to ask the City Council for money to fund a plan that their own community relations worker had already proposed. Alarmed by the hostility toward whites that he saw rising among black youths, he wanted authorization to recruit and pay a corps of responsible young black men who would identify, and help cool, potential hot spots. They would be on the alert for allegations that the police were not acting properly; they would cope with rumors. After listening patiently to him, and to me, the majority of the committee members still decided that things were not really that bad in Tampa and that they could not justify a request for the money needed.

A little over a year later, the committee was forced to eat its words. Racial violence did break out, for the reasons and in the areas where the staff member had foreseen it might. He received national publicity for organizing a corps of black youth called "white hats" because he gave them white construction helmets to wear on the streets. The city ended up paying much more for the "white hats" and the cost of the mini-riots than they were asked to put up in the first place.

My only direct challenge to segregation—not a bold or dramatic one—took place during a speaking engagement in Miami. This time, an association of nurses had asked me, C.U. Smith, and Victoria Warner, also of the Florida A and M faculty, to present a panel discussion of desegregation during one of the sessions at their annual convention. The three of us were good friends.

Although the Civil Rights Act of 1964 was still in the future, some hotels on the perimeter of the South were beginning to relax their rules against having black guests. Therefore, Chuck, Vicky, and I all had rooms reserved for us at the convention hotel. We checked in just after lunch, gave our program during the afternoon, and returned to our rooms after agreeing to meet in the dining room for dinner. A few minutes later, Chuck called me in my room to say, "Lewis, we've got a problem." He explained, "The hotel was sold recently; and the new owners have told the nurses they'll honor our room reservations, but aren't ready to serve blacks in the dining room. The association is protesting, and Vicky and I are going to wait for the outcome." He concluded, "You can go on and eat if you want to." I immediately replied, "I'll wait with you." He then said, "Come on down to my room—we've got a bottle of bourbon to enjoy while we wait!"

We waited and waited—it must have been nearly three hours, perhaps more. It is fortunate that we were not too drunk to get to the dining room when a call finally came informing us that the hotel management had relented: We were expected in the dining room. When we got to the door, it became obvious that it was Smith and Warner who were expected, not me. The headwaiter, correct but unsmiling, led them to a table without noticing that I was trailing behind. When we reached the table, he exclaimed, "You can't eat with them!" Chuck said, "Either he does or we don't eat." The manager must have been watching from the entrance, for he quickly appeared and precluded a "scene" by telling the headwaiter to seat us. We all ordered big, luscious steaks. I had never felt closer to my black friends than I did as we enjoyed our meal, trying to appear as casual as possible while conscious of the stares of the other diners. As we walked out of the dining room, Chuck remarked, "I hadn't thought of making a federal case out of eating here, but that steak would have been worth one!"

I thought of that headwaiter's exclamation, "You can't eat with them!" many times after the Civil Rights Act forced reluctant restaurateurs to serve black patrons. A story circulated, and I'm not sure if it is apocryphal, of a black man and his white friend who took a seat in a restaurant. The manager came over to their booth and declared, "I'll serve the nigger because the law says so, but it doesn't say I have to serve nigger lovers!"

The tremendous problem of the bad fit between changing national policies and local attitudes and practices was impressed on me when I served on a panel at an AFL-CIO regional meeting in Miami. Don Slaymon, educational director for the national union, presided. The other panelist was one of my heroes, Charles Morgan, Jr., already famous for having been ostracized and run out of Birmingham for taking a moderate position during the intense controversies there. The audience comprised business managers and officers of union locals from all over the South. Our task was to convince these local leaders that it was both feasible and in the best interests of their members to conform to the national union's liberal, inclusive policy on race. I don't think we were very persuasive, even though the audience was interested and courteous, as well as highly amused by Charles Morgan's folksy, southern style of speaking. Again it took the Civil Rights Act to provide these leaders with an incentive to catch up with their national leadership.

In my daily life in Tallahassee, and I was at home more than on the road, I was also reminded of how slowly changes at the top were reflected in communities, particularly in the South. Kay and my children lived from day to day with the controversies that kept the citizens of my home town constantly on edge, wondering when more "trouble" would erupt. It seemed to them that I was away most of the time.

Whether I was at home or not, Kay was very busy. She had been teaching in an elementary school since 1955; her work, feeding three children and chauffeuring them to after-school activities, left her little free time. After the hate calls in 1960, she had another reason to regret my frequent absences—the fear that more calls might come during a night when she was alone with the children.

Her school was all-white throughout her tenure, which ended in 1965. This suited the principal and most of the teachers fine; some of them said they would resign before teaching black children. It was an idle threat, for when the school was finally integrated, after Kay's departure, none of them carried through. Most of them were very dependent on their meager stipends. The $4400 a year that was Kay's top salary was a boon to us, but not a necessity. This made a great deal of difference in her relationship to the principal.

We suspected that he became unhappy about having her on his faculty after I achieved notoriety during the sit-in crisis. He never challenged her on the issue of desegregation, but he was a lazy and authoritarian administrator. With her high principles and her feeling of independence, Kay was very often the only teacher who would question his high-handed decisions, many of which resulted in more work for the teachers. She usually found herself with no support when she spoke up in a teachers' meeting. Much to her disgust, however, a few teachers would sidle up to her afterward and whisper, "I certainly agreed with what you said!"

While the *Brown* decision had no impact on the school for many years, another decision of the Supreme Court did, exacerbating the hostility between Kay and the principal. One of the high points of the day for him was the minute or so every morning when he or one of his staff recited a prayer, which was piped into every classroom. After the "prayer in schools" decision in *Engel v. Vitale* in 1962 the superintendent ordered this practice stopped throughout the school system. Kay openly expressed her delight at the ruling, for we both believed it was right. This was the last straw for the principal and he started making things worse and worse for her. At the end of her ninth year of teaching, she resigned, no doubt to his delight.

I will never know just how much my unpopularity with the segregationists in Tallahassee affected the lives of my children. They had thoroughly assimilated the inclusive attitudes that Kay and I had tried to teach them. They were ready to live by their principles, but they never became activists. Kit went away to college in 1961. She spent one year at an all-women's institution, Converse College, and then returned to Florida State University, living on campus until she graduated. During her first year, she did hear that the alumnae of a sorority that was considering her warned sorority members that her father was of questionable character, and a young Tallahassee man who dated her told her that an uncle had asked," Why are you going out with that commie's daughter?"

All three of our children graduated from Florida High School, the FSU demonstration school. There were no black students there while Kit attended; the first black to attend, a girl, entered during Lew's senior year. Our older son would have little contact with black peers until he entered the U.S. Military Academy. After his return from Vietnam he shared an apartment with another USMA "grad," LeRoy Outlaw, a captain in the field artillery who was black. Their accents were so similar that when we would call the apartment long-distance, we wouldn't know which one was answering the phone. LeRoy got a tremendous laugh when Kay would say, "Hello, this is your mother!"

Johnny, who graduated from high school in 1965, had the earliest experience with black friends. By the time he was playing varsity football and baseball, he was friendly with four fellow athletes who were black. We often sat with their parents at games. One young man, a "scat-back" for whom Johnny blocked as fullback, was particularly close to him. As graduation approached, Johnny decided he wanted to have a swimming party for a few friends and their dates. This was possible because we were partners in a neighborhood cooperative swimming pool. At the time, the public pools were closed because the city fathers did not want to integrate them. Johnny invited his black friend Keith to come to the party and bring his girl friend. The boy liked the idea but encountered stiff resistance from his parents. Fortunately, his father, a dean at Florida A and M University, was a friend of mine. Kay and I found a solution. We invited the dean and his wife to join us as chaperons for the party, and they accepted. As a result, we staged what was probably the first desegregated swimming party in Tallahassee.

During his last summer at home, Johnny had an experience that give him great insight into the grim realities of race relations. He decided to get a job and earn some money even if he had to work as a common laborer. His first job was at a black powder plant in a rural county south of Tallahassee. Not only was the job dirty and dangerous, but his fellow workers were truly sinister Florida Crackers who talked as if they were Ku Klux Klansmen, which some of them may well have been. He was not upset at all when he was laid off after two weeks. He promptly obtained another job as a laborer for a plumbing contractor, digging ditches and "tying iron." One of his fellow laborers was an old black man, old enough to draw social security but still compelled to work to support himself and his wife. My son was indignant when he learned that he, an inexperienced teenager, was earning as much as this veteran worker. In many conversations, he learned a great deal about the hardships this man had endured throughout his life.

We first began to follow the old southern custom of hiring a black woman to do housework when Kay started teaching. During the nine years that we did so, we were often reminded of how much we were still captives of traditional southern culture and our own upbringing. We sometimes were unwittingly offensive, as in the case of Margie's name.

One of our most faithful maids was Roberta. She enjoyed watching soap operas while she ironed. It was fortunate that my schedule was such that I could pick her up for work in time to get her to our house before her favorite shows started. She had refused to work for another family because they would not let her watch television. We rejoiced with Roberta when she married a man with a good job with the city, and we helped them purchase their first house. Even after we left Tallahassee, we exchanged Christmas cards for several years. She was added to our Christmas list which included my mother's devoted employee, Pearl, who had worked for her until Mother died. Every year, we sent a Christmas card and a check to Mrs. Pearl Easly, in Macon, until one year the envelope came back as undeliverable. She always replied with a barely literate "thank you" letter asking about our children and telling us a little about her life in retirement. The Old South died hard for blacks and whites who had loved each other even within the cage of white supremacy.

The racial scene in Tallahassee was still not peaceful. The public swimming pools were closed. There were many weeks when we discouraged our sons from attending movies because CORE had picket lines around the segregated theaters. Although Florida State University had finally admitted a few black students, off-campus establishments and downtown businesses were still segregated. Only after the passage of the Civil Rights Act of 1964 did the owners cave in, appearing almost relieved that they were no longer caught between civil rights demonstrators and segregationist customers. Now they could say, "It isn't my choice—it's the law."

As demands and opportunities arising from the national race relations industry took more and more of my energy, I became less active on the local scene. The activities of the Tallahassee Council on Human Relations seemed less meaningful to me as I saw militant blacks in CORE taking over more and more of the initiative in promoting change. I did work within the university to try to facilitate the integration of the new black students into the life of the institution.

With C.U. Smith, I embarked on a project, sponsored and funded by the Committee on Sociological Resources for Secondary Schools of the American Sociological Association, to produce a teaching unit entitled *Leadership in American Society: A Case-Study of Black Leadership*. It was one of a number of units designed for use in American high schools. To develop our unit, we enlisted the aid of social studies teachers in FSU and FAMU demonstration schools. There were some rumblings of discontent in the predominantly white high school when students were given material portraying Frederick Douglass, Booker T. Washington, W.E.B. DuBois, and Martin Luther King, Jr., as examples of great American leaders. The test of the materials went on, however, and our unit, completed with the aid of James M. Fendrich, a colleague at FSU who took over my role when I went on leave to UCLA in 1965, proved to be one of the most successful in nationwide tests. It was especially effective in stimulating interest among black students.

Just two months before the course of race relations would be changed by the passage of the 1964 Civil Rights Act, I was invited to be on the program of the annual forum of the National Conference on Social Welfare. The meeting was in Los Angeles. My topic was hardly specific; "Current Issues in Civil Rights."

Already, however, I was beginning to understand the changing nature of the problem and the issues. Foreseeing the imminent triumph of the civil rights movement, I declared, "There is growing evidence that no matter how successful the 'black bourgeoisie' may be in breaking down legal and traditional forms of segregation, the Negro masses are in danger of becoming an urban proletariat trapped behind economic and educational barriers." I did not realize then how great this danger was—the word *underclass* had not yet achieved currency—but I was talking about what would be the racial crisis of the 1980s.

One of the most memorable parts of my visit to Los Angeles was a luncheon for some of the speakers, hosted by Nathan Cohen, president of the National Conference. One of the guests was Whitney M. Young, Jr., recently appointed as executive director of the National Urban League. I had first met Whitney when he was dean of the School of Social Work at Atlanta University. During one of my visits to AU he had given me a guided tour of the black belt of Atlanta and filled me in on the black power structure in the city. After he went with the Urban League, he had visited our FSU research office in Jacksonville during a fund-raising campaign among the white businessmen of that city. Grigg and I had persuaded him to come to Tallahassee to discuss our research, and Kay and I had the honor of having him as our house guest.

Just before going to the Los Angeles conference, Whit had been testifying before congressional committees at hearings on the legislation that would become the foundation of President Lyndon Johnson's War on Poverty. We were all impressed by his observation that one of his hardest tasks was to convince congressmen that they should think of this legislation not as laws to help black people only, but to help all poor people. In a few months "Appalachian whites" would come to symbolize the poor white people he was talking about.

Whit also told an amusing and illuminating story of his introduction to New Rochelle, New York, where he and his wife, Margaret, moved when he took the job with the Urban League. Before taking office he was featured as their "man of the day" by the *New York Times*. A few days later, a delegation of white citizens of New Rochelle called on him to invite him to buy a house in that suburb. In spite of the fact that they really wanted to use him as a very acceptable token, he did buy in a previously all-white neighborhood. After moving in, he was horrified one evening when a strange white man came to his door and asked if he would be interested in joining the "white birch society." Conscious of the then prominent John Birch Society, his first reaction was that this must be an especially racist local branch whose representative had thought he was white. He was greatly relieved when the solicitor explained that the society was devoted to saving the white birch trees in the region!

In July 1964 Congress passed the most far-reaching civil rights act in the history of the nation. It and the events of the next two years would change both the pattern of race relations in the United States and my personal diagnosis of the course of black protest and white resistance.

At first, I shared with many other supporters of the civil rights movement the feelings of triumph at the passage of the act. I rejoiced to see segregation in public accommodations begin to crumble, at least in the urban South. I fervently hoped that the equal opportunity provisions of the law would quickly lead to more than token employment of blacks, particularly in academia.

One part of the act had a very personal impact on me. The non-controversial Title X created a federal Community Relations Service. Its mission was one of education and conciliation. Representatives would go into communities threatened by tension over desegregation and work quietly, often behind the scenes, to rally the forces advocating obedience to the law. Often individuals who desired peaceful progress toward compliance were so intimidated that they did not know who their allies were; CRS representatives would try to get them together. CRS was placed in the Department of Commerce, not the Department of Justice, to convince people that it was not a law-enforcement agency, but a conciliation service.

President Johnson asked former governor LeRoy Collins to be the director of this agency. Collins accepted, even though he was well aware that doing so might prove to be a political liability if he reentered Florida politics. He asked my good friend John A. Griffin to serve as his assistant. John immediately started recruiting a corps of consultants. Charles Grigg, C.U. Smith and I were among them.

Early in the autumn of 1964 this group of consultants met in Washington for an orientation and training session, which turned out to be another thrilling experience for me. When we all came together the first morning I met people I had known of for years as "white liberals," struggling to bring peace and justice to the South, but stigmatized by both their neighbors and the federal government. I felt almost as if I were part of an underground that had suddenly emerged from hiding. I knew that for many years J. Edgar Hoover's FBI and various intelligence agencies of the federal government had viewed the liberalism of any white southerner as a possible indication of subversive tendencies. While doing disaster research, I had been required to obtain the highest levels of security clearance from the Department of Defense and the Atomic Energy Commission. Friends who had been questioned by agents investigating me would tell me of the intense interest displayed in my interracial activities and my liberal views. According to some friends, even Kay was suspect. Now the federal government was paying the expenses of scores of people like me to come to Washington and was promising to pay us consultant fees and *per diem* for going into communities to represent it. While we would not work under the Department of Justice and were forbidden by law to reveal anything we discovered in a community to law-enforcement agencies, the Civil Rights Division did send Burke Marshall and

John Doar to speak to us about their role in enforcing the Civil Rights Act. With the victory of the civil rights movement, the race relations industry had become legitimate, no longer shady and suspect.

It was on my way home from this meeting that I came closest in my life to knowing what it is like to be black in America. For some reason, C.U. Smith and I were booked on the same flights to Atlanta and Tallahassee; Grigg didn't go back with us. During the flight to Atlanta we were concerned about reports of a hurricane that was approaching Florida's Gulf coast. When we landed about 7:00 p.m., there was a rainstorm over Atlanta, and we learned that all flights south were canceled. The latest weather reports indicated that the hurricane might hit our home town within the next hour or two.

Both of us had families waiting for us, and without hesitation we decided to rent a car and head south. As we drove farther south in Georgia, the night seemed to get darker and stormier. In a small town near Albany, we stopped at a filling station to change drivers—C.U. took the wheel. A minute or two later, as we drove through pitch-black darkness, he said, "Lewis, I don't want to scare you, but a car full of white men has been following us ever since we stopped back there." He may not have wanted to frighten me, but he assuredly did. I suddenly experienced the fear that so many black people, including my good friend, had known for so long. There was nothing we could do but proceed at a steady but legal speed, while C.U. kept his eye on the rearview mirror. We both thanked God when the car turned down a side road a few miles farther on. The rest of the journey was uneventful, but we remained tense. Not until we drove into Tallahassee and learned that the hurricane had passed to the west of the city did we relax.

As cynical as I am about sociology and its claims to being scientific, I have frequently felt that most of us complete research by reaffirming our preconceptions, even though we may have stated them as hypotheses to be tested. Nevertheless, I feel that the studies I conducted between 1957 and 1965 did produce surprises that cumulatively led to a major change in my assumptions about race relations. This shift in my attitudes would be as great as the one that led to my "conversion" from being an orthodox Cracker twenty-five years earlier. Now I would cease to be a liberal, optimistic integrationist and would view black-white relations from a pessimistic, radical, and pluralist perspective.

My life would also move in different geographical directions beginning in 1965. A year earlier, Ralph Turner had invited me to be a visiting professor at UCLA for the academic year 1965–1966. This would enable us to collaborate more easily on the second edition of *Collective Behavior*. Kit was graduating from Florida State in June 1965 and had already signed up to work for the army Special Services Division as a service club hostess in Germany. Lew had been accepted at West Point and would begin his plebe year in July. Johnny was just entering tenth grade, so it seemed to be an optimum time for him to interrupt his schooling at Florida High School for a year.

Kay, Johnny, and I planned to make a leisurely trip to California in August; except for my wartime travels, none of us had ever been west of the Mississippi River. As we were making preparations to be away for a year, I encountered my erstwhile enemy, the bank president who had tried to have me fired. He was now president of the Florida Senate. When I told him I was going to be away for a year, he exclaimed, "Oh, you're going to have a sabbatical." In spite of his political influence on higher education in the state, he did not even know that the universities in Florida did not offer their faculty members sabbatical leaves.

Even before leaving Tallahassee for Los Angeles, I had started writing a new book in race relations. It would reflect much more of a conflict approach than had *Racial Crisis in America*; I was already thinking of using the word *revolution* in the title. *The Negro Revolt* had already been preempted by Louis Lomax, and William Brink and Louis Harris had written *The Negro Revolution in America*. What I had in mind, however, was not what they meant by "revolution." In *To Be Equal* Whitney Young had written, "The Negro is in revolt today not to destroy the fabric of our society nor to seek an insulated compartment in it, but to enter into full partnership in that society". I would disagree with this also.

Most of the writing on my book would be done in Los Angeles, the locale of the latest of the "long, hot summers." The city was a new world for me and my family, and my work on the book would lead me into new ways of thinking about the future of black-white relations.

Chapter 11

THE COMING OF THE
REVOLUTION

A Right Wing Paradise—Visit to the White House
The Impossible Revolution?—A New South

The idea of looking at the black protest movement of the 1960s as truly a revolution came to me in the spring of 1965. I was preparing my notes for a class in race relations at FSU. Already intrigued by the expressions of black discontent with the amount of progress since the apparent victory of the civil rights movement, I noted that Martin Luther King, Jr., was speaking increasingly of appealing to a "higher law." "Higher than what?" I asked myself, "Had not the highest court in the nation interpreted the fundamental document, the Constitution, to give blacks full equality, and had not both the executive and legislative branches finally acted to implement the new interpretation?" To appeal beyond these authorities was the language of revolution. Blacks were no longer simply asking that the nation "complete the unfinished business of the American Revolution." They were no longer asking that the wayward South rejoin the rest of the nation. They were challenging the values and authority of the federal government; they were attacking white America, not just the Jim Crow South. I remembered that during the famous 1963 March on Washington John Lewis had been restrained by other civil rights leaders from asking in his speech, "I want to know: Which side is the federal government on?"

I had also been very interested in the story of Elijah Muhammed, Malcolm X, and the Lost-Found Nation of Islam in America, the so-called Black Muslims. When Whitney Young spoke to business leaders in Jacksonville when we had our office there, he warned them, "If you will not support organizations like the Urban League you may find that you will have to deal with the Black Muslims." I remembered this as a realistic warning of a major shift in the black protest movement if blacks found that even their moderate, nonviolent appeals for inclusion in American society were rebuffed. The events in Selma in the spring of 1965 convinced me that white resistance remained powerful and violent. Even though Martin Luther King, Jr., had received the Nobel Peace Prize in 1964, he still was no hero to most white Americans, and it was clear that in the South he was widely perceived as a subversive revolutionary. Then, as we were making our final preparations to move to Los Angeles, rebellion set Watts on Fire and frightened the nation. My mother-in-law called Kay to plead with us not to go to California; she was sure we wouldn't be safe. She could not have been more wrong, although we did not realize this until we arrived at our temporary home. I could not have found a more peaceful locale in which to write about revolution in America than Pacific Palisades, California.

Kay and I felt ourselves extremely fortunate that Arlene, the wife of our friend from Chapel Hill days, Harold Garfinkel, had found a house that we could rent near them and the Turners. All we knew about Pacific Palisades was that a number of UCLA faculty members lived there and that the name sounded pleasant. We did not know that Ronald Reagan, then a candidate for governor of California, lived there and that his political views were representative of the culture of the community. When Johnny registered to be in the tenth grade at "Pali High," we learned that it was almost a lily-white school. Little Florida High School in Tallahassee had more blacks among its 200 students than Pali did among its 2200. There was one Japanese-American boy on the football team. One of the team members' parents told us we were very fortunate to live in the "Pali" district because many other schools were much more "cosmopolitan." I had never before heard this term used as a synonym for "desegregated."

The first day I went shopping in Pacific Palisades, I was horrified to find racks in drugstores selling literature of the John Birch society. In Tallahassee one had to go to the American Opinion Bookshop to find this right-wing garbage. As Kay had the opportunity to meet some women who were not faculty wives, she found them reacting favorably to her southern accent; they were sure that she was a fellow conservative. They trotted out their anti-black prejudices and let her know how much they sympathized with the white people of the South, particularly since Watts had shown how terrible blacks really were. We heard rumors of how some white people in communities such as Palisades had armed themselves in case the blacks started to invade their territory. Kay quickly found herself limiting her social life to our UCLA friends.

Johnny found himself being stereotyped in another way. Big and strong for his fifteen years, he looked like the football player he was. He spoke with a slow southern drawl. Despite the fact that he earned an almost straight-A average in ninth grade, he was assigned to the lowest section of every subject he was to take. In only two or three weeks he was reassigned, after he convinced some of his teachers that he was being exposed to content that he had already covered the year before. His mathematics teacher was struggling to introduce the "new math." Johnny knew more about it than she did, having studied it the year before in a southern school that was obviously suspected of being inferior.

Despite this unexpected culture shock, Pacific Palisades was an idyllic spot in which to live and work. While Ralph and I did some work on our revision, my major effort was devoted to working on the book that I had now decided to call *The Impossible Revolution*. As I have said, the title *The Negro Revolution* had been preempted, although I felt that other people using this term did not believe it was truly a revolution. Reviewing their usages, I thought, "This is a revolution but one which most Americans don't believe could happen—even some who call it one. So why not call it the "impossible revolution"? Later, Peter Rose, editor of the Random House series in which the book appeared, persuaded me to add a question mark at the end.

I had hardly gotten my classes at UCLA under way when the race relations industry broke into my routine again. President Johnson had decided to call a White House Conference on race relations, to be devoted to the theme "To Fulfill These Rights." This phrase was derived from the theme of a similar conference called by President Truman, "To Secure These Rights." Now I found that through the good offices of John Griffin and Governor Collins, of the Community Relations Service, I was invited to participate in a *planning* conference for the main conference. I did not understand the difference at the time. It was enough for me that I received an invitation to the White House. The first event of the conference would be a greeting by the president in the East Room.

Once again, I felt that I had been invited to Olympus. Gathered in the East Room were not only old friends from the civil rights movement but also celebrities on whom I had never laid eyes, such as Vice-President Hubert Humphrey, the attorney general, and A. Phillip Randolph. Morris Abram, whom I had known at the University of Georgia, was very much in evidence as one of the co-chairs of the affair. Then LBJ made his entrance to welcome us to the conference. Afterward, I had the thrill of speaking to him personally during the reception that followed.

The work of the conference started the next day, at the Washington Hilton Hotel. At the first plenary session I realized that something was wrong. Randolph was to be the main speaker, but it was something said by Berl Bernhardt, executive director of the conference, that made headlines. One of the major events in race relations of the previous year had been the release of a report written by an assistant secretary of labor, Daniel Patrick Moynihan, *The Negro Family: The Case for National Action.* This report had been a major source of the inspiration for the conference. But on this occasion, Bernhardt, before introducing Randolph, declared facetiously, "I have been reliably informed that no such person as Daniel Patrick Moynihan exists!" What had been going on, I wondered?

I learned the answer later when I read the excellent book *The Moynihan Report: The Politics of Controversy,* coauthored by my former student, William L. Yancey, and Lee Rainwater. In the weeks before the November meeting, many blacks interpreted the report as an attack on the Negro family. This led to pressure on the White House to renounce it. Copies were not even among the literature made available to participants in the conferences, even though there was a section devoted to "the family" in which Moynihan was a participant. Most of the agenda papers given in that section were attacks on his report.

I was assigned to the section or "task force" on "The Community: Institutions and Social Action." In this, as in the other groups, the dominant tone was one of angry criticism of the federal government. It was demanded that the very administration that had called the conference do far more to help the black community—still called the "Negro community" in 1965.

A. Philip Randolph had opened the conference with a call for a $100 billion dollar "Freedom Budget" to abolish Negro ghettoes. Civil rights workers who had been brutally assaulted in the Deep South attacked the Department of Justice and the FBI for not having done more to protect them and bring their persecutors to justice. On every hand there was anger at the proposition that the Negro family was deteriorating. Hylan Lewis contributed an agenda paper in which he contended that Moynihan had portrayed all Negro families as being like the poorest, most disorganized segment. His was the most even-tempered, scholarly critique offered; many others were demagogic in style and content.

In my task force, Lawrence Landry, a militant black leader from Chicago, forcefully voiced the indignation felt by many blacks over the fact that President Johnson had reversed the decision of his commissioner of education to withhold federal funds from the Chicago school district. The commissioner had met Mayor Richard Daley in a head-on confrontation over school desegregation and had lost. Blacks felt that, once again, the party politics of powerful whites had been placed ahead of the welfare of blacks.

Another target, much to my surprise, was the federal anti-poverty program. Impatience with the slowness of the program to bring change to the ghettoes was coupled with outright rejection of government management. One black woman declared, "Just give the poor people in the ghetto the money; they know how to organize and use it." A black leader employed by the city of Los Angeles as a human relations worker suggested what amounted to a form of reparations. A really effective step to improve the economic condition of black Americans would be, he said, for General Motors to turn over one of its divisions, such as Chevrolet, to blacks! After a few minutes of discussion in this vein, Richard Cloward, who happened to be sitting next to me that day, said disgustedly, "This is unrealistic. No government is going to subsidize the creation of new political power in the nation." I thought at the moment, "How right he is. These people are talking revolution at a conference financed by the very government they are attacking!"

Landry was the angriest and most radical member of my task force. He even charged that the conference was being run by whites and Jews. What stuck with me most was an outburst in which he shouted, "The federal government is the enemy!" He had answered the question that John Lewis had not been permitted to ask publicly. I would use his assertion as a chapter heading in my book.

The press called the planning conference a failure, some reporters labeling it a "revolt against the White House." Obviously, the Johnson administration was gravely disappointed in the outcome. The full conference, "To Fulfill These Rights," held in June, was downplayed. Most of the social scientists invited to the planning conference, including me, were omitted from the guest list. SNCC boycotted the conference. CORE was represented by its new president, Floyd McKissick, who denounced the affair as a hoax. The race relations industry was being rejected as a helpmate to the black revolution.

I returned to Los Angeles even more convinced that I was going to be writing about a social movement that could now be properly termed a revolution. Some critics of the ideas Ralph Turner and I had advanced in *Collective Behavior* have given the impression that my writing in *The Impossible Revolution?* was independent of, or even contradictory to, our approach. On the contrary, one of my principal justifications for using the word *revolution* was Ralph's proposition that one of the most critical factors affecting the nature of a social movement is the public definition. My reading about different revolutions had brought home to me how often the stated goals and tactics of movements changed dramatically as the leaders encountered opposition to their initial, moderate demands for change. Frustrated reformers, loyal to the existing establishment, would become revolutionaries as they were rebuffed and reviled as subversive and disloyal. I had witnessed firsthand this sort of labeling of the civil rights movement by authorities and most of the white public in the South. Now I was becoming increasingly persuaded that there was little real sympathy in other regions for the plight of black Americans, and that most of the so-called gains of the movement had come as a consequence of coercive tactics that created embarrassing crises for presidents, who would rather have seen the issue go away. Now President Johnson, the most sympathetic occupant of the White House, was sending the message, "I didn't mean we'd go *that* far." Moreover, as CORE leaders were the first to charge, he was now giving higher priority to the war in Vietnam than to the promise to fulfill the rights of black Americans.

Events during the year following the planning conference reinforced my convictions. During the famous "Meredith March" through northern Mississippi, Stokely Carmichael shouted down Martin Luther King, Jr., with the slogan "Black Power." The Black Panther Party for Defense and Justice was formed in Oakland, California. SNCC and CORE excluded white members. Even King, while remaining faithful to his philosophy of nonviolence, was constrained to explain and even apologize for the violence that the new breed of black leaders advocated and that the crowds in the ghettoes sometimes perpetrated.

I was fortunate in being able to keep abreast of what was happening in black-white relations through reports by Jack Nelson, correspondent for the *Los Angeles Times*. I was pleased to find that this California newspaper employed a reporter who not only knew the South well but also very sensitive to the complexities of race relations. Later I learned that he was another white southerner whose blinders had been removed. I would meet him in 1987 at a conference in Oxford, Mississippi, "Covering the South," a reunion of reporters who had covered the civil rights movement. Nelson himself was the organizer.

Shortly after my return from Washington, I met the black writer who had preempted the title *The Negro Revolt*, Louis Lomax. We were both speakers at a UCLA student-faculty retreat in the mountains outside Los Angeles. He was flamboyant and at times demagogic, but I liked him personally and found that we shared many ideas about the black protest movement. He informed me that he had a nightly television program on one of the Los Angeles stations and would like to have me come and talk about the White House Planning Conference.

I was excited about the invitation, but should have been forewarned as to what might happen. Friends at UCLA told me how he came to have the program. Another channel carried a show hosted by Joe Pyne, an abrasive white journalist who loved to get liberals on his stage so he could berate them. He had invited Louis to be a guest one night and found that Lomax could not only take abuse, but could dish it out. The manager of a competing station was so impressed that he invited the black journalist to host a show of his own.

Louis did invite me to appear, though not in order to ridicule me. I made two long, late-night trips across Los Angeles to his studio only to find myself standing in long lines with other participants waiting to appear. When I finally made it to the stage after the second trip, less than five minutes remained on the program. Louis took up most of the time with his introduction, so I was able to utter only a few sentences that made no sense without some follow-up. I never saw Louis Lomax again, for he was killed in an automobile accident a few months later.

By the end of my year at UCLA, I had almost finished my book. Now I had a subtitle which was more descriptive than the title: *Black Power and the American Dream*. It was well that I had gotten so much done during the year, for I returned to a busy scene in Tallahassee. During my absence from Florida State University, Meyer Nimkoff, suffering from acute depression, had committed suicide. During the year, I had made a return visit to discuss assuming the chair of the department, which I agreed to do. Charles Grigg remained director of the now-flourishing Institute for Social Research and, soon after my return in the fall of 1966, took on the additional job of associate dean of the College of Arts and Sciences. We would both be very busy, for sociology was prospering at FSU, and we were deep into recruiting new faculty and graduate students.

Tallahassee was changing under the impact of the 1964 Civil Rights Act and the 1965 Voting Rights Act. Blacks were becoming more active in politics, registering and voting in greater numbers than ever. King Solomon Dupont, a Baptist minister who had been one of the "protest Leaders" during the bus boycott, made a strong, even though unsuccessful, try for election to the City Commission.

Under the threat of loss of federal funds, school districts throughout the state were at last beginning to desegregate—more than a decade after the Supreme Court had declared segregation unconstitutional. Johnny's football team now had several black members. Ironically, teams from some of the rural, "red-neck," counties had the greatest number of black players. Unlike the urban school districts, it was difficult for them to evade the spirit of the law by tokenism. With only two high schools, one white and one black, some counties found it legally and economically more feasible simply to close the black school. The athletic coaches were the first people to find profit in what was generally regarded as a deplorable necessity.

Still, things that were not so obvious were going on. Black children were still pioneers in the desegregated schools and were subject to untold numbers of slurs and harassments. The Florida High School football coach displayed a tag with a Confederate battle flag on his car, despite the fact that his black players and their parents might find it offensive. At least the team's nickname was the Demons (for demonstration school), not the Rebels. The traditional May festival had been abandoned because the public high school had been forced to admit black students. Many restaurants complied with the public accommodations clause of the Civil Rights Act, but a few tried to evade it by using the old northern device of calling themselves "clubs." One new, popular establishment had opened as "The Confederate Inn", but was now "The Confederate Club."

In spite of the progress being made toward desegregation I found C.U. Smith upset by some developments. On the one hand, many doors were now open to him that previously had been closed. The visibility he gained from his work with me on the research for the attorney general had promoted his fortunes both on his own campus and in off-campus interracial activities.

But on the FAMU campus he found a countercurrent—a growing spirit of black nationalism and separatism among the students. He felt himself under attack for "trying to be white." Even his style of dress was criticized, as middle-class black students began to adopt the denim uniform of lower-class blacks or the leather jackets of the Black Panthers, and as Afro hairstyles became popular. On more than one occasion he said to me in anguish, "These kids are throwing away all the things I fought for in the fifties."

Although I felt my two years as chair of the department at Florida State were generally successful, my proudest accomplishment involved Smith. Grigg and I succeeded in persuading the administration to appoint him Adjunct Professor of Sociology—the first black faculty member at the university, albeit a marginal one. He would continue in this status and over the years taught many classes in race relations on the predominantly white campus.

Chuck's appointment led to an amusing social incident. Since he was technically a member of the faculty, his wife, Marilyn, was entitled to belong to the Faculty Wives club, although she did not become active in it. When the time

for the annual spring dance sponsored by this club approached, some members
who had been active in the Council on Human Relations were determined that
the Smiths would attend. I am not sure how Marilyn felt about being an ice-
breaker, but C.U. jumped at the opportunity, for he was always ready to take
another step toward integration.

The committee of wives charged with finding a site for the dinner dance
found themselves faced with a serious problem. The dance had not been held on
the campus since the retirement of Doak Campbell, the staunchly conservative
Baptist president who would not tolerate alcohol at any faculty affair. The law
still prohibited serving alcoholic beverages on the campus, but the faculty was
now free to eat, drink, and dance merrily off campus. The large restaurants and
clubs that could accommodate the dance, including the American Legion Hall
and the Elks Club, were not interested in hosting an integrated dinner dance.
Finally, irony of ironies, the owners of the Confederate Club decided they
wanted the business badly enough to comply with the law and serve blacks.

The dance went off without incident. The faculty couples who were friends
of the Smiths had a large table together, and we really didn't care whether other
couples disapproved of our "socializing with blacks," as we were sure a few did.
What was amusing was the attention the white waitresses showed Chuck Smith.
The service he received was excellent. It appeared that there were sexual
overtones in their excessive attention, or so he suggested to me later. I agreed.

In January 1968 *The Impossible Revolution?* was published by Random House.
Prentice-Hall, publisher of *Racial Crisis in America*, was eager to have this book
as a sequel, but I found Peter Rose to be such a congenial, helpful editor that I
went with Random House. The book turned out to be more radical and
pessimistic than I would have predicted when I started writing it. It was almost
as if I ended up writing from the perspective of a Black Power advocate, and the
work proved more popular with blacks and white radicals than with some of my
liberal friends. Many years later, I would still get some satisfaction from a
statement by William Strickland, a black political scientist and ardent black
nationalist. In introducing me to an audience discussing the candidacy of Jesse
Jackson for the Democratic nomination in 1984, he said, "Many blacks will agree
with me that there have been few white scholars who understood the Black Power
movement as well as did Lewis Killian."

My being able to take the role of angry blacks was profitable, for many copies
of the book sold in black colleges. Yet I have always been deeply concerned over
why I was able to adopt this perspective so successfully. True, even before I saw
the black protest movement as a revolution, during the heyday of the civil rights
movement, some of my black friends had complimented me on my ability to see
things from their viewpoint. I seemed to be even better at understanding and
explaining the rejection by blacks of America as a white man's society. Was it

because I was still at heart a Cracker who felt uncomfortable with integration in spite of my professed belief in it as a value? Did I secretly feel relieved that there was not so much pressure for me to challenge my white friends now that so many blacks were implying that they really didn't want to mix with us? These doubts still haunt me. Certainly I developed a double consciousness during this period, still working for the goal of assimilation, but wondering all the while whether the black nationalists were not right in regarding it as an impossible dream. Nevertheless, I know that, deep in my heart, I still cherished the goal of a color-blind society, even though I knew that with my background I could never be completely color-blind myself. I was constantly reminded of this by the fact that Kay still found it easier to relate to black people simply as persons than I did. To do so remained an unusual but exhilarating experience for me.

As much as I loved the South, living in California for a year had been exciting. Had I been offered the opportunity to remain at UCLA, I would have been sorely tempted to accept. When I returned to Tallahassee, though, I fully expected to remain there for several more years. I thought I would occupy the chair of sociology for at least three years.

Except for the excursion to California, I had been tightly bound to Tallahassee for thirteen years. One bond was the welfare of my children. They were all happy and successful in school, and I did not want to dislocate them. But by 1966 Kit had graduated from college and had been working for the army in Germany for a year. Lew had completed his first year at West Point. Only Johnny held us in place.

Equally important as a tie to north Florida had been my feeling that it was my duty to remain in the South to do what I could to fight against segregation and discrimination. Now, as the ugly face of northern racism was bared and the black protest moved to New York, Boston, and Chicago, I felt that I could carry on the struggle elsewhere if I so desired. The South had not joined the nation, as optimistic liberals had hoped. It didn't need to. The rest of the nation had been shown to be no better than the South when it came to the treatment of black Americans.

I continued to be embattled after my return to FSU, but race was not the issue now. Just as things seemed to be going well in the department and the university, a crisis developed in the state's educational system. Support for the public elementary and secondary schools had been stagnating so that at the beginning of the school year hundreds of teachers had sent signed but undated letters resigning their jobs to the Florida Educational Association (FEA). The organization was not a union at that time, and there was no right for teachers or other state employees to strike. After a couple of months of the reign of Claude Kirk, the state's first Republican governor since Reconstruction, the situation had deteriorated to the point that the officers of FEA exercised their option to date and submit the letters of resignation to the county school boards. A de facto teachers' strike was under way.

I am sure that Kay would have gone out with the other teachers had she still been employed. Many of our friends did so, and we contributed to the relief fund that was started to help them meet their living expenses. There was no strike fund, for the FEA was not a union; and theoretically this was not a strike. The pressures, economic and social, on the teachers who had "resigned" were tremendous. For the first time in all my years in Tallahassee, I took part in a march on the capitol. We wanted to see the state and county school administrations meet the teachers' demands and rehire them.

I felt, as did many of my colleagues, that the faculty of Florida State University should come out very strongly in support of the calls for greater support for the schools. There was no doubt that conditions were deplorable. I knew of only a few faculty members who were not in sympathy with the teachers.

The politically sensitive university administration did not want to see the institution take a position that might anger the governor. In fact, the chancellor of the system had passed the word down that restraint should be shown. Charlie Grigg and I parted company on this issue. The president of the university was compelled to call a general faculty meeting because of the evident widespread concern. A small group of deans, including Charlie, got together before the meeting and drafted a resolution that was considered politically safe. I, in the meantime, had drawn up a much more strongly worded statement, which some of my friends agreed to support. When the general meeting was convened, the two resolutions became the subject of heated debate. Mine prevailed, much to the chagrin of the administrators.

My anger peaked during a conversation with the vice-president for academic affairs. The public schools were in danger of losing their accreditation because they were being staffed by "scab" teachers, many without licenses. The Grigg family was investigating a private school in Georgia to which they might send their sons. Plans for a new private school in Tallahassee were suddenly being brought to fruition. I was despairing of how I could recruit new faculty members in this sort of climate. The vice-president said blithely, "Just tell them they can enroll their children in the new private school."

Impulsively, I said to my secretary, "Find the last job offer I've gotten!" During the previous months I had received several invitations to apply for positions but had refused all of them. She came up with a letter from the University of Connecticut asking if I would be interested in applying for the headship of sociology. Now I dashed off a letter saying that I would consider the invitation if the position was still open. It was, and to the chagrin of Kay and Johnny, I entered into serious negotiations with "UConn."

That I would suddenly consider leaving the South surprised many people besides my family. After I made the decision to do so, Bob McGinnis, of Cornell, a former colleague at FSU now doing research on the mobility of sociologists, told me that I would be one of the last he would expect to move at this stage of my career. Guy Johnson, who had just retired from the University of North Carolina, told me that he wished he had known that I could be moved from Florida State. He also asked if I had been approached by the department at Chapel Hill at the time of his retirement and expressed disappointment that I had not. He said he had recommended me as his replacement in the field of race relations.

What were the factors, other than my anger at the way things were going in Florida, that entered my decision to accept the headship at Connecticut? As I have said, I had reached a point at which I no longer felt the compulsion to remain in the South that had bound me for so many years. Perhaps it was also that I had often fantasized that it would be romantic to live for a while in a Currier and Ives setting; at the time of my first interview at Storrs, the countryside was beautifully white. My assessment of the University of Connecticut as a growing, progressive institution was a major factor. Everett Hughes and David Riessman both commended it to me when I asked for their advice. The fact that the administration had a faculty council on human relations that dispensed funds for special projects in race relations seemed a good omen. In contrast to FSU, which appeared to be in retreat from the halcyon days of Bob Strozier's presidency, UConn looked like an institution that was willing to look ahead, not back. After I accepted the position there, I found reinforcement in the fact that, unbeknown to me during my candidacy, the Sociology Department had hired as a full professor John E. Leggett. I had met John briefly during my year in California, while he was at Berkeley, and I knew of his radicalism. I thought, "This is a bold administration that will take on a sociologist who is already notorious for his participation in the Free Speech movement and the grape strike in California."

In the few months after I announced my intention of leaving FSU, things there got worse. The teachers' strike ended in a draw; almost none of the teachers' demands were met, but all of them were allowed to return to work. Now, however, a crisis arose within the university. A student wrote a rather good short story for a student literary magazine, and it was accepted with the approval of the faculty advisers to the publication. The story involved a black veteran returning from Vietnam and included a great deal of black vernacular language, including "motherfucker." The issue was printed and appeared in the campus bookstore. In the meantime, a minor staff member involved in the technical production placed a copy on the president's desk, opened at the page with the offensive word. The president made a unilateral decision to have the student magazine withdrawn from circulation immediately. Within a day or two, the Free Speech Movement came to staid, traditional Tallahassee with the "Pig-Knife" controversy—that was the title of the short story. Once again, a majority of the faculty rose in protest, but the president was supported in his action by the Board of Regents, the local chamber of commerce, and many alumni.

The accumulation of anger over the teachers' strike and then the "Pig-Knife" issue put me in a good mood to say farewell to Tallahassee in August 1968. By now, Kit had returned from Germany, married an army officer, and moved to Alexandria, Virginia. Lew was returning to the Military Academy, and Johnny was enrolling at Cornell with the intention of majoring in biology and playing football. The pain of leaving many good friends of long standing, white and black, was eased by the excitement of entering on our great northern adventure, whatever it might hold for each of us. I would soon find that I had misjudged the University of Connecticut and would suffer great mental anguish as a result.

12   **TROUBLES AT THE NORTH**

New Challenges at Work—"Dow Off Campus"—Protests at
Sociology Meetings—Back to Race Relations

Storrs, Connecticut, I found, is not a town but one of a series of small centers
made picturesque by white-steepled churches, old houses, and taverns that look
colonial whether they are or not. The stone fences creeping up and down the
rolling hills sent me to my favorite collection of poems by Robert Frost. Kay and
I learned to tell the difference between a saltbox house and a garrison house, and
we spent happy afternoons exploring old graveyards with their quaint head-
stones. The weather was beautiful, and we eagerly awaited the advent of our first
New England autumn.

As always, it was exciting to make new friends. We also discovered old
friends in Storrs—Joe Zygmunt, who had also been a student of Herb Blumer at
Chicago, and John and Ellen Greene, whom I had known during army days in
Iran. Challenged by my new job, I was in a near-manic state. I wanted to be a good
leader and administrator at Storrs but also to involve myself with the sociologists
scattered about the branches of the university. They were technically members
of my department but were really very much out in the cold.

I was teaching one course and was committed to working on not one but two
books. Ralph Turner and I were still struggling with our long-overdue second
edition of *Collective Behavior*. Now, however, I was under contract to Random
House to write a volume on white southerners as an ethnic minority. Stimulated
by the ethnic revival going on in the world, Peter Rose had launched a series
called "Ethnic Groups in Comparative Perspective." I was intrigued when he
asked me if I could analyze my own people as an ethnic group. The venture was
made even more attractive by the fact that Peter was located only about fifty miles
away, at Smith College in Northampton, Massachusetts. I had enjoyed working
with him long-distance when he edited *The Impossible Revolution?*.

I was not facing up to the fact that I was over-committed, nor was I paying
sufficient attention to omens of possible trouble within the university and
particularly within my own department. What threatened involved race relations
only peripherally, even though these were the days of the Black Power move-

ment. Perhaps Florida State, despite the furor over the "Pig-Knife" issue, was too remote from the centers of campus rebellion for me to realize what might happen.

I should have gotten an inkling just before the beginning of the first semester, when I attended the American Sociological Association convention in Boston. Black-white relations were an issue during the meetings, and a Black Caucus had emerged in the association. It was not very much in evidence, however. Much more visible were the radical sociologists who were in a white-hot fury over U.S. involvement in Vietnam. At a plenary session, two of the speakers were Whitney Young, now with the Urban League, and Wilbur Cohen, Secretary of Health, Eduction, and Welfare in the Johnson administration. Young's speech was well received, but Cohen was the target of a radical protest. He was denounced from the floor as being "secretary of disease, ignorance and warfare." Many members of the audience stood with their backs to him throughout his address. This happened in Boston on the same night the police in Chicago were rioting against demonstrators outside the Democratic National Convention. The next day, at the business meeting of ASA, there was a flood of rhetoric aimed at President Johnson, Hubert Humphrey, and Mayor Daley. The society voted to move the 1969 convention from Chicago, where it was scheduled to meet.

It did not take me long after my return to Storrs to realize that the movement that had erupted in Boston was simmering on the UConn campus. There was a Students for a Democratic Society (SDS) chapter; John Leggett was soon meeting with them and regaled me with stories of their debates and their apparent inability to get anything started. John was smiling and jocular. A faculty member who was in his sixth year at UConn, David Colfax, seemed morose and preoccupied. He had not seemed so when I first interviewed for my job, but between that time and the fall, he had changed drastically. I was disposed to like him on the basis of our first contacts, and I was very interested in some research on school desegregation that he and some colleagues were just completing. Dave had been promoted to associate professor in his fifth year of employment, before he had to be considered for tenure. He seemed to be one of the rising young stars of the department.

I had to find out from one of his close friends what had caused the change in him. Alarmed and angry about the escalation of the Vietnam war, a position that was not unusual for an academic, he had burned his draft card in a demonstration in Hartford. The sequelae of this event were disastrous for Dave and the university. His draft board in Pennsylvania changed his classification to 1-A, even though he was thirty-two years old, married, and a father. He received hostile letters and telephone calls. Then, late one afternoon, an anonymous caller informed him that a bomb would go off in his house that evening. Dave sent Mickey, his wife, and the children to stay with a friend and called the state police to come to his house. According to my informant, when the officer arrived he showed no sympathy, but instead berated Dave for his political views. After an angry exchange of words, the patrolman "scratched off" in the gravel driveway, showering with rocks the man he was supposed to help. Dave picked up a stone and hurled it at the rear window of the car. He ended up under arrest and served a ten-day jail sentence for his actions.

The bomb threat was probably the work of a member of the Nazi-style Minutemen. Within a month after my arrival in Storrs, state and federal officers raided a house less than thirty miles away containing a small arsenal and quantities of Minuteman literature. Dave had good reason to be frightened; New England had its merchants of hate just as did the South.

Colfax and his associates in SDS, students and faculty, became more, not less, active in the face of public and official persecution. One proposal brought to me by some students involved race relations. It was ill conceived but caused me some momentary worry. SDS wanted the Department of Sociology to introduce a course taught by a black instructor immediately, but there were no blacks on our faculty. The student spokesman assured me that they had a candidate, a graduate student who had been a civil rights worker, who was available to teach as an adjunct. Although I had no idea how I would get authorization to hire him in case he presented even minimum academic quali-fications, I agreed to interview him. I did not want to appear to be a tradition-bound administrator unwilling to adjust to changing times, nor a white southern racist, so I did not reject the proposal out of hand, as impractical as it seemed.

The person who appeared in my office was a pleasant, not very well-spoken, seemingly confused young black man, who was a part-time student, not a graduate student at all. We had an interesting conversation about the civil rights movement, but it was evident that he had no interest in trying to teach a course. He indicated that he would be willing to talk about his experiences to an occasional class if invited. Apparently, he was an innocent pawn of white radicals attempting to strike a symbolic blow against what they perceived as racism.

Another project was bold and symbolic, but, I thought, feasible. Colfax and Jack Roach, a tenured faculty member, had been working with a black nationalist group in Hartford. With some white students, they were helping blacks renovate a rented building to serve as a community center. The project proposed to me would make the university a partner in the activities of the black group. The university would provide funds for a series of speakers who would appeal to blacks in the ghetto but would also speak on the Storrs campus. It would be a joint university-ghetto intellectual experience, although the ideational content would be radical. It was our hope that the University Council on Human Relations would help support the project financially. As department head, draped with academic respectability, I was to present the proposal.

The existence of the council, with funds at its disposal, seemed to indicate a commitment by the university to social action going beyond lip service and theoretical discussions. My meeting with the council was the beginning of my disillusionment with the faculty and administration that was so anxious to appear liberal. I received a courteous, attentive hearing from the assembled faculty members until I named some of the speakers who were being considered. One was Julius Lester. I knew little about him except that I had found his book *Look Out, Whitey, Black Power's Gonna Get Your Momma* helpful in understanding the Black Power movement while I was writing *The Impossible Revolution?*. His name evoked an angry outburst from a Jewish faculty member who had been identified to me as one of the leading faculty liberals and a favorite of the university president. He informed the council that in writing about the New York teachers' strike, Lester had made anti-Semitic statements and that he would have no part of providing him a speaking platform. All I could say was that as a white southerner I had long been accustomed to verbal assaults by blacks and that perhaps he too would have to get used to being one of their targets. He had, however, succeeded in smearing our proposal as irresponsible and perhaps dangerous. We received no promise of funds. When I got to know Julius a few years later at the University of Massachusetts, I realized that this brilliant writer would have been a serious, stimulating lecturer no matter how controversial his ideas. During the time I knew him, he was an outspoken critic of black anti-Semitism and ultimately became a convert to Judaism.

The first major crisis of the year would lead to further disillusionment, for it would force me into the position symbolized by Voltaire's declaration "I despise what you say but I will fight to the death for your right to say it." I found myself defending my radical colleagues, even though I found many of their words and acts personally distasteful and morally questionable.

The first eruption of what proved to be a year-long cataclysm came on a beautiful morning late in October. SDS members and allies, student and faculty, invaded a room where recruiters from Dow Chemical were interviewing students interested in employment with the manufacturer of napalm, among other products. The demonstrators announced that their intent was simply to debate with the recruiters about the morality of their work. The "debate" persisted until it constituted a disruption of the activity. The provost of the university appeared and invoked the authority of the Board of Trustees and the administration in ordering the demonstrators from the room. There was no question that he recognized many of the faculty members. The protesters withdrew slowly, with Colfax being one of the last to move toward the exit, engaging in an angry, defiant shouting match with the provost before he left.

He, Leggett, and Roach returned to the Sociology Department and informed me that I might expect them plus several other members of the sociology-anthropology faculty to be dismissed in view of what the provost had said. Although such was not the intention of the administration on that day, their prediction was partially accurate.

The conflicts during the ensuing months became a worse nightmare for me than my times of trials and troubles during the civil rights movement. Then I had felt that I knew on which side right lay. My doubts concerned strategy and tactics. Now I found myself on the horns of a moral dilemma. Still a reserve officer, with a son at West Point, loyal all my life to the nation for which my father had died, I had come slowly to question the rightness and wisdom of our intervention in Southeast Asia. While I could understand the nationalism of Ho Chi Minh, there was nothing about the philosophy nor the tactics of the North Vietnamese and the Viet Cong to lead me to view them as crusaders for freedom. Certainly I was not about to join the radicals in their demonstrations; but I saw enough merit in their arguments, and I felt sufficient empathy with their anger, to go a long way in defense of their right to protest. They, the administration and many faculty colleagues forced me to go a long way, indeed.

As in the early 1960s the process of polarization proceeded while I witnessed it from what had become no-man's land. Again, no middle ground was countenanced. The radicals were determined to continue their protests, and the interference they encountered drove them to bolder, deliberately outrageous actions. The administration was equally committed to stopping the demonstrations or reducing them to innocuous verbal protests. The viciousness of their actions also escalated.

The next big confrontation involved the Grumman Aircraft Company. By the time potential job applicants attempted to enter the small building where the recruiters waited to interview them, the demonstrators had completely blocked access. When a handful of campus police tried to clear a way to the door, they had to struggle hand-to-hand with some students. The next thing that happened was that a host of state patrolmen, armed with heavy billyclubs, descended on the crowd to disperse it and make arrests. I saw one sociology graduate student with blood running down his face from a head wound. Leggett and others were arrested, even though they were not in the crowd surrounding the building but were bystanders. John was not an entirely innocent bystander, for earlier in the morning he had harangued the crowd but had left to teach a class before the confrontation with the police. Then why had he been picked up later? Anticipating that there might be "trouble" on the campus that morning, state police forces had assembled in a state institution several miles from the campus to look at slides taken by police agents during previous demonstrations and meetings. Hence "agitators" such as John had been targeted in advance. Leggett was never prosecuted nor, so far as I know, were any of the other people arrested, but the message was clear: The "establishment" in Connecticut was prepared to use brutal, police-state tactics to repress dissent that went beyond words.

There were more demonstrations at recruiting sites, then a "strike" to shut down classes for a day, and finally the occupation of the Executive Office Building for several days. No one else was physically injured, though. The demonstrators became more scrupulously nonviolent in their confrontations with the authorities, and the police no longer used their clubs.

I was still disgusted by some of the tactics of the protesters. While I was all for free speech, I found the "filthy speech" puerile and nauseating. Some student speakers shouted "fuck" so often you would have thought their generation invented sex. A philosophy professor announced that he was going to pour gasoline on a dog and burn it to death in the middle of the campus. He would show, he said, that many Americans would get more upset over the burning of a dog in the United States than over the burning of people in Vietnam. He was right, for the response to his announcement was sufficiently strong to cause him to desist.

Some events had an amusing aspect, although even these redounded to the disadvantage of the perpetrators. Few people caught up in the controversy had any sense of humor left. Both incidents that I remember involved Jack Roach. During a demonstration outside the Executive Building, a television cameraman kept focusing on Jack. He appealed to the newsman to stop his intensive coverage of his activities. Finally he got rid of the unwanted attention by starting to "moon" the camera.

Another demonstration took place while the Board of Trustees was meeting in a closed session in the same building. By this time, there was widespread speculation that the board might be considering disciplinary action against the three sociology professors; they had become symbols of resistance. The secrecy of the board proceedings had itself become an issue for the protesters. During the course of this meeting, a security guard came out and told Roach that the board would like him to appear before them. Jack told the messenger, "Tell the board they can go fuck themselves!" Apparently the guard relayed the message verbatim to the board, for it was later used as one justification for disciplinary action.

The controversy divided faculty, students, and the department itself. Faculty meetings became ordeals. Old wounds, supposedly healed before I took the headship, were reopened. Old slanders, long ago disproved, were repeated. Worst for me was the attitude of Colfax, Roach, and Leggett. One day they met with me to say that even though they liked me and thought I was a good head, they had decided that they must destroy the University of Connecticut, beginning with the Department of Sociology and Anthropology. I had no fear that they would be able to destroy either, but they did make the task of building a better department more difficult. As a new head, I was eager to fill the faculty positions that had been made available to me by the dean. Whenever we brought a candidate to the campus for an interview, they insisted on taking him aside and telling him all that was wrong with the university.

SDS had prepared elaborate charts showing the involvement of UConn with the military-industrial complex through its investments and through research contracts and grants. Whether companies producing supplies for the military would continue to recruit on campus remained the basic issue. The administration was unyielding in its policy of continuing the traditional practice not only of permitting recruiting but also of providing space for the activity. An anthropologist, Norman Chance, had been employed as a full professor at the same time I was with the understanding that the following year he would become head of a newly formed, independent Department of Anthropology. In a sense we were co-heads for the year. Concerned to prevent further damage to the existing department, we undertook the futile mission of serving as mediators. We finally came up with a proposal to which Leggett, Roach, and Colfax gave assent, although we had no way of knowing how well they could sell it to their SDS compatriots, who shifted from day to day before the winds of participatory democracy. At least we thought our idea might serve as a talking point for the initiation of a dialogue between the protesters and the administration. Our suggestion was to remove from the campus all recruiting by outside agencies, even the Peace Corps. We felt that a case could be made that agencies wishing to recruit employees could be asked to pay the cost of renting "hiring halls" off campus. The fact that the university had always provided the space did not mean that the practice couldn't be changed for the sake of restoring harmony within the institution.

Norman and I received no response to our suggestion from the administration, but only requests to bring our defiant faculty members to their senses. The message seemed clear: If they would stop encouraging protests, all would be forgiven. I'm not sure this was true, for I came to distrust the administrators and to suspect that the business people on the Board of Trustees were really calling the plays. Neither Norman nor I wanted to become or even appear to become mere agents of the authorities, despite our dual identities as both heads and faculty members.

There were several items when I was convinced that administrators were lying to me. My clearest sense of betrayal came when Norman and I were informed by our dean that representatives of the Board of Trustees were willing to talk to us before reaching a decision as to what actions they would take toward dissident faculty members. We thought we were finally making progress as mediators. Told to meet the representatives at the Faculty Club, we proceeded there, followed by a small crowd of protesters, including the three from sociology. When we entered the club, we found the dean and another member of the administration waiting. They informed us that the board had already concluded its deliberations and adjourned. Then they insulted us by suggesting that we could slip out a back door and thus avoid facing the group that was eagerly awaiting the results of our "negotiations." Indignant, we declined their offer and went out to face the disappointed insurgents.

Perhaps it was at this point that I began to doubt the wisdom of remaining at the University of Connecticut, although the unending controversy had already begun to make me almost physically ill. I still think of the bitter joke of an administrator at another university, who asked a fellow dean, "Do you throw up before breakfast or after?" Many times I had asked myself, "What am I doing in the middle of this mess—these are not my people?"

I seriously considered an offer from Tufts University but decided against that move. When Peter Rose discovered that I might be moved, he passed the word to Everett Lee, then chair at the University of Massachusetts. I was invited to interview there and commenced the process. On the day I was to go for a final interview, I awakened to a heavy snowfall. Still torn by doubts about whether to wash my hands of the department at UConn, I took the bad driving conditions as a sign that I should stay put, so I withdrew from my negotiations with UMass.

In the meantime, ironically, I had been busy preparing a recommendation for tenure for David Colfax. I could not overlook the fact that just two years before, he had been deemed worthy of a promotion. I knew he was a popular teacher. After his promotion, he had continued to be active in research, although the administration tried to convince me that it was his colleagues, not he, who had been doing the work. He had not been actually charged with any professional misconduct, nor had he been convicted of any crime since the misdemeanor of throwing the rock at the patrol car. Hence I decided to write a positive recommendation.

A short time later, the administration and the board acted. The College of Arts and Sciences "took care" of Colfax. The Dean's advisory committee turned down my recommendation on the grounds that Dave was not academically qualified. Leggett's case was simple; his appointment, like my own, did not include tenure for the first year, so it was not renewed.

Jack Roach presented a more complex case. He already had tenure as an associate professor. No personnel action was pending for him, unless he was to be given a raise or a promotion, both very unlikely. In his case, the Board of Trustees took an unprecedented and incomprehensible action: They declared that he was on indefinite probation, forbidden to say or do anything that might disrupt the university. He remained on probation, receiving no promotion and no raises for seven years, until he won a suit against the Board in a federal court. He was retroactively promoted and awarded pay increases.

I was just about to go to my first Eastern Sociological Society meetings and, in August, I would be attending the ASA meetings. At this point, I concluded that I could not defend the administration's actions before my colleagues in the profession of sociology. I knew I would be called on to do so if I remained as head. That day, I called the University of Massachusetts and asked if I could reopen my negotiations with them. In a very short time I was given an appointment in Amherst as full professor with tenure, with the understanding that I would not be asked to serve as chair of the department. I submitted a brief and simple letter of resignation to my dean at UConn.

Once again, Kay and I prepared to move north—but this time by only forty-two miles. By June we had purchased a home in Amherst and were ready to move in by early July. We were both eager to leave Storrs, Kay even more than I. I recall my year at the University of Connecticut with little pleasure and a great deal of pain. I felt that I had failed in the mission of building a better department there, and I wondered if I had "chickened out" too soon. There were times when I asked myself, "Did I let the radicals intimidate me? Did I go too far in my defense of their right to continue their protests?" Such doubts were accentuated by the realization that I had enjoyed my new reputation as a somewhat radical sociologist, acquired after the publication of *The Impossible Revolution?*. Had I been afraid that if I cooperated too much with the administration, I might be denounced as merely another southern conservative who had been misjudged? I will never know the answers to my questions, but I knew that I was relieved to be out of a no-win situation.

In the meantime, I was kept busy with professional activities. I was able to concentrate now on writing *White Southerners*. Moreover, I was scheduled to be the author on "The Author Meets the Critics" session at the eastern meetings. *The Impossible Revolution?* already selling at an encouraging rate, was the topic. Although the session was thoroughly enjoyable, I remember little about it except the praise given my work by a young black sociologist who would soon be my colleague at UMass, William Julius Wilson. This was the beginning of a long, rewarding relationship, personal and professional.

Like the ASA meetings of the previous summer, the Eastern Sociological Society convention was made exciting by outbursts of "insurgent sociologists." One episode reached the heights of absurdity while demonstrating how much of the insurgent activity was expressive, not instrumental. Several sessions were organized as "rap sessions," rather than conventional "papers sessions." In the spirit of participatory democracy, a theme was announced, but there was no presider, no speakers, and not even any chairs in the meeting room. I went to one such session with the theme of race relations. The most active participants sat in a circle on the floor, while the rest of us stood around them. Their awkward attempts to focus on the theme were not helped by the actions of a student from the Boston area who, I was told, was known there as "The Ghost." He wandered around the room interrupting the discussion by announcing loudly, "They leave their mothers in the Bronx and go to college and fuck!" This would get some laughs and an occasional expression of agreement that student radicalism was not really serious, but it did not advance the discussion of the theme. Finally, a young black man, one of the few blacks in the room, stood up and said, "You white radicals aren't serious—if you were, the first thing you'd do would be to throw 'The Ghost' out and get on with your rap!" At this point, several white sociologists seized the offender and started to evict him physically, tearing his coat in the process. The "rap session" ended in chaos.

At the American Sociological Association meetings in San Francisco the following August, the self-styled insurgents were even more disruptive. Again, the issue was the conflict in Vietnam, not race relations. The spirit of Black Power was very much in evidence, however. A few black sociologists whom I had known by other names appeared on the program with new African or Arabic names. During some sessions, Black Panthers from the San Francisco Bay area were present in berets and black leather jackets. The Black Caucus, just becoming active the year before in Boston, now evolved into the Association of Black Sociologists, and a group of black members staged a conspicuous walk-out during the business meeting. C.U. Smith refused to join them. He told me later that he had fought too hard to create a racially inclusive society to join a group that was exclusive, even if it were black. Within a few years he would take the lead in forming the Section on Racial and Ethnic Minorities in the ASA. I was proud to be associated with him in this endeavor and was a charter member of the section.

The disruption of the convention came on the night of the plenary session, at which the president gave his address. Ralph Turner was president. Ironically, his topic was "The Public Perception of Protest." On the day of the session the news came that Ho Chi Minh had died. Just as we were convening in one of the ballrooms, in marched a group of insurgent sociologists, led by a woman, Carol Brown, with Dave Colfax close behind her. They seized the podium and the microphone and announced that it was not fitting that sociologists should continue with "business as usual" when a great world leader had died. They would, instead, conduct a memorial session to honor Ho Chi Minh.

Pandemonium reigned for a few minutes. There were expressions of support for the demonstrators but more shouts of anger at them. One woman started singing "God Bless America." Brown continued to read a prepared speech despite the din.

Ralph reacted quickly. He made no effort to challenge the protesters but arranged with the hotel management to have another ballroom set up for the session as quickly as possible. In about half an hour someone shouted the announcement that the plenary session would start immediately in the new room. Now I found myself in a novel role. Lest the demonstrators attempt to again deny Ralph his platform, some of his friends organized a bodyguard. Three or four sociologists—one of them, I remember, was Dick Hill of the University of Oregon—stood at the door. Allen Grimshaw, of Indiana, and I stationed ourselves near the podium to protect the microphone in case any of the insurgents got through the door. No such attempt was made, however. While the protesters droned on with their memorial, before a dwindling audience, Turner gave his presidential address to a packed room.

Ralph told me that shortly after he returned to Los Angeles, one of his graduate students called him to say that he had been among the disrupters of his session. He wanted to reassure his professor that there was nothing personal about his actions, that he was acting purely on principle. Ralph informed him that he could not accept this as an apology. For him, he said, this was a once-in-a-lifetime event and that there was no way he could take it but personally. I was reminded of the assurance of my three faculty members that they thought I was a great guy but, as a matter of principle, they had to try to destroy my department. It is real individuals who are hurt by actions taken for great, abstract causes, and none of us likes to be told that we are expendable.

Even before the fall semester began at the University of Massachusetts, I was able to become involved with race relations again. Peter Rose was conducting a summer institute for junior bank executives. He invited me to participate as a discussant in a session where one of the speakers was Robert Allen, a black nationalist with a Ph.D. in economics. He was one of the leaders of the Black Economic Development Conference, the body which had produced the "Black Manifesto" read by James Forman from the steps of Riverside Church in New York a few weeks previously. It was a demand for reparations to be paid to the black community by the churches of America. Allen spoke eloquently and presented impressive statistics on discrimination and its consequences, but his nationalist solution went too far for me or the bankers. He argued seriously for the establishment of a black "Republic of New Africa" in five states of the southern United States; all assets, public and private, would be expropriated and turned over to the new government. A year or two before I had heard Milton Henry, a militant black from Detroit, argue for such a separatist solution to the nation's racial problems. He did so with angry rhetoric, surrounded by fierce-looking bodyguards dressed in African garb, as was he. It was something quite different to hear the proposal advance by an obviously well-trained economist dressed in a business suit. My task as a discussant was easy; I had no difficulty in pointing out the impracticality of his ideas. "Hamming it up" a little, I did draw on my southern background to explain that it would be quite out of character for white southerners meekly to obey an order of the federal government to give up their property. It was good to be engaged again in a discussion, no matter how bizarre, of something other than the Vietnam issue. It was also interesting to observe the reactions of a group of fairly conservative whites to this extreme expression of black nationalism.

An amusing by-product of James Forman's attempt to seize the pulpit of Riverside Church occurred at the Episcopal church in Amherst that summer. On one of the first Sundays Kay and I attended service, an Amherst college student suddenly rose in the middle of the liturgy and marched to the front of the church, accompanied by a young black man. He announced that his black friend wanted to read a manifesto against racism. I don't remember the content of the message, but I do remember how silly the two young men appeared when no one, clergy or laity, offered any challenge to their "seizure" of the chancel. After being heard politely, they marched out of the church and the service continued. Perhaps they got some personal satisfaction from trying to imitate Forman, but they had little or no impact on a congregation that already considered itself very liberal. A wealthy parishioner had even paid the rector's way to fly to Selma in 1965 to join the famous march for a day.

Early in the fall I would speak from the pulpit of this church, but at the behest of the rector. After protests at the General Convention by black churchmen supporting the BEDC's demand for reparation, the national church had decided to take up a special collection to be used for the betterment of race relations. This was not a satisfactory response to the demands, for the money was not to come from the budget of the church but only from whatever funds the special collection produced, and it was not to be turned over to BEDC but dispensed by the church itself. Our rector apparently did not feel equal to the task of making a plea for these funds, and having learned of my background in race relations, asked me to do the job. I never got any feedback from my talk and was never even informed how much money the parishioners put in the collection plate that Sunday. I felt my plea was quite eloquent, elucidating the need for black pride and self-determination as well as the justification for some sort of recompense to blacks for past injustices. In explaining why the BEDC had asked that the money be turned over to them rather than dispensed by a white or even an interracial agency, I quoted the line from a then-popular advertisement, "Mother, I'd rather do it myself!" Regardless of what I may or may not have accomplished, I found it highly amusing that I, with my deep southern accent, should be the one to preach to a liberal "Yankee" audience on what they owed to blacks.

When the fall semester opened at the University of Massachusetts, I found myself in a very different milieu from the one at Storrs. The Vietnam conflict was an issue, but race relations loomed even larger. The year before, black students had seized an integrated dormitory and moved the white occupants and their belongings into the street. Rather than confront the black students with police power, the administration had negotiated a settlement with them. All the students, black and white, were reassigned to other dormitories, and the building was renamed New Africa House. It would serve as an Afro-American cultural center and would house the newly created W.E.B. DuBois Department of Afro-American Studies. Over the years I would get to know several members of the faculty of this department and eventually would become an adjunct professor in it, but this first year I was just another white professor on a campus where the spirit of black nationalism was strong. During the next year I would feel that I had changed from a "nigger lover," as I had been known in the South, to just another "honkie."

13 ON BEING A HONKIE

*Teaching About Black Power—Encountering Black
Hatred—A Comparative Perspective*

The academic year 1969–1970 was one of intense interest in race relations, but also one of strong passions. Many blacks openly displayed their hatred of "honkies," as whites were called after Stokely Carmichael popularized the epithet. An amazing number of white students seemed to revel in an orgy of self-hatred. White coeds walked about campuses proudly displaying their copies of Eldridge Cleaver's *Soul on Ice*, in which he described how he vented his rage at white America by raping white women. Walls were plastered with pictures of Huey Newton, head of the Black Panthers, with black beret and submachine gun; the slogans read, *Free Huey*! Bobby Seale, another Panther leader, sat bound and gagged in a Chicago federal courtroom during the trial of the "Chicago 8" for alleged conspiracy to cause the riots during the 1968 Democratic convention. In September Angela Davis was appointed to the faculty at UCLA; the Board of Regents tried to fire her when she proudly admitted to membership in the Communist party. A federal court stopped them, but the administration of Governor Ronald Reagan continued to seek ways to get rid of her. While the Black Panthers thrilled many black college students and their white sympathizers, they frightened other Americans including "the pigs": the federal, state, and local police forces. Although we did not know it then, the federal police conspiracy, COINTELPRO, was counterattacking against revolutionary black nationalism with informers and agents provocateur.

Given such a milieu it is not surprising that my first class in race relations at the University of Massachusetts contained 475 students. Bill Wilson taught another section of the same course with an enrollment of 250. This was one of the most popular courses in the curriculum, eagerly sought by idealistic and angry young people, who hoped they might find some clues as to how to save the world or, at least, take vengeance on "the establishment." The large enrollment in my section was accounted for partly by advantageous scheduling but also by the fact that my reputation had preceded me to Amherst. The previous year *The Impossible Revolution?* had been used in some large introductory sociology classes. According to Wilson, many UMass students thought I was black.

As usual in any course, the first week was marked by "drops and adds." I will always wonder how many of the drops occurred when students discovered that I was not black but a "honkie" with a southern accent. I know that over the years some students did drop the course for just this reason. One black woman was honest enough to come to me at the end of the first class and say, "I'm dropping this class because I don't think I can learn anything about race relations from a white person with your accent." I persuaded her to wait to hear my first couple of lectures before withdrawing. She did, and remained in the class.

I surprised her and many other students with my sympathetic interpretation of black nationalism. Apparently, I did, in the jargon of the day, "dig" the Black Power movement, but I still wonder why I did. Was it that I had developed, in my sociological training and experience, an unusual ability to "take the role of the other"? Having been converted from white supremacist orthodoxy, did my new vision enable me to see with extraordinary clarity the pain we had inflicted on black people? This interpretation would go directly against one of the major tenets of black nationalism: that no white can ever understand how it feels to be black.

After the Black Power movement overshadowed the theme "black and white together," I was bewildered and bereft, as were many white liberals. Blacks were telling us they did not want to be, indeed could not be, our brothers and sisters. We did not have *soul*! Integration was a meaningless goal, and white liberals were especially hated because we had teased them with the promise but were not willing to "go all the way." A political scientist at Smith College, Stanley Rothman, may have come closest to explaining my position in his comments on an essay on white southerners that I wrote for *Through Different Eyes*, edited by him, Peter Rose and William J. Wilson. Rothman observed:

> The essay by Lewis Killian, although concerned primarily with Southerners, catches the poignancy of the liberal dilemma quite well. He himself now feels, albeit reluctantly, that, given the impossibility of meaningful integration, he must become a white supporter of black nationalist aspirations.

Even accepting Rothman's analysis of my sympathy for black nationalism, I still wonder why I embraced it so enthusiastically, as I feel I did. Was it that it gave me some distinction among sociologists or that it garnered respect from blacks who would reject me as a liberal integrationist? One of the epithets directed at whitewardly mobile blacks during this era was "Oreo"—black on the outside, white on the inside. I often asked myself, "What do you call the white counterpart of an Oreo, and what makes one?" I knew what white segregationists would call me—a "nigger lover"—but to my black friends I was a different kind of "honkie," even though I could not be a "soul brother."

I struggled with such self-questioning as I prepared lectures for my huge class and then found myself eloquently explaining the spirit of black nationalism to a predominantly white audience. This would be the largest class I would ever teach, although the course drew from 150 to 250 students for the next three or four years. Then the classes began to dwindle, not because I had lost my fire but because students began to think more about how they would make a living than how they could improve humanity's lot. The black students who still hungered for courses in race relations usually took them in the Afro-American Studies Department, where the spirit of black nationalism survived even after the Black Power movement had faded. Other black students, like white ones, were flocking to the School of Business. These doldrums of social reform from the campus were several years away, however, as I began a new phase of my career in the Pioneer Valley of western Massachusetts.

My ill-deserved reputation as a radical opened other doors in Amherst. Not long after I began to get the lay of the land, I was called by another faculty member already known to me by reputation. He invited me to join a "radical faculty association." I knew that he was from a group almost totally preoccupied with the issue of Vietnam and blindly committed to doctrinaire Marxism. I declined his invitation by saying that I wasn't sure I would fit their definition of *radical*.

I also found myself on the invitation list for black speakers brought to the campus by the students' Distinguished Visitors Program. It was at a dinner honoring Claude Brown, author of *Manchild in the Promised Land*, that I really felt most like a "honkie." Kay and I attended the dinner at the Lord Jeffrey Amherst Inn and found ourselves part of a small minority of whites. The atmosphere was frigid, and at times we noticed glances that appeared hostile. We were sitting within easy hearing distance of Brown and a member of the Afro-American Studies faculty, Michael Thelwell. "Mike," as we eventually came to know him, wore an expensive suit with a bush jacket; throughout much of the meal he toyed with a miniature scimitar he always carried. We could overhear his conversation with the guest of honor, but there was no way we could become part of it. It did not take me long after this encounter to find out all I could about Thelwell. He was Jamaican, and although he had lived in the United States since the early 1960s and was seeking citizenship, he was still being harassed by the Immigration and Naturalization Service. He was one of the early members of the Student Non-Violent Coordinating Committee and had risked his life in Mississippi during the civil rights movement. He became a convert to Black Power along with his friend and coworker Stokely Carmichael. A brilliant young writer, he had joined the University of Massachusetts faculty at the same time I did. During the year I was at Connecticut, he had been a fellow at the Institute for the Humanities at Cornell and had witnessed the takeover of the student center by armed black students. He knew, as I did, that the principal reason blacks armed themselves was the threat of attack by members of certain fraternities. This I had learned from our son Johnny, who was a freshman at Cornell that year.

Mike came to Amherst burning with anger at whites—a categorical hatred, even though, like the most prejudiced whites, he made a few exceptions. It would be many years before he mellowed a bit, and I became one of the exceptions. We continued to have many differences over the years, but I treasure a copy of his excellent book *Duties, Pleasures, and Conflicts*, with the inscription "For Bro. Lewis K—keep on keeping on Bro, with fraternal good wishes. Mike".

In this initial encounter, Mike and other black dinner guests froze me out. Not long afterward, I felt the heat of a vicious verbal assault by a black student. Although some students of race relations deny that there can be such a thing as "black racism," I feel that I saw it in action at a conference on Black Studies on the campus of Amherst College. The black Amherst students who organized the two-day event invited me to speak on a topic I knew was booby-trapped: "What Can White Professors Contribute to a Black Studies Program?"

I knew that the answer was supposed to be "nothing," but I brashly accepted the assignment. During the first day of the conference, I received ample confirmation that the atmosphere, intellectual and emotional, was distinctly anti-white. Harold Isaacs of MIT, a distinguished historian and student of race relations, gave a talk embodying universalistic values and deploring the rise of what he called "tribalism" in ethnic relations, not only in the United States but in other countries. The response of his audience was definitely "tribal." He seemed bewildered by the reception, but I had anticipated it. Being forewarned did not reduce the anxiety I felt when my turn came, and I rose to address an audience composed largely of young, angry black nationalists.

I started by acknowledging that many of them might feel that there was no place in a Black Studies program for a white professor. Then I boldly proceeded to tell them that I thought there could be. My talk was organized around two themes. The first was that even if blacks now felt that whites were not merely outsiders but antagonists, they still might consider the wisdom of the adage "Know your enemy." Hearing white perspectives on black-white relations might help them to do this. Then I moved on to the "insider-outsider" issue. To dispose of this by simply saying that no white could ever understand the black experience was greatly to oversimplify the issue, I argued. No individual could ever experience the world just as another person did because they never lived in the same skin, heard with the same ears, or saw through the same eyes. Therefore, we were all outsiders, in a sense, and the black experience was not even the same to all blacks. At this point, I saw some head-nodding by a few older black people in the audience. I concluded with the suggestion that since even people who were outsiders to one another could still have some similar experiences, we could all learn by sharing those things we did have in common.

The assault came as soon as the question period began. A young woman from Hunter College rose and angrily declared, "The first sentence the speaker said was true, but the rest of his speech was shit!" I have forgotten just how I replied, but whatever I said was inadequate. Bill Wilson, sitting by me on the platform, rose in all his blackness to defend me. He informed the audience that many students at UMass who had read *The Impossible Revolution?* thought I was black until they met me and that therefore I must have some understanding of the black experience. My assailant answered rather lamely that maybe I was persuasive in my writings, but I surely wasn't when I spoke. Maybe it was my southern accent as well as the substance of my remarks that infuriated her. After this exchange, the discussion was fairly calm and even a little constructive.

Becoming part of the Amherst scene involved many relationships besides black-white ones, of course. Even in these, our southern accents played an interesting and sometimes amusing part. This historic little New England college town was a novelty to Kay and me, and although I was known by my writings to some of the sociologists we met, we were perceived as *auslanders* in many encounters.

Geographically, the town is located in what is known as the Pioneer Valley, the area lying on both sides of the Connecticut River north of Springfield. Academically, the University of Massachusetts is part of a five-college consortium including Amherst College, Smith College in Northampton, Mt. Holyoke in South Hadley, and Hampshire College, just coming into being on the outskirts of Amherst when we arrived. There were opportunities to meet a great variety of people, most of them connected with academia in one way or another.

Our formal introduction to the university came at the reception for new faculty members and was good for a story that Peter Rose found very appropriate for his introduction to my book *White Southerners*. We went to the reception with our new friends, Hans Speier, newly appointed as a distinguished professor, his wife, Margit, and some friends of theirs who were also of European origin. All of them, with their pronounced Middle European accents, preceded us through the receiving line and were greeted cordially but with no unusual comments. We, too, were given a warm welcome; but the president added, "My, you must feel a long way from home!"

As seems to be the case with many white southern women, Kay drew more attention and evoked more stereotypes because of her accent than I did. Ironically, she had picked up her accent from me over the years of our marriage; when I met her, she spoke with the northern accent of her parents. I ascribe a good part of the reactions she encountered to the Amherst milieu.

From the beginning, and even now, I have thought of this community as a liberal Shangri-La, not really in touch with the rest of America. One of the first things I noticed was that people who, by their dress and manner, would have been regarded as eccentrics in Tallahassee were commonplace here. It also came as a surprise to us that almost every Sunday morning there would be one or another small group of demonstrators on the town common, parading with their signs as if the eyes of the world were on them. In 1969 most of the signs expressed criticism of the federal government and our involvement in Vietnam. When the 1972 presidential election came, the town overwhelmingly supported George McGovern. After the election, I summed up my perception of the political outlook with the observation, "Massachusetts was the only state which voted for McGovern, but Amherst was the only town where people expected him to win."

In this milieu, speaking with a southern accent and having a son who had just graduated from West Point triggered many negative reactions, or so we believed. Kay felt that she received a cold shoulder from many women when she tried to become a part of such groups as the League of Women Voters. She remains convinced that one woman who eventually became one of her best friends was very hostile during their early association in a women's hiking group. This woman, a "Smithie," was the wife of a retired army officer but was deeply involved in the peace movement. Initial conversations made Kay feel that she must dissuade her of the notion we were both southern racists and unmitigated hawks. Typically, my wife decided that she would break down the barriers and make this woman get to know her better. Her success was phenomenal, and Alice and her husband became treasured companions over many years.

Interestingly, Kay's southern style evoked a different reaction from salespeople in stores and blue-collar workers, such as plumbers and electricians, who came to our house. Sometimes a sales clerk might ask, "Where are you' all from?" but never in an unfriendly manner. The men more typically would start a conversation with, "You're from the South, aren't you? I was stationed at Ft. Jackson when I was in the army." Lavish praise of the friendliness of southerners would follow.

My "networking," to use modern sociological jargon, consisted of getting acquainted with a stimulating variety of academics in the valley. Bill Wilson quickly became a good friend and colleague. I had known Hans Speier's work because of my reading for collective behavior. It was thrilling to learn that he would be not only a colleague but also a neighbor. Charles Page, also a fairly recent addition to the UMass faculty, introduced me to many Smith College faculty members, for he had been head of the Sociology Department there for many years. During our sixteen years in Massachusetts, he and his wife, Leonora, introduced us to many outstanding scholars whom they entertained in their Northampton home.

Two students of race relations were major attractions affecting my decision to move to Amherst. I felt that Milton Gordon's book *Assimilation in American Life* was one of the most significant works in the field, and it was a privilege to be on the same faculty with him. Peter Rose, across the river at Smith College, was still working with me in bringing *White Southerners* to publication.

Even before the book was finished, Peter invited me to speak about it in his classes in race relations at Smith. Twenty years later, he reminded me of an exchange with black students in one of these classes that had been recalled for him by one of these students, who was now a faculty member at the college. She told him that she had felt very hostile toward me when he introduced me to speak, with my southern accent, about white southerners. My opener was a question, however: "How many of you know what pot-likker is?" All the white students looked mystified, but the black ones knew and started laughing. This woman told the class what it was, but then I surprised her by asking, "Are you a dunker or a crumbler?" This really broke her up, for it is an inside joke among pot-likker *afficionados*. When you eat the delicious and nutritious juices of cooked vegetables such as greens or black-eyed peas, do you dunk your cornbread in the liquid or do you crumble it? She and the whole class quickly got the point that southerners, white and black, had much in common. Then we proceeded to discuss amicably the similarities, differences, and conflicts between them.

Actually, we were not the only southerners in the Sociology Department when we arrived in 1969, and yet others were added. The chair of the department, T.O. Wilkinson, had grown up in Jacksonville, and his wife was from Vidalia, Georgia. Although T.O. had lost his southern accent, Edie sounded just as southern as we did. They had been in Amherst for so long and had been so active in town politics that people seemed to have forgotten about their origins, and they certainly did not make anything of it.

Only a year or two after we came, a young man who had just finished his Ph.D. at Chapel Hill was hired. Wade Clark Roof and his wife, Terry, were both South Carolinians. Although they were young enough to be our children, we found that we had much in common and became fast friends. Clark had been a Methodist minister and held a degree from Yale Divinity School. One year as a pastor in South Carolina during the civil rights movement was enough to cause him to follow the path taken by many sociologists over the years, from the ministry into sociology. His primary interest was in the sociology of religion, but he shared my interest in race relations both personally and professionally. The Roofs became neighbors, and we shared many southern meals together. Clark was a fisherman and when he would return with a mess of bluegills, we would fry them and make hushpuppies just as though we were having a Deep South fish fry.

Another newcomer in 1969 shared my ideas, my joys, and my tribulations for all the years I was in Amherst. This was Michael Lewis, who had just come from the faculty of the University of Illinois. Mike had been a student of Charles Page at Princeton. He and I thought very much alike about sociology and social problems, but when we disagreed, we never pulled any punches. Our arguments were a rewarding aspect of a deep friendship.

My first three years at Amherst were exciting and satisfying ones, filled with new intellectual adventures and enlivened by new friendships. I worked with challenging students, including several black graduate students. Now, perhaps because I was located in the Northeast rather than in the South, new opportunities opened for me and I began to gain a broader perspective on race relations.

Just before we moved to Amherst, I received an invitation to participate in a UNESCO "meeting of experts on the role of the mass media in a multi-racial society," to be held in Paris in December. I really didn't know what this meeting was all about, but I had a good idea why I had been invited. Harry Alpert, an eminent American sociologist, was director of the Division of Social Sciences. We had met while I was working with the Committee on Sociological Resources for Secondary Schools, and he also knew of my contributions in the fields of collective behavior and ethnic relations. I was asked to present a paper on "The Mass Media and Minority Protest Movements." In a multinational workshop, I was to speak for the United States.

I did my job well without realizing what was probably expected of me. My paper concluded with a staunch declaration of "First Amendment fundamentalism," opposing government censorship of any kind. I wrote, "One of the first signs that a ruling group fears a revolution is its attempt to restrict freedom of expression. Perhaps its willingness to broaden freedom of speech and of the press would be a sign that it does not deserve a revolution."

What I did not know was that the governments of many Third World countries represented wanted UNESCO to adopt a policy endorsing censorship. As one African delegate epitomized their position, "We are tired of American film distributors flooding our country with Tarzan pictures in which the white ape-man is the hero and our people are the villains." He reflected the perspective of new nations, with undemocratic regimes, highly nationalist, and eager to restrict what they regarded as imperialist propaganda. This was one of the early skirmishes in a long battle within UNESCO that ended in a defeat for the viewpoint I represented. This controversy was one of the factors leading to the withdrawal of U.S. support for UNESCO over a decade later.

I began to get the sense that this was a carefully staged event on the afternoon of the first day. To my utter astonishment, one of the delegates moved that the Soviet representative and I be elected co-presidents of the meeting. We were elected by acclamation and took turns presiding over the remaining sessions.

The papers and the discussions were interesting, even though often filled with rhetoric. One of the most interesting and dramatic speakers was the poet Andrew Salkey, who was from London but who represented Jamaica, from whence he had migrated. Our rooms adjoined in the little hotel where we were housed, and we spent two pleasant evenings together. He was the first Jamaican I had ever known, and I found both his accent and his viewpoints interesting. He was enamored of Castro and had recently visited Cuba with a delegation of artists and writers. He enlightened me about the varieties of Caribbean nationalism, and from him I first heard about C.L.R. James, the West Indian Marxist who strongly influenced the American black nationalist James Boggs.

Two of Andrew's stories I still remember. One, told during a late supper at the restaurant in the Eiffel Tower, alerted me to the fact that there was rising black consciousness in Britain, just as in the United States. It seemed that Andrew's wife was an Englishwoman. He said, "I thought we were getting along fine until one night I went down to the pub and the boys there told me I had a problem because my wife was white!" He remained married, nevertheless, but not long afterwards he moved to the United States.

The other story was told during the session at which Salkey presented his paper. Much of the essay was an attack on the policies of the British Broadcasting Corporation. Andrew appeared occasionally on their telecasts and was an adviser on coverage of minority affairs. When Martin Luther King, Jr. was to pass through London en route to Stockholm to receive the Nobel Peace Prize, Salkey asked to be allowed to interview him for the BBC. According to him, the official whom he asked denied any air time for King, saying, "Not our problem, not our man, not our prize!"

As the conference progressed through three and a half days of long sessions, I recognized that the issue of censorship was central. The Soviet delegate was walking a fine line between appearing democratic by opposing censorship but without offending the Third World delegates. I realized that all our debates were pointless. While I certainly had no instructions from my government, I was not about to back down from my initial position. The Russian, who was a Jewish journalist, kept insisting that an exception must be made in the case of "racist propaganda" and he kept reminding us of Nazi anti-Semitism. The recommendation adopted at the end of the conference, probably drafted by the UNESCO staff, represented a compromise. Recommendation 8 ended, "We recommend that UNESCO follow the general principle of seeking ways to enhance freedom of production and distribution of information by and to all peoples—particularly to those peoples for whom opportunities for production are now restricted." But there followed Recommendation 9, "Nevertheless, the media should not be used for racist propaganda."

We never undertook to define or delimit "racist propaganda," but it was evident to me that it might mean different things to people in the various countries represented. I have often reflected on the irony of the fact that anti-Semitism was already growing in the Soviet Union at the time my Russian-Jewish co-president was denouncing it. I wonder if he knew what his government was up to.

Despite my feeling that this carefully managed workshop was a rather fruitless exercise, hearing the divergent viewpoints of people from such a variety of societies was a tremendously rewarding experience. It helped prepare me for the research I would do later in Great Britain.

About a year and a half later, I took part in another conference with a much
clearer theme: "Black Sociologists." My friend from student days in Chicago,
Morris Janowitz, now on the faculty, invited me to do a joint paper with C.U.
Smith on "Black Sociologists and Social Protest." The conference was at the
Kellogg Center in Chicago, on the very site where my family and I had lived in
veterans housing. James Blackwell, of the University of Massachusetts at
Boston, collaborated with Janowitz as organizer.

By this time, the Black Power movement was on the wane but black
consciousness was not diminishing, as the title of the conference suggested.
Whites were in the minority, but it was a pleasure to me to be with many of my
black friends and colleagues, such as Frank Edwards, James Conyers, Butler
Jones, Jacqueline Jackson, and Bill Wilson. I received some rough treatment
from several of the black participants, however, particularly Blackwell.

Smith and I collaborated on our paper over several months. In our division
of labor I was to write the introduction, a historical portion, and the conclusion.
C.U. volunteered to do a mail survey of black sociologists to ascertain the extent
of their participation in protest during the Civil Rights Movement. I completed
a first draft of the introduction and the historical portion fairly early and sent it
to my friend, but I received no feedback from him. Shortly before we were to
meet in Chicago he gave me a summary of his findings from the survey. I was
able to compose a conclusion that we could use in our oral presentation, but I was
eager for Smith's reactions to what I had written. I had not portrayed black
sociologists as particularly militant during the history of the discipline in the
United States, arguing that they had been in part hostages to the requirements for
mobility in a white-dominated profession. In particular, I stated that at the 1968
and 1969 American Sociological Association conventions, they had not been the
vanguard in the demands for reform but had lagged behind the New Left radicals
and the emerging Sociologists for Women in Society, even though the Association of Black Sociologists had been formed during the 1969 meetings.

Alas, I never received a critique of my portion from Smith, and it turned out
that my draft contained at least one egregious historical error. On the basis of the
draft, which I amended in my oral presentation, Blackwell became furious with
me and never missed a chance to take a dig at me throughout the conference. I
could understand why he was angry, for he had been one of the founders of the
Association of Black Sociologists, but I felt that such treatment was not fully
justified. I was especially put out that Smith bore none of the contumely heaped
on me. Moreover, Janowitz and Blackwell chose to deal entirely with me during
the editing of the paper for publication, but when the volume was published, C.U.
was listed as the senior author.

The conference ended on an amusing but controversial note. As a white
scholar, I was happily on the sidelines. Kenneth Clark was invited to be the
speaker at the concluding banquet. He flew in from New York on the afternoon

of the event and attended none of the sessions. He shocked the conferees and organizers by condemning the whole affair as an exercise in black separatism and emphasizing the need to treat black sociologists as sociologists, not as blacks. No one should have been surprised. Not long before, he had resigned from the Board of Trustees of a college because they decided to approve having an all-black dormitory on the campus. He was a dedicated integrationist and was not into the spirit of black consciousness.

During the summer of 1972, Kay and I enjoyed a wonderful break from life in Amherst, and I had the opportunity to observe at close hand ethnic relations in Hawaii, often represented as an inter-racial paradise. A "golden people" reflecting the amalgamation of all the races was alleged to be emerging. Being lucky enough to obtain an appointment for the summer semester at the University of Hawaii's Manoa campus, in Honolulu, I was able to teach a class in minority relations with white *kamaainas* who had been born in the islands, *haoles* from the mainland, Chinese-Americans, a black air force captain, and a Hawaiian with an English name. From them and from everyday observation, I soon learned why sociologists like Andrew Lind and Clarence Glick had protested against what they saw as wishful thinking about the extent of integration.

Since my graduate school days, I had read how one immigrant group after another had progressed from the cane and pineapple fields to positions higher in the occupational and social structure, exemplified by the Chinese in business and the Japanese in the professions. Now I learned that there was at least one new group at the bottom of the heap, although the opportunities for agricultural laborers had markedly decreased. Every few days, the *Honolulu Star-Bulletin* would report that whites driving or traveling by bus along certain roads on Oahu had been attacked by Samoans. Driving through the area where these incidents occurred, I saw miserable slums populated by dark-skinned migrants from American Samoa, the newest minority.

I also learned that the integration of the earlier groups was not nearly so complete as often represented in journalistic accounts. One of the earliest groups of immigrant laborers were Portuguese from the Azores and Madeira Islands. They were white in appearance, European in culture, and by 1972 were far removed from the plantations. Yet I still could hear the derogatory ethnic term "Portegee", which was applied to them during the many years when they were regarded as a separate "race," and I learned that they still ranked below *haoles* economically, although they were better off than most of the nonwhite minorities.

One question on the final examination I gave in my minority relations course demonstrated how sensitive the issue of race could be and how the very low proportion of black Americans in Hawaii did not eliminate prejudice against them. I asked the students to write an essay on the problems that would arise if the federal government were to subsidize the migration of low-income citizens from inner-city areas on the mainland to Hawaii. They were well able to pose the same sorts of resistance and problems of adjustment studied in our analyses of immigrant minorities and their reception on the mainland. I was dumbfounded, however, when several of the students who were residents of Hawaii were so angered by the idea that they could not see the question as hypothetical. They thought I was in favor of such a plan! The Hawaiian student was particularly indignant and wrote a bitter answer declaring that he wished that Hawaii had never become a state and was still an independent kingdom. Despite his English name and his distinctly Caucasian physiognomy, he was psychologically as Polynesian as the "white Indians" I had known in Oklahoma had been Cherokee or Osage.

I returned from Hawaii with an even more comparative perspective on ethnic relations. How meaningless was the concept of "race" as designating real biological divisions of the human species became even more evident, and M.F. Ashley-Montagu's intriguing title *Man's Most Dangerous Myth: the Fallacy of Race* took on deeper meaning for me. Even as I felt how unnecessary ethnic classifications and conflicts were, I was conscious of how pervasive and compelling these socially constructed compartments were in the human drama.

When we returned to Amherst after an idyllic summer, I found myself not rested but tense and anxious. Immediately after I got back, I became embroiled in a controversy in my parish, where I now occupied the top lay position of senior warden. This was the beginning of a conflict between myself and the rector that eventually led to my leaving this parish and attending a Lutheran church for seven years. In addition, I started thinking about writing some sort of sequel to *The Impossible Revolution?* These factors are not enough to explain, however, why it was that, by early December 1972, I went into a deep depression. It had been coming on for nearly two years. I had begun experiencing "lows" during which I felt powerless and useless, could not be truly interested in any activity, and could work only by driving myself. During many of the months when Ralph and I were finishing the long-overdue revision of *Collective Behavior*, I had been depressed. Reluctantly, at the urging of our family physician, I started sessions with a psychiatrist. Whether because of the therapy or because of spontaneous recovery, the depression lifted, and in the fall of 1972 I was back in my old pattern of anxious, compulsive, frantic activity. I was still taking medication, however, and seeing my psychiatrist periodically.

Just before the beginning of the Spring semester I was feeling so low that I could hardly drag myself out of bed in the morning, even though I couldn't sleep. I became frightened that I might commit suicide. Then my psychiatrist left town for a long vacation, and while he was gone, my supply of medicine ran out. On a dismal Saturday morning I hit such a low that Kay persuaded another psychiatrist to see me on an emergency basis. He convinced me that I should commit myself to the psychiatric ward at Franklin County Hospital, in nearby

Greenfield. It was run as a "therapeutic community" under the direction of a very fine psychiatrist, Stanford Bloomberg.

East Spoke, as the ward was called, worked superbly for me as a crisis-intervention center. Within two weeks, my depression had been replaced by a new outlook on myself and on life. I was in such a euphoric state that I immediately sat down and wrote an introspective account of my experience as a mental patient. Then I got together with Dr. Bloomberg and we crafted a patient-psychiatrist analytical essay that was published in the journal *Psychiatry*, under the title "Rebirth in a Therapeutic Community."

Ironically, before the article reached the press over a year later, my depression had returned. I was far from being "cured"; I had merely taken the first step on a long journey to a state in which I could cope with the compulsions and guilt that would lead to my "crashes." There were two or three subsequent periods during which I had to fight the desire to retreat to East Spoke again, and I continued in outpatient therapy for nearly three years.

Yet during both my low times and the intervening months of remission, I continued to be productive. I never missed a class, except during the two weeks at the beginning of the semester when I was hospitalized. I prepared several articles for publication as chapters in edited books and did revise *The Impossible Revolution?* by writing a new, additional last chapter and retitling it *The Impossible Revolution, Phase 2*.

The pessimism about the future of race relations in the United States that informed the new chapter was as profound as the personal despair I felt when depressed. After all the courage and conflict, the sacrifices and the suffering, of those who from 1954 through 1972 struggled to bring about a new era of racial democracy, neither racial injustice nor racial conflict now ranked high on the agenda of white Americans. Vietnam, Watergate, the energy crisis, inflation, and the destruction of the ecosystem were the new issues. Lyndon B. Johnson, the great ally of the civil rights movement, had deserted the cause when he shifted his attention to Southeast Asia. Richard Nixon had been more concerned about winning white votes from George Wallace than in appealing to black voters; the door of the White House was once again closed to black leaders. In my judgment the problems that, in the words of the Kerner Commission, were leading the United States to become two societies, one white, one black, separate and unequal, had not been solved but had only been pushed out of the national consciousness. True, segregation by law had been abolished, but separation and inequality continued to increase as the gulf between whites and blacks and that between "qualified" blacks and those trapped in the inner-city ghettoes widened. Once again, as I had in the first edition, I went out on a limb and made dire predictions. First, I predicted a further decline in the economic welfare of the large number of black Americans not fortunate enough to have the education, training and self-confidence to enable them to move into the black middle class, training and self-confidence to enable them to move into the black middle class, which, according to optimistic observers, was steadily expanding. But, perhaps overly impressed by the rhetoric of the Black Power movement, I suggested that the current absence of a great deal of overt racial conflict was only a lull between storms and that a third, even more violent phase of "the impossible revolution" would emerge. My most pessimistic prediction was a reiteration of the one I had made in 1968 in the words, "Given a choice between a massive freedom budget and a police state, the American electorate is more likely to choose the latter."

My prediction of further declines in the economic status of black Americans proved all too accurate. The political battle cry "No new taxes" drowned out appeals for humanitarian domestic programs despite the interlude of the Carter years. Automation and the export of jobs to Third-World countries made sociologist Sydney Willhelm's bitter question, "Who needs the Negro?" seem even more relevant.

That renewed black violence erupted only in sporadic instances, such as in Liberty City, Miami, mystified me. What had happened to the desperate anger so eloquently expressed by Huey P. Newton in his book *Revolutionary Suicide*? Where were the "angry black ideologists" I had said were waiting to renew the revolutionary attack as soon as large numbers of blacks once again lost faith in white promises?

The least dismal answer that occurred to me was that they had been coopted. This was certainly true of some of the leaders of the civil rights movement, and it appeared that many bright young black men and women were, like their white counterparts, more interested in making the most of the opportunities now open to them than in fighting the battles of their less fortunate brothers and sisters. Two legacies of the Black Power movement, black consciousness and the concept of ethnic group rights, appeared strong, but the potential for violence reflected in the slogan "by any means necessary" was not being realized.

Other possible explanations were more terrible to contemplate. One was that the most effective antidote to black revolutionary action was the drugs that were flooding the ghettoes. The black "soldiers" whom Sam Greenlee imagined fighting the police and National Guard in his frightening novel *The Spook Who Sat By The Door* were instead killing each other in gang wars. My other thought was that perhaps the repression that played such a major part in bringing about the end of the Black Power movement had indeed driven home the lesson that black defiance of white power is suicidal. Could it be that just a demonstration of the capacity of white-dominated governments violently to suppress effective black protest was sufficient to make the police state which I had predicted unnecessary?

These questions remain unanswered as I write many years later. They were not on my mind during the years immediately after the publication of *The Impossible Revolution, Phase 2*, in 1975, for I still had a good deal of confidence angry with me for my devotion to the role of Cassandra. Her anger was exacerbated by the psychological torture to which I subjected her during my periods of depression. She would have been justified in leaving me during these dark years, but her devotion was such that she never took a vacation from me. Although she was bewildered as to what to do to help me, her succor and faithfulness played a major part in enabling me finally to learn to cope with my illness.

One other activity I undertook even while still in therapy was preparing an application for a Guggenheim fellowship. Entitled to my first sabbatical leave during the academic year 1975–1976, I felt that if my half-salary were supplemented by a Guggenheim or a Fulbright stipend, we could do something we had long dreamed of—spend a year in England. To my surprise and delight, I was awarded a handsome Guggenheim fellowship to do research on black power in Britain, something I knew very little about even though I had done a good bit of library research in preparing my research proposal. Uncertainty as to what sort of research I would actually be able to carry out did not diminish my joy at the prospect of getting to know the land from which my mother's parents and ancestors had come. Kay and I were about to enter a drastically different phase of our life, and I was to gain an even broader comparative perspective on ethnic relations. Once again, luck was with me, and my first year abroad since World War II proved professionally fruitful as well as personally enjoyable.

| Chapter | **14** | **A NEW PERSPECTIVE: RACE IN BRITAIN** |

Looking for Black Power—Community Relations—School Busing In England—An Academic Lynch Mob

My knowledge of race relations in Great Britain was sorely limited when I started preparing a research proposal. I knew that Enoch Powell had become a symbol of right-wing resistance to the immigration of dark-skinned people from the West Indies, the Indian subcontinent, and Africa to Britain, as had so many since 1949. I had heard of the National Front, a right-wing organization with racist and fascist leanings. During the early 1970s race riots in a part of London called Notting Hill had made headlines even in the United States. It was evident that tension and a potential for further conflict must exist, but I knew next to nothing about the actors. My first task was to scour the library for books on race relations in Great Britain.

One of the first books I located was not only of great help but also a great ego-booster. Entitled *Community Action and Race Relations: A Study of Community Relations Committees in Britain,* it constituted a very critical analysis of the Community Relations Commission (CRC) and the local Community Relations Councils that had been created by the Race Relations Act of 1968. Much to my surprise and pleasure, the two British authors, M.J. Hill and Ruth M. Issacharoff, had read *Racial Crisis in America* and found my analysis of the weaknesses of biracial committees in the United States to be applicable to Community Relations Councils. Both, they concluded, served as buffers to prevent ethnic conflict, rather than as agents for reform. Both the Community Relations Commission and its more powerful counterpart, the Race Relations Board, were seen by them as agents of a government dominated by whites. Even though the government was in the hands of the Labour party, the leaders appeared no more desirous of real change in the racial order than were their Tory opponents.

This valuable work provided one part of the structure of my research proposal. The other came from a very suggestive, but less accurate work written in a jail cell by a Nigerian named Obi B.J. Egbuna. It was entitled *Destroy This Temple: The Voice of Black Power in Britain.* Egbuna had been jailed for his activism in support of Black Power; he was subsequently deported. I later found that he greatly exaggerated the strength and significance of the Black Power movement in England, but his book influenced me to put together a proposal to study the interaction between the militants of whatever Black Power movement there was and the race relations bureaucracy. These were not, of course, the only sources on race relations in Britain that I read, but they were crucial to my plans for research during my year in London.

Late in the summer of 1975, Kay and I took up residence in a flat in Putney, near Wimbledon, in southwest London. Together we started to learn firsthand about British culture. I began my on-the-scene investigation of a situation that I knew only through an inadequate reading of the literature.

My mentor at Chicago, Everett Hughes, had served as a reference for me when I applied for the Guggenheim fellowship. When I informed him that I would indeed be undertaking to carry out my research project in London, he provided me with introductions to two people at the Community Relations Commission. One was Mark Bonham Carter, the director. The other was Sheila Patterson, an anthropologist and editor of a journal subsidized by the commission, *New Community*.

Hence one of my first visits to the West End took me to the commission's offices "in" Bedford Street, as the British would say. During the ensuing months, I would spend many hours in the crowded, somewhat shabby quarters then occupied by CRC. On one of my early visits, I had difficulty getting in the front door. The National Front was staging a demonstration against the agency; I had never before met any members of this infamous organization face to face. Fearful that the protestors might gain access to the interior, the guards, universal in British government offices, had locked the door and were carefully screening everyone who entered.

Thanks to my first visit, my bona fides had been established. Bonham Carter had received me graciously and offered access to the resources of the commission. Sheila Patterson's small office was next to the library. I was excited not only at learning of the existence of *New Community*, a journal devoted entirely to ethnic relations in Britain, but also at the wealth of materials in the library. This included files of a multitude of publications of ethnic organizations and, most significantly, a directory of organizations concerned with ethnic relations throughout the United Kingdom. This listed not only all local Community Relations Councils but also many groups who were quite hostile to the whole community relations approach. I was confident that, so armed, I was ready to start my field research.

None of the organizations was labeled Black Power, nor did any have the term in their titles, but I felt that I could make a pretty good guess as to which would be in conflict with the Community Relations Councils. Many of the addresses were in Brixton, the area of London with the highest concentration of West Indians. It had been the subject of *Dark Strangers*, an anthropological study of immigrants in London by Sheila Patterson. Although the Brixton market was widely known as a West Indian market, the area was not like an American black ghetto. The proportion of blacks was only about 30 percent.

When I started pounding the pavements of Brixton, I was impressed by the contrast with Putney, which was almost lily-white. That the level of living was lower was evident from the shabbiness of many of the houses and the quality of the stores.

My hopes began to fade with my very first visit to the area. At address after address, I would find an empty store with no occupants, black or white. Looking through the windows of some, I could see on the floor mimeographed sheets, which indicated that there had been some activity there at some time, but I found no tenants and certainly no Black Power organizations.

I still had some hope when I visited another office, not in Brixton but in Penton Road, many blocks to the north. Several militant-sounding organizations were listed at the address, but I was hoping to get an interview with a man named A. Sivanandan, director of the Institute of Race Relations (IRR). Even in a short time, I had learned a good bit about him and his "institute." The Institute of Race Relations had once been a well-funded research organization dominated by a council composed mostly of white academics and business tycoons. It published a journal called *Race Today*. In 1972 there had been a revolt by staff members of the institute against the council, centering on the radical ideological tone of the journal, which did not accord with the liberal, moderate views of council members. The staff won a Pyrrhic victory. At a meeting of all 400 members of the institute, they gained majority support, but the defeated council members resigned, withdrawing their financial backing.

One of the leaders of the revolt was Sivanandan, a Sri Lankan, who was the librarian. The library was the major asset remaining after the dissolution of the council. It became, in effect, the institute, with the erstwhile librarian as the director. Sivanandan also continued as editor of the journal, and subscriptions became the major source of income for the shrunken organization.

When I sat down to interview this militant leader, my hopes rose again. He was a fierce-looking man with long, bushy hair; he seemed to exude nervous energy. To my delight his greeting to me was, "Killian—oh yes, racial crisis in America." What a thrill to find that my book was known not only to academics in England but to a leading activist. Alas, I did not really get an interview during the time I met with Sivanandan. My opening question evoked an hour-long monologue on the evils of capitalism, the exploitation and oppression of Third World people both in their own homelands and in Great Britain, and the hypocrisy of the British government and its race relations agencies. For all his militant oration, he gave me no information about a Black Power movement or any movement organizations in the country.

One thing I did conclude from my aborted interview and several hours of browsing in the institute library. Apparently, Sivanandan and the IRR had come to constitute a facade for a social movement that had no army of followers. In the library I found names and announcements of meetings of numerous protest groups devoted to ending the oppression of a large variety of Third World people. There was even one supporting the aspirations of the Maori of New Zealand. I was confident that I had already learned enough about race relations in Britain to be sure that there could be no more than a handful of Maoris in the country. All the announcements indicated that the organizations met in Pentonville Road, and Sivanandan was named in all of them. Fifteen years later, the institute still survived, and "Siva," as he was known to friends and enemies, still edited the journal, now called *Race and Class*, but he had never become a British Malcolm X or Stokely Carmichael, much less a Lenin.

Now, terribly discouraged, I made one more effort to find if there were any significant remnants of the Black Power movement that had enjoyed a flurry of activity and publicity in the early 1960s. There had even been a Jamaican militant who called himself Michael X, but he had been exposed as primarily a racketeer and had returned to Jamaica, where he died a common criminal. Was there someone like him still trying to gather a following in one of the areas where blacks from the Caribbean or browns from the Indian subcontinent were concentrated? Certainly some of the Community Relations Officers (CROs), the field workers and front-line troops of the Community Relations Commission, would know.

The two CROs I first interviewed proved to be excellent choices. Shortly after I left England, the Community Relations Commission published a monograph comparing the functioning of three different but representative Community Relations Councils. Two of the three were the ones I had chosen quite by chance.

The first was in the borough of Wandsworth. This area had been the major recipient of the influx of East Indians from Africa who had fled Uganda following Idi Amin's ascent to power. The CRO was a white former minister, Charles Boxer. In talking to him, I began to sense how difficult the job of the CRO was. He seemed tired; our conversation was frequently interrupted by telephone calls about problems of various sorts. It was from Boxer that I first heard the term "race relations industry." As he confirmed my hunch that whatever Black Power movement had existed in Britain had by now largely dissipated, he remarked, "A lot of the leaders have been coopted by the race relations industry." Intrigued by the latter concept, one that I had never heard before, I asked him to explain what it meant. He told me that it was a term frequently used by a conservative writer for the *London Daily Telegraph* who wrote under the pseudonym "Peter Simple." To my surprise, Boxer went on to say that many of the very people whom the columnist so often derided had taken over the term and applied it to themselves and their agency. He also said that some radical blacks also used "race relations industry" pejoratively, even though it had been popularized by a right-wing newsman.

This chance discovery of a new term gave my research a new focus. Hereafter, in my interviews with CROs and other functionaries of the Community Relations Commission, I would explore their reactions to it.

My last venture in quest of the elusive Black Power movement took me to the Community Relations Office in the borough of Brent. It had a fairly high concentration of West Indians, although not as many as Brixton. If there had been a current Black Power movement, the CRO, Philemon Sealy, would no doubt have been high in the ranks of its leadership. He contrasted sharply with Boxer. A Trinidadian, he let me know quickly that I should not refer to him as a West Indian and certainly should not mistake him for a Jamaican. In is role as CRO, he attempted to be a leader of the minority community in his borough, not just a mediator between them and the white-dominated borough council. As a result, he often found himself in conflict with the council, which provided much of the funding for his work.

The story was the same in Brent as in Wandsworth, with no Black Power organizations to be found. Once again, luck came to my rescue. Shortly before my first visit to Sealy, I had read in a newspaper about a case before the Race Relations Board involving the busing of minority students to schools outside their district or "catchment area." I asked Phil if he knew anything about this, and his answer was a rich one. Not only did he tell me about a controversy that had been going on for several years over what was called "dispersal," the British equivalent of busing, but he informed me that a friend of his, Jeff Crawford, was the person who had brought the case to the Race Relations Board. Now my further research would concern yet another topic that I had never envisioned in my original proposal. The "race relations industry" and "school dispersal" kept me busy for the rest of the year and resulted in two articles.

In exploring the connotations of the "race relations industry," I was constantly reminded of how difficult it is for us to do good even when we are sincerely trying. Although I had read the criticisms of the Community Relations Council in the book by Hill and Issacharoff, I was still very favorably impressed that the British government had such an agency devoted to improving ethnic relations. In 1964 I had been thrilled by the creation of our own Community Relations Service, but it had been only a trouble-shooting agency, while the Community Relations Commission supported eighty-five local officers working full-time. But I had perceived our agency as an extension of the civil rights movement and had rejoiced in the thought that the movement had succeeded in getting the federal government to take up a task it had begun. Turner and I had defined the "institutionalization" of a social movement as constituting one form of success. This seemed a good illustration. I would soon begin to realize how limited was the success in both the United States and Great Britain.

As I read the literature about race relations in Britain in daily newspapers, social science studies, and the angry publications of protest groups, I found that both the Community Relations Commission and the Race Relations Board, another government agency, were besieged by critics on both the right and the left, both white and minority. "Peter Simple," writing several times a week in one of London's three major newspapers, certainly must have struck a responsive chord with many white Britons, just as he would have with many white Americans. His sarcastic attacks on the race relations industry were diabolically clever. He wrote regularly of "Ethnic House," which he said was the headquarters of "a growth industry—Britain's economic growth point No.1." He sneered at the many people who pursued "careers in race relations." In one column he offered an overview of what he felt they existed to do, "to question, test, tabulate, chide, lecture, warn, issue reports and more reports, research studies and more research studies." To him workers in the industry did not solve problems, they invented them. He reflected the opinion that the government should not spend thousands of pounds each year paying "do-gooders" to search for discrimination where it did not exist or to remove it where it was justified.

Militant members of ethnic minorities were sure that discrimination existed and wanted something done about it, but their attacks on the race relations industry were just as vehement. Sivanandan suggested that the industry, with all its branches, had been created by a conspiracy of white liberals, old India hands, and black moderates, who feared drastic, revolutionary changes in the racial order. He even gave a date for the founding, 1963, when a private foundation brought together a group of what he called "race professionals" to conduct a survey of race relations in the nation. Many of the intellectuals involved in this survey were indeed active later in the Community Relations Commission and the Race Relations Board, and a number of them were Sivanandan's opponents in the fight within the Institute for Race Relations.

Sivanandan was not alone in his view of the industry. One black writer charged that government agencies had been deliberately created by the Labour government to contain and divert minority protest, not to improve the conditions of the minorities. Another, who had once been employed as a Community Relations Officer, asserted that the community relations program had not the slightest reference to the needs or desires of the black community. These militant minority writers were united in their indictment of the industry. It was created by white politicians; it could not and would not do anything of which they did not approve; hence it failed to attack in a meaningful way the economic, educational, and social discrimination suffered by minority groups. Worse yet, it served as an obstacle to radical reform by creating the illusion that the government was doing something and by defining the problem of race relations as one of helping "immigrants" fit into British society.

I expected to find the workers in the race relations industry angry and defensive about these criticisms, particularly the weekly jibes of Peter Simple. I found that Charles Boxer was right; many of the workers used the term themselves and were quite cynical about their work. One official, an Indian, characterized what he and his co-workers at the Community Relations Commission did as "a lot of busywork without any impact." It was not that these workers felt that they were doing no good at all, but they seemed to agree with their militant critics that they were not able to attack the real problems of discrimination and inequality in a radical manner. I wondered how many of them would have continued in the field if they could have found better jobs or if they had been able to convince themselves that minority protest movements could accomplish anything.

My research ultimately led me to do some soul-searching. A Jamaican CRO showed me how broad the meaning of the term race relations industry could be. He started our interview by declaring that he was definitely part of an industry. Then he turned the spotlight on me, saying bluntly, "When you called, I knew you were an American and a sociologist and I almost refused to see you. We have been studied until I think black people are the most researched people in Britain. Students go to the universities and they all do their research on race relations. Some people even get jobs on the basis of being experts on black people."

Shocked, I realized that he had virtually described my whole career as a sociologist, from the day I accepted the Phelps-Stokes Fellowship for research in race relations. Late, as I pondered this revelation, the doubts that had tormented me during the years of the civil rights movement returned. Had my liberal, social-engineering approach been appropriate for situations that demanded revolutionary action? Had the written manifestations of my "expertise" ever had a chance of affecting the political power struggle that drove race relations? Was the truth about my writings that they had been addressed more to my fellow academics as I struggled for professional recognition than to the people who were really doing something about discrimination?

Within the next year, I completed the most cynical essay I have ever written, "The 'Race Relations Industry' as a Sensitizing Concept." I presented my conclusions about the race relations industry in Great Britain and then, looking at the U.S. scene through a new lens, I realized that America had a race relations industry older and larger than that of the United Kingdom. It dated back to the establishment of the Bureau of Indian Affairs in 1824. After the War Between the States, another federal agency was added, the Freedman's Bureau, but it was short-lived. With the end of Reconstruction the government almost got out of the race relations business, although its policies strongly affected the plight of minorities, particularly blacks. During this period of neglect, a body of "race professionals" developed in the academic world. This important part of the industry grew without federal subsidies but was handsomely financed by foundations. These included the Phelps-Stokes, Rosenwald, Sigmund Livingston, Field, Taconic, Rockefeller, and Ford Foundations. I had been a beneficiary of five of them.

I discovered that black Americans such as Lerone Bennett, Jr., and Vernon E. Jordan had written critically of a race relations "establishment," which they charged favored whites and a few blacks known to have influence in the black community. Bennett called it a "black establishment," but pointed out that often the top people in it were white.

It was after passage of the Civil Rights Act of 1964 that the federal government again became a major partner in the industry. Now I recognized that while the expanded industry might be viewed as a continuation of the civil rights movement, with its emphasis on integration, it was not an extension of the more radical Black Power movement. It was far more likely to benefit middle-class blacks than to help the black masses escape from poverty and de facto segregation. I found myself echoing many of the charges leveled by black critics at the British race relations industry but with the U.S. civil rights bureaucracy as my target.

The pessimistic conclusion to my article was as much an indictment of myself as it was of the race relations industry. I wrote, "Crusaders for better race relations, like all crusaders, often fancy themselves as pure in heart and noble in purpose. Yet contemplation of the possibility that race relations may become an 'industry' sensitizes us to the fact that individual motives may be quite mixed and that the organizational structures within which even 'good works' are done may be constraining."

Anomalies in social phenomena have long intrigued me. I have found that examining them often reveals unrecognized complexities and facets of things taken for granted. Hence my interest was aroused when I read in the London press that minority groups in several parts of England had been campaigning against the busing, or as the British called it, "dispersal," of schoolchildren. The situation in Boston, where white parents were fighting against busing and defending the neighborhood school, was fresh in my memory. Why was it that in Britain the minority parents were the protestors? My research disclosed another illustration of the psychological principle that the ground against which a figure appears can change how it appears to us. Largely because of its political background, busing appeared to minority parents in England as discrimination against their children, not as governmental intervention on their behalf.

Unlike blacks in the United States, ethnic minorities in Britain had never asked for busing or even racial balance as measures to improve the education of their children. It was white parents and school administrators in certain districts who, in the early 1960s, became concerned that the increasingly high proportion of Indian, Pakistani, and Afro-Caribbean students in the schools was lowering the quality of their children's education. A few local education authorities started "dispersing" the minority children, busing them to schools with fewer of their number. In 1965 the Conservative government issued a policy statement to the effect that when the proportion of "immigrant" children in a school exceeded one-fifth, it would be wise to institute dispersal.

Nothing was ever said about busing white children to maintain this sort of racial balance, and no white child was ever bused. The number of minority children affected was actually very small, but they were concentrated in a few districts. At first, few minority parents were disturbed by the new practice. Some even accepted the rationale advanced by the government that dispersal would be educationally good for their children because they would acquire the English language and culture more readily, accelerating their progress toward assimilation. By the early 1970s, after minority parents had seen their children bused year after year, they began to voice the same complaints that white opponents of busing in the United States had angrily advanced. Their children had to leave home too early in the morning and spend too much time on the buses. When they got off the buses at the distant schools, they felt like outsiders and were treated as such by the other children. The schools were not close enough to their homes for the parents to get there quickly in an emergency. In other words, these parents wanted their children to go to neighborhood schools. Minority protest organizations and left-wing groups, including one local Communist party branch, took up their cause. Their complaint was finally accepted by the Race Relations Board, and dispersal was declared by this body to constitute discrimination when based solely on race or ethnicity. The ruling was hailed as a victory for ethnic minorities.

If at the same time the U.S. Supreme Court had handed down a ruling that school boards should be color-blind in their assignment of children even if this resulted in racial imbalance in the schools, this would have been denounced as a racist decision. My research in England brought home to me how much the context influenced the evaluation of policies and practices, even the evaluation research done by sociologists. For several years, only the rare white liberal sociologist or black American challenged the assumption that only the resistance of racist whites kept busing to achieve racial balance from being a boon to black children. The U.S. Civil Rights Commission had dismissed many of the same kinds of complaints raised by minority parents in Britain as "fears and myths" when brought up by whites in America. The advantages of the neighborhood school figured prominently among these so-called myths. My previously existing sense that the controversy over busing centered more on its symbolism than its actual effects was reinforced. How little immunity sociologists had from involvement in such symbolic, political conflicts was forcefully brought home to me by a controversy back home.

During the year Kay and I spent in England, I returned to the United States twice. I was serving the first year of my term as a member of the council of the

American Sociological Association. Lewis Coser, another member, was also spending the year in England, at Cambridge. Both of us flew back to Washington for meetings of the council. The new president of the association was Alfred McClung Lee. His election, after his name had been put on the ballot as a result of a petition, was a victory for the self-styled "humanistic," action-oriented wing of the association.

When I returned for the first council meeting, I learned that Lee and a number of other prominent social scientists, including Tom Pettigrew and Kenneth Clark, were on a crusade to discredit James S. Coleman because of his "white flight" hypothesis. Not only had he published a scholarly paper in which he concluded that school busing could be a factor leading to the flight of white families to suburban areas, thereby increasing school segregation; he had also appeared before the Massachusetts legislature to discuss his findings.

Here was internecine conflict in the top ranks of the American race relations industry. Jim Coleman, widely known both inside sociology and among laypeople for the famous "Coleman Report" done for the federal government, had been seen as a champion of desegregation. It mattered little that his research had shown that only under certain conditions would desegregation benefit black children educationally or that he himself had complained that people were drawing unwarranted conclusions from the report. He had been regarded as an ally by long-time advocates of desegregation-no-matter-what, such as Clark and Pettigrew. Now he had become a heretic in their eyes. He had declared, "I believe it of central importance to insure that desegregation becomes a beneficial policy, rather than merely a symbolic victory which harms as much as it helps," and he had said that in some cases busing was harmful.

Within twenty-four hours of Jim's appearance before the legislature, Pettigrew and several other social scientists held a press conference in which they announced that they had examined the data Coleman presented in his paper and had found his conclusions unsupported. They were particularly critical of his having testified before a policy making body.

When I got to the council meeting, I learned that Al Lee wanted us to censure Coleman for unethical conduct. He had already asked the Committee on Freedom of Research and Teaching to investigate, but it was clear what he believed the result should be. I felt I was being asked to take part in an intellectual lynching. I knew that Coleman's conclusions could be challenged and would be, just as every important social science research report becomes the target for other "scientists". This did not mean, however, that his conduct was unethical or that his research was dishonest. Of course, I could not forget that Lee had attempted to have me censured for my research for the Florida attorney general. It, too, had violated the liberal ethos of the sociological profession.

Happily, all my colleagues on the council vigorously opposed the president's efforts. The controversy did not die easily, however. Some of Lee's written attacks on Coleman were so vicious that Jim threatened to sue him for libel. When I returned to Washington several months later for the next council meeting, I found that Lee wanted the association to help finance his defense if Coleman did sue. Again he lost. It was not surprising to me that in his presidential address the following August he complained that he had been forced to work with an uncooperative council. This whole episode served to exacerbate my growing cynicism about sociology and the race relations industry.

My experience in studying ethnic relations in another country made me more strongly aware of another bias in American research, including much of my own. This was the tendency to regard the assimilation of minority groups into a uniform American social order as the desirable end-point of progress. It is true that in *Racial Crisis in America* I had pointed out that integration demanded that blacks give up their identity and any distinctive culture they might have. In England I saw minority groups for whom multiculturalism, not assimilation, was the goal.

Minority parents had been told that school dispersal would be beneficial to their children because it would help them acquire English culture. The Indians, the Sikhs, and the Pakistani rejected this "benefit" in their protest against dispersal. They wanted good education and equal economic opportunity for their children, but they did not want them to have to give up their ancient cultural traditions in order to enjoy them. The Sikhs did not want their sons to have to give up their sacred turbans in order to comply with school dress codes. The Moslems wanted their daughters protected from Western ways of treating females. All the groups, including the Afro-Caribbeans, complained that the school lunchrooms failed to make sufficient concessions to their food preferences, too often serving what they considered a bland English diet.

Although these very different groups were united in their conviction that they were victims of prejudice and discrimination, they had difficulty in making common cause. From Phil Sealy, in Brent, I learned of the many divisions among the black people called "West Indians" by the British. This was a white name for a collection of diverse people, just as "Indian" is a term applied by white Americans to people who call themselves Cherokees, Creeks, Apaches, Wampanoags, Mohawks, or other tribal names. Trinidadians felt they were different from "Badians," from Barbados, and even more so from Jamaicans, whom they regarded as arrogant. To them it was a sign of white British ignorance that all were lumped together as "West Indians." Then there were the "black Britons," growing in number as new generations of black babies were born in England and were not immigrants. That the British so often called all dark-skinned people from the former colonies "immigrants" was viewed as the most damning evidence of their insensitivity and prejudice.

Phil Sealy had in his office a file of minutes of various conferences in which the various minority groups had tried to form alliances. All had failed. Most interesting to me was the fact that there was a great deal of fruitless debate as to what any united organization should be called. All were agreed that "immigrant" was unacceptable. The Afro-Caribbeans argued for "black," but this was unacceptable to the Indians and Pakistanis. They were brown and lighter, not black. There were indications that they also considered themselves culturally superior to the black descendants of British slaves and did not want to be perceived as similar despite their common position of inferiority in Great Britain.

As I learned more of the reality of ethnic relations in Britain, I had a preview of trends that would soon become more evident in the United States, Puerto Ricans, Chicanos, Cubans, and other Latinos would find it difficult to join forces with blacks and even with one another. In some places, such as Miami, they would be in conflict with the black minority. The diverse Latin American groups would be lumped together as "Hispanics" and treated in many statistical tables, official and unofficial, as if they were third "race." Puerto Ricans would be under pressure to become "Americanized," even though they are born U.S. citizens in a territory in which Spanish is the native language. In the 1980s we would see the growth of a Moslem minority, adding to the religious diversity previously oversimplified as "Protestant, Catholic, and Jewish." After almost a lifetime of research, I found ethnic relations growing more and more complex, perhaps unfathomable.

Although we lived there for less than a full year, Kay and I fell in love with England and particularly London. Aided by a Continuing Education course called "Knowing London" that Kay took, we came to know our temporary home better than we did any American city. I continued to be stimulated by my sociological study of ethnic groups and patterns of ethnic relations that seemed so much like those I had known in the United States but that were actually so different. Although my research had not been faithful to my original proposal and had often been unsystematic, I had acquired a comparative perspective unattainable through reading. In spite of all the reasons we had for wanting to return to our native land we were saddened by the conclusion of our sojourn in England and were determined to return there as soon as we could.

Return we did, four years later, this time because I worked out an exchange of positions, houses, and cars with an English sociologist. On this trip I went to teach, not to do research, but my education about the multicultural society developing in Great Britain continued. It started on the day of our arrival in London. John Downing, the lecturer at Thames Polytechnic with whom I exchanged, lived in a part of London called Stoke-Newington. Kay and I arrived at Victoria station after a long rail and ferry trip from Heidelberg, where our daughter, Kit, and her family were living. After piling our many suitcases into a taxi, we told the cabbie where we wanted to go. His gruff reply was, "You don't want to go there—nobody but blacks live in Stoke-Newington." I replied, "We have to. We're exchanging houses with a man who lives there." He snorted, "You must live in Harlem then." Had the law permitted him to refuse our patronage, I am sure he would have dumped us and our luggage on the sidewalk at that moment. He gave us a fast ride to our new "home" with no further conversation and sped away as soon as he had unloaded us and received the fare.

We soon found out what he meant by "blacks." There were some Afro-Caribbeans in the area, but most of the residents were Pakistanis, Bangladeshis, and Greek and Turkish Cypriots. It was true that only a small minority of our neighbors were white English families, most of them old residents. The majority of the communicants at the Anglican parish church we attended were Afro-Caribbean.

Our second year in London was a memorable experience, sometimes frightening but mostly interesting and pleasant. Our black next-door neighbors warned us of the danger of being mugged day or night, and we lived cautiously. These neighbors, Ruel and Patricia, had both come to England from the island of Monserrat as infants. Their speech was thoroughly English, but they could hardly be said to be assimilated. Their close friends were all black, and Ruel regularly smoked "ganja" (marijuana) with his buddies. We soon developed a relationship that was both friendly and symbiotic. They knew the neighborhood, and we had a washing machine that we shared with them. During the course of the year, we rejoiced with them at the birth of their first child. They named the little boy Charlie because Ruel, who had ambitions as a musician, so admired the American jazz musician Charlie Parker ("Bird").

Other close friends acquired that year included our butcher and his family. John Morgan was a white blue-collar Englishman but was probably the richest person we knew during our two years in London. We learned much about social class in England from him. It took us about four months to convince him that despite the fact that I was a college professor and we were his customers, we would enjoy having him and his family as friends. At first we saw him only in the neighborhood butcher shop. Like nearly all the merchants in the neighborhood, he would not have thought of living there. After we succeeded in breaking the ice, we enjoyed many social occasions with the Morgans. Our main problem came to be finding affordable ways to reciprocate for their lavish entertaining.

Once again, in 1981, we experienced a bittersweet departure from England. I have kept my interest in ethnic relations there and for several years served as a member of the editorial board of *New Community*, contributing articles on race relations in the United States. During our two years in Britain, I became well acquainted with British sociologists Michael Banton, John Rex, and Sheila Allen, leading figures in the study of race and class. My correspondence and occasional visits with them have served to sustain my comparative perspective, as well as my interest in the changing scene in the United Kingdom.

With some of my heart remaining in England, I found my attachment to the University of Massachusetts weakened on our return. New England had never really seemed like home to Kay and me; we were still southerners. From 1981 onward, I began to think more and more about retiring early and returning to north Florida.

Chapter **15** PHASING OUT: DISILLUSIONMENT
AND RETIREMENT

Conflicts with Graduate Students—Fighting the Union—
W.J. Wilson, Race and Class—Defending Collective
Behavior—The Last Hurrahs

Although I still had at least eight years to serve until retirement, my attachment to the Sociology Department at Massachusetts diminished after I returned from my first year in England and even more so after my second year abroad. The department had become bitterly divided. Professional disagreements between faculty members often were transformed into personal antagonisms accompanied by extreme rudeness. The infighting was vicious, and I started withdrawing from faculty politics. At one point I became so disgusted during the annual dogfight over the composition of the Personnel Committee that I introduced a motion that shocked even my best friends. I moved that the members of the committee be selected by chance. So distrustful were many faculty members of the judgement of their colleagues that my motion passed.

Other conflicts contributed to my disaffection. Some were with graduate students, collectively but not individually. My relations with most of them were cordial and satisfying, but the Graduate Student Association had come to be dominated by a clique of student politicians. They seemed to be more concerned with asserting what they perceived to be their rights than in meeting the faculty's demands for high-quality work. I wondered if I were becoming an anachronism as I persisted in regarding them as apprentices, not as colleagues or junior professionals. To my chagrin, many of my fellow faculty members did treat them almost as if they were colleagues. I had never felt that I was a particularly hard teacher, but I could not adopt the attitude that admission to a program of study should carry a guarantee of completion. It came as a shock to some of my graduate students that I would actually give a grade of *C* when I knew they were supposed to maintain a *B* average.

The most painful, time-consuming battle and the one which made me wonder even more how much longer I should stay in the academy was over the unionization of the faculty. I could not bring myself to accept the notion that a union was compatible with professionalism. Moreover, it appeared to me that a majority of the proponents of unionization were among the most mediocre

196

members of the faculty, and I knew some whom I thought would have been fired if they had not held tenure. What I felt most strongly was my resolve never to engage in any "job action" that would deprive my students even temporarily of the services I was dedicated to providing.

I was on the losing side of a bitter battle that went on for over two years. During it, I made many enemies, and my relations with some friends were strained. Fortunately, I did not have to join the union, even though the university became a "union shop." The contract included a conscientious objector clause. Under it, I was permitted to pay the equivalent of the dues into a scholarship fund rather than into the coffers of an organization I abhorred. Again, however, I wondered if I were becoming a conservative old curmudgeon unable to adjust to changing times and shifting values. Since my undergraduate days I had been an ardent supporter of the labor movement, in a period when the CIO was equated with communism in the South. I had been horrified by the chicanery and violence employed by the textile industry to keep unions out of cotton mills in my native state. I had seen National Guardsmen manning machine guns around mills in Macon to keep striking workers off the premises. Now I found myself opposing the organization of my own workplace and being thrust into an uncomfortable alliance with some ultra conservative colleagues. That I lost the battle was less painful than that I had felt duty bound to enter the fray.

Unhappy with the conflicts and pettiness I saw around me in Amherst, I turned my attention increasingly to professional activities beyond the campus. My four-year term on the Council of the American Sociological Association bound me more closely to the larger community of sociologists, as did my participation in the meetings of the International Sociological Association in Uppsala, Sweden, and Mexico City. At the sessions sponsored by the Research Committee on Racial and Ethnic Relations, I exchanged ideas with sociologists from many nations. Again, my knowledge of the complexities of ethnic relations both at home and abroad deepened. I was struck by what I saw as the provincialism of many American students of the subject, particularly those who treated prejudice and discrimination, now summed up in the word "racism," almost as if they were peculiar to the United States and South Africa.

A meeting that proved to have special significance for my thinking took place in New York City. It was a joint Indo-U.S. Seminar on Ethnicity and Social Change, sponsored by foundations in both India and the United States. The participants included not only sociologists but lawyers, political scientists, and economists from both nations. From the Indian delegates I learned of a problem that was new but of great significance to me. It involved a new vocabulary, including such terms as "scheduled castes," "depressed classes," "protective discrimination," and "reservations policy." These were all used in discussing the Indian counterpart of affirmative actions.

As I look back it seems that I have favored the spirit of affirmative action at least since 1964. Shortly before the passage of the Civil Rights Act of 1964, I was invited to address the National Council on Social Welfare on the topic "Current Issues in Civil Rights." My thesis was that once we secured the right of black citizens to equal opportunity, the next task would be to equip them with the skills necessary to attain the goals set before them. This was precisely the theme of President Lyndon B. Johnson a short time later in his famous address at Howard University. My plea was for special educational opportunities to enable blacks to become qualified for jobs heretofore barred to them.

Later, as a consultant to the Community Relations Service during the few months it was headed by Governor LeRoy Collins, I had to study the text of the act thoroughly. The most important assignment I took for the CRS was speaking to citizens' groups, particularly in the South, about what to expect from enforcement of the new law. I learned that while the text stated that employers should "take affirmative action" to make equal opportunity truly available to minority workers and women, it nevertheless explicitly forbade preferential treatment of workers because of race or sex to remedy any numerical imbalance in the workforce. The history of the congressional debate strongly suggested that the bill would not have passed had not the sponsors, especially Senator Hubert Humphrey, declared in no uncertain terms that any attempt to achieve racial balance under Title VII would run afoul of this very title. Such action would constitute a failure or refusal to hire some individual because of his or her race, color, religion, sex, or national origin. It seemed clear in 1964 that equal opportunity did not mean or require preferential treatment, as "affirmative action" was later widely believed to do. Like the *Brown* decision ten years earlier, the new law called for color-blindness, not color-consciousness. It was an affirmative response to the plea of Martin Luther King, Jr. that people be judged on the content of their character, not on the color of their skin. Affirmative action, as originally used, meant making extra efforts to make sure that minority-group members knew about job openings, not to hiring them in order to meet numerical goals, guidelines, or quotas.

By 1974, it was evident that this earlier meaning was no longer widely understood or accepted. The University of Washington denied a white Jewish student, Marcus DeFunis, admission to its law school while admitting black applicants who were technically not as well qualified. DeFunis brought the first court case charging that preferential treatment to increase minority representation constituted reverse discrimination.

I followed this case with close attention and a heavy heart. It grieved me to see the Jewish Anti-Defamation League and the National Association for the Advancement of Colored People, long-time allies in fighting ethnic discrimination, opposing each other in the case. It was clear that a double standard was being sued in screening white and minority applicants to the law school. I anticipated that the Supreme Court would rule that DeFunis had been denied admission because of race, in violation of Title VII of the Civil Rights Act and perhaps in contravention of the Fourteenth amendment. By the time the case reached the highest court, however, the law school had found a place for the plaintiff, and the justices were able to avoid a decision; the case was declared moot. I remained deeply troubled by an editorial in *Crisis*, the official journal of the NAACP. The editor wrote, "The university is trying to rectify more than three and one-half centuries of white-imposed discrimination against the non-white peoples of this nation. While Mr. DeFunis personally had nothing to do with this long-enduring conspiracy to deprive black folk of their rights, he is a member of the white majority which initiated and maintains this conspiracy." Thus DeFunis was being pronounced guilty simply because he was white.

The terms of what would be a long, heated controversy had been laid down. The legal issues would be raised in case after case, and the Supreme Court would no longer be able to avoid making decisions that would profoundly influence the course of ethnic relations and politics in the nation.

During the ensuing years, I wrote several articles in which I addressed these issues directly or indirectly. One, "Affirmative Action and Protective Discrimination: A Comparison of the United States and India," grew in large part out of my reading about the Indian situation after attending the Indo-U.S. seminar. After India became an independent nation in 1947, its constitution mandated "reservations" for members of "depressed classes," including primarily the "scheduled castes," better known as "untouchables." While it was designed to abolish untouchability, making it illegal to discriminate against the exuntouchables, the constitution guaranteed what came to be called "protective discrimination" for the same people. Quotas of seats in the parliament, of places in institutions of higher education, and of government jobs were established; these were the "reservations." As do advocates of affirmative action in the United States, supporters of the reservation policy argued that it would be a transitional remedy, necessary only until untouchability had been abolished in fact as well as in law. Thirty years later, untouchability seemed to be increasing, not diminishing, as both individuals and groups were petitioning the Indian courts to declare that they should be included among the "scheduled castes" so that they too could benefit from the reservations. The block of ex-untouchable representatives in the parliament was strong enough to fight off any attempts to phase out the reservation policy but not to extend it, as many would like to have done.

The issue divided the nation. New epithets, such as "reservation wallahs," were applied to the beneficiaries of the policy. Citizens who could not enjoy the benefits complained and sometimes even rioted because they felt that their opportunities were being limited. Protestors included members of castes just above the "depressed classes" category as well as the most-favored Brahmins. Critics of the policy also pointed out that it was the better-educated and more affluent ex-untouchables who benefited most from reservations, while the ones who needed help most gained little. As a result, the gap between the more fortunate and the masses was widening, just as some observers believed the gulf between "qualified blacks" and lower-class blacks in the United States was doing. I found particularly significant a study by an American anthropologist, Leila Dushkin, showing that opinion polls in India revealed a widespread belief, particularly among better-educated people, that the number of persons receiving preferential treatment was much larger than the statistics indicated. I saw the same sort of misconception emerging among white Americans, sustained by "affirmative action horror stories" and the subtle hints by some politicians that whites were becoming a disadvantaged ethnic group compared with the "special interests" that wielded so much power in the national Democratic party. This was a decade before David Duke, in Louisiana, and Jesse Helms, in North Carolina, would brazenly use affirmative action as a very effective campaign issue. I found it surprising that with the United States moving apace toward a policy of compensatory discrimination, American social scientists paid so little attention to the Indian experience.

Before my paper comparing the two situations was published, in 1981, I presented it to two audiences in England. I thought my analysis was a very pragmatic comparison of the evolution and consequences of very similar policies in two nations. I studiously avoided debating the abstract morality of color-blindness versus compensatory color-consciousness. The reactions of a minority of members of my British audiences demonstrated that even to suggest that preferential treatment might have unanticipated consequences which would defeat its purpose was enough to evoke accusations of racism. When, as a guest of Michael Banton, I gave the paper at the University of Bristol, the audience included an Indian student and two English faculty members, a married couple who had just returned from a lengthy visit to the United States. The Indian summarily dismissed my analysis with the declaration, "The Brahmins will never give up their privileges unless they are forced to." The Englishman said rather calmly, "Your observations differ from those of the people we talked to in the United States," mentioning particularly a well-known advocate of affirmative action. His wife, however, became so angry that at one point I thought she was going to slap my face. She accused me not only of being racist but also of being a male chauvinist, even though I had not spoken at all about the benefits women were receiving from affirmative action, which happen to be greater than those enjoyed by blacks. So vicious was her verbal assault that Michael was moved to assure the audience that I was respected even by many black sociologists in the United States.

Thus it was in England that I had my introduction to the sort of impassioned, moralistic, and polemical debate that usually arose from any attempt to examine the realities of affirmative action as it came to be understood by the 1980s.

Nathan Glazer, a sociologist long identified as an objective student of ethnic relations, whose conclusions brought him to a liberal, antiracist position, was discredited because of his arguments against what he called "statistical equality" in his book *Affirmative Discrimination*. Just as in 1954 it had been against the ethos of American sociology to hypothesize that gradualism might have some advantages in connection with school desegregation, now it was not "politically correct" to question color-conscious preferential treatment from a moral, legal, or pragmatic standpoint. I had long disagreed with Glazer's optimistic view of the American economic system and his extension of what is called the 'immigrant analogy" to the plight of blacks in the modern industrial era. In a review of his later book, *Ethnic Dilemmas*, I described Glazer as a political liberal turned neoconservative but not neoracist. Yet he has been so often attacked as being a white Jewish racist that I have found myself hesitating to quote some of his cogent analysis lest I become a victim of guilt by association. As was true of Jim Coleman during the white-flight controversy, Glazer was set upon by an academic lynch mob. He would not be the only victim of liberal intolerance.

A prominent Jewish American who had been something of a hero to me since student days at the University of Georgia was another. Morris B. Abram had been a year or two ahead of me at the college. As an undergraduate and as a law student, he was what we then called a BMOC: "big man on campus." Even as a student, he was an outspoken advocate of interracial and interfaith democracy. As a young lawyer in Atlanta, after serving on the staff of the prosecutor at the Nuremberg trials, he lead the fight to abolish the notorious county unit system of electing members to the state legislature. He had been denounced as a liberal "nigger lover" for doing so, since the system gave the rural supporters of such demagogues as Eugene Talmadge disproportionate power. After leaving Georgia victorious in his fight, he went on to a distinguished career as president of the American Jewish Committee, president of Brandeis University, and adviser on civil rights to President Johnson. In 1979 I was shocked to learn that Morris had withdrawn his support for Jimmy Carter because his fellow Georgian favored the goals and guidelines of affirmative action. Although I agreed that this policy had become a betrayal of the goal of a color-blind America for which white southern liberals had risked much in the 1950s, I could not imagine myself supporting Ronald Reagan simply because of this one issue. Morris felt so strongly, however, that following the defeat of Carter, he accepted appointment to the Civil Rights Commission after Reagan had reorganized it. In the storm of denunciation that followed, his record as a liberal was completely overlooked, and he was excoriated as one of the new-style racists.

On one occasion in Amherst I avoided exposure to liberal and, in this instance, black intolerance. While the case of Alan Bakke was before the Supreme Court, an association of black students at the University of Massachusetts decided to have a panel of speakers discuss the two sides of the issue of numerical set-asides for minority applicants to universities and professional schools. The event was to take place in an atmosphere already inflamed by charges that Bakke's supporters were white racists and that he himself must be a Jew (he was not), since several Jewish organizations were submitting *amicus curiae* briefs in his support. I received a call asking me to present the pro-Bakke side. I declined as politely as I could and immediately called my friend Milton Gordon to advise him that he should do the same if invited. The organizers finally got a young lawyer from Boston to take the unpopular view. I attended the program and even though I had anticipated what would happen, I was still shocked by the viciousness of the attack on the white lawyer, much of it in personal rather than intellectual terms. At the end of the program, I approached the podium to offer my apologies to him for the treatment he had received while on our campus. As I came within earshot, I could hear him explaining to the other panel members that he personally agreed with their anti-Bakke position but had only been doing what he was asked to do. They expressed their amazement that he had performed the task assigned when he did not believe in it; apparently they knew little if anything about legal debates. I left the auditorium, thankful that I had not been as naive about black bigotry as had he.

During the summer in which the Supreme Court finally handed down its historic but ambiguous decision in *Bakke*, Kay and I were in Pensacola. We were enjoying the beach apartment we had just purchased as a possible retirement home, and I was working on my part of the third edition of *Collective Behavior*. Somehow I learned that a relatively new organization called the Black United Way was having its national convention in Atlanta. The program included a number of well-known black speakers as well as a then-little-known disciple of the late Elijah Muhammed, Minister Louis Farrakhan. I decided that we would drive to Georgia and see what the program was like. It turned out to be, on the whole, a revival of the spirit of black nationalism. Farrakhan offered the most eloquent expression of this spirit, and his speech was wildly applauded. The conference was overcast by a pall of gloom, however, because the court had just ruled that the numerical set-asides by the medical school of the University of California at Davis violated Title VII of the Civil Rights Act. Alan Bakke was adjudged to be a victim of reverse discrimination, and the medical school was ordered to admit him. In a session devoted especially to this case speaker after speaker, including the famous Julian Bond, deplored the Court's ruling as a reversal of the gains of the civil rights movement. But there was one speaker, a young lawyer who had once been a member of the Black Panthers in Oakland, who disagreed with the prophets of doom. He declared that blacks should be rejoicing because although the court had ruled out specific numerical set-asides—quotas—it had stated emphatically that race could be considered by colleges as one factor in selecting applicants for admission. This, he argued, was a victory for blacks. The Court's rulings in several subsequent cases proved the accuracy of his analysis. I thought to myself that he was the most perceptive of the speakers, but I was deeply concerned that the highest court seemed to be moving in the direction of a color-conscious stance, with race once again being legitimated as a salient characteristic of American citizens. My dilemma was that while I knew that ethnicity did have high salience for perhaps a majority of people in the United States, I could not feel that it constituted progress for the highest court to retreat from the principle proclaimed in 1954, that the Constitution should be color-blind.

During the next few years, this dilemma became so painful that I lost my enthusiasm for teaching courses in race relations. So emotionally involved was I in the issue that I no longer had confidence that I could present an even-handed analysis, and I did not enjoy coping with students, black or white, who were sure that there was only one side. At the same time, another controversy in the analysis of ethnic relations was giving rise to an equally bitter intellectual and personal battle. I was deeply involved not only because of my intellectual convictions but also because William J. Wilson's newest book was at the center of the controversy. The mob was now pursuing him in full cry.

My close association with Bill in Amherst lasted only two years. During that brief period we formed a friendship that has endured years and miles of separation. We have been true colleagues, stimulating each other through the exchange of our writings and interacting during occasional visits at professional meetings.

I learned early of two of Bill's ambitions. One was to be known professionally as a theorist, not as a specialist in race relations. The other was that he be judged as a sociologist, not as a black sociologist; he did not want to be an "affirmative action candidate" for jobs or honors. Events soon proved that he could not overcome the salience of his blackness. Between 1969 and 1971, the UMass campus was rent by numerous protests in which black students were usually allied with radical whites. Bill, as a very popular professor who was black, was repeatedly drafted by the administration to mediate in the conflicts that arose. Dedicated to his teaching and very active in research and writing, he found these demands onerous but inescapable. His workload was overwhelming.

To say that he was pleasantly surprised when the University of Chicago invited him to be a candidate for a position is an understatement. Yet his joy was not unalloyed. His main reservation, I believe, was his concern that he not be considered just because he was a very promising young black scholar. The Department of Sociology at Chicago had never had a tenured black professor. Of course, the University of Massachusetts was willing to go to great lengths to try to keep him, including promotion to full professor and a handsome increase in salary. He would not bargain; he made it clear that a promotion would be premature at this stage of his career. After all, he had just been awarded tenure.

His situation was complicated even more because during his discussions with Chicago, he was approached by Harvard about becoming head of a new Black Studies program. This was exactly the kind of position he wished to avoid, so he had no difficulty in resisting the lure of the Ivy League.

Bill did accept an offer from Chicago, but only provisionally. He agreed to a trial year as visiting associate professor before establishing any permanent tie. He left Amherst in 1971, to return only for visits to give lectures and once to receive an honorary degree. Within five years he not only became the first black scholar to be a permanent member of the Sociology Department at Chicago but also was elected chair.

During the first American Sociological Association meeting after publication of his book *The Declining Significance of Race* (1978), Bill was invited to be the guest speaker at the dinner meeting of the Sociological Research Associates. Some sociologists, particularly the members, would consider this a high honor. SRA is an elitist, almost secret, organization with no publicly stated criteria for membership. Members nominate prospective members, and a committee decides which of them will be invited to join.

Although Bill Wilson would later become a member and eventually president, his reception at his first SRA meeting was almost a "roast." When he finished his presentation, several black sociologists vied to be the first to query him. Their questions were delivered in tones that were cold if not hostile; this was true even of gentle, courteous Frank Edwards. Other questioners made it clear that they thought his thesis "the declining significance of race" was dangerous and ill considered. Although Bill was treated courteously, this gave just an inkling of painful encounters soon to come.

Not long afterward, I was on the firing line with Bill during one of these encounters. At the next meeting of the Eastern Sociological Society, he was invited to be the author in the traditional "Author Meets the Critics" session. Besides myself, members of the panel were Doris Y. Wilkinson, Jim Geschwender, and Charles Willie. Geschwender was an old friend, and I had known Wilkinson when she was in the ASA office but I knew Willie only by his writings. I should have anticipated fireworks when I saw that here I was, a white, liberal male on a panel with Jim, a Marxist; Doris, a black woman; and Willie, a black man. All three took their charge to be critical in its most negative sense. Jim, from his Marxist perspective, attacked Bill for his conception of class. Wilkinson, gently, and Willie, polemically, attacked him for suggesting that race was in any way declining in significance. They spoke, as many other critics were already doing, as if Wilson had claimed that race was now of no significance.

Later, Willie would seek to build himself a position of glory in sociology as Bill's chief opponent, once representing himself as being to Wilson what W.E.B. Du Bois had been to Booker T. Washington. By the time he had finished speaking on this occasion, I was so furious that I spoke not just to Bill's analysis but to the criticisms. Recalling the title of a paper written by E. Franklin Frazier, "The Negro's Vested Interest in Segregation," I asserted that it now appeared that some blacks had a vested interest in the existence of racism. At one point, Willie was so incensed at what I said that he rose halfway out of his seat and shouted, "No!" I was convinced by this experience that even some sociologists who had read beyond the title of Bill's book were exploiting the fact that it could so easily be misinterpreted or misrepresented.

Bill has admitted both privately and publicly that he had misgivings about the title *The Declining Significance of Race* from the first. He had been about to call his work "The Transformation of Race Relations" but then decided that "the declining significance" would signal more dramatically a new approach and get people to read the book. As I stated when introducing him for his presidential address to the American Sociological Association in 1990, the title did attract attention, and it did sell books. It also led to the author's being accused of being an Uncle Tom, of literally taking money from white conservatives, and of writing the book in order to get tenure at the University of Chicago, even though he was already chair of the department. So popular did Wilson-bashing become that even graduate students wanted to write theses devoted to refuting his ideas. One announced to me that he was "proving Wilson wrong" in a term paper that, incidentally, he turned in over a year late. Many black sociologists attacked him. The Association of Black Sociologists voted to censure him at the same time that the American Sociological Association was honoring him with the Spivack Award for the best book of the year on ethnic relations. I found that my old, dear friend Chuck Smith was so angry at Bill's book, or at least at the title, that I could not discuss it with him.

The worst ordeal I saw Bill endure lasted for two days. In March 1979, the director of Afro-American Studies at the University of Pennsylvania organized a two-day symposium on the topic "The Declining Significance of Race?" with Wilson as principal participant and, it turned out, target. The list of speakers was so impressive that I decided to attend the event at my own expense. What I witnessed appeared most of the time to be another intellectual lynching. All the charges that had been leveled at Wilson during the previous year were repeated, even though he had already refuted most of them. Black Nationalists attacked him viciously, not surprisingly. Marxists were equally vehement, however. When I had an opportunity to ask why they were not pleased that Wilson was focusing on class rather than race, the reply was that he was wrong for using a Weberian rather than a Marxist conception of class.

Philip Foner, a white Marxist historian, did not even attend the conference but sent a paper to be read. In it he used an anecdote that many people in the audience felt was insulting to black women. The depth of the feeling against Wilson was demonstrated when a black woman angrily demanded to know why he had not attacked Foner for his comments. She disregarded the obvious fact that Foner was not even present and that it was he, not Bill, who had insulted her.

I was fascinated by the whole orgy of criticism. Although I did hear a few excellent discussions seriously examining Wilson's work, instead of treating him as a traitor to his race, I was beside myself with anger for most of the two days. Much of the time I sat next to Bill as he suffered being a whipping-boy. At one point I whispered to him, "I hope Penn is paying you enough to put up with all this crap." With a wry smile he replied, "How's a thousand dollars a day?" I felt a little better for him at that point, but still knew that he was deeply hurt by the treatment he was receiving. Some of his remarks when he had the floor were bitter, but neither then or at any other time did I ever hear him publicly raise his voice in anger.

The attacks on him continued over the ensuing years. Entire sessions at sociological meetings were devoted to critiques of his ideas. After the furor over the words "the declining significance of race" seemed to have subsided his use of the concept "the black underclass," became the new target. The angriest I have ever seen Bill was on the first day of the ASA meetings in Atlanta in 1988. He was scheduled to be on another "Author Meets the Critics" session, with his latest book, *The Truly Disadvantaged*, as the focus. The day before, he had taken part, by invitation, in a session of the Society for the Study of Social Problems on the topic, "The Underclass." He was offended and furious at what had happened and felt that he had been deceived by fellow sociologists. He had found that the papers of all the other participants were written, not about the underclass, but as attacks on his use of the term. He told me, "I expect to be attacked in a session like the one coming up, but I should be able to take part in a serious discussion of an important problem without being a target. I was badly misled as to the nature and intent of that program."

For years I have studied and taught Wilson's theories and the data he advances to support them. I find them persuasive and hear many other analysts of American society saying very much the same thing, but without acknowledging that they are agreeing with him. The reaction of so many social scientists to his work has been less perplexing than infuriating. The jealousy of some black sociologists for the public and professional recognition Wilson has received has been nakedly displayed. I find it easy to understand that it disturbs many of them for him to suggest that for well-educated black Americans, the burden of race is not so heavy as it once was and that some have "never had it so good." Wilson has openly stated that while he believes that affirmative action is needed, he feels that it should not be the central political and economic issue for blacks. More important, he contends, is the question of how to rescue poor blacks, as well as the poor of other ethnic groups, including whites, from the poverty that is oppressing more and more of them. As for Wilson's white critics, some of them friends of mine, I cannot help but feel that many are seeking to curry favor with that apparent majority of black sociologists who have been his enemies.

Yet for all my intellectual agreement with Bill's analysis I once again find myself questioning the basis for my convictions. How much are they based on the cogency and validity of his work and how much on the fact that he is such a much-admired, much-loved friend? He and Chuck Smith are among my oldest and dearest friends, yet they disagree with each other, and I am caught in the middle. I did gain a large measure of confidence in my evaluation of Bill and his work when he was elected president of the ASA and when his presidential address on the concept of the underclass seemed well received. Whether out of true intellectual conviction or profound loyalty, I remain convinced that he is as right as any sociologist can be. I know him well enough to be sure that he accepts the fact that his theories are incomplete and need constant testing. The prodigious amount of research that he and a generation of students trained by him are doing testifies to this.

My modicum of faith in the objectivity and integrity of sociologists was eroded by the assaults on Wilson and, before him, on Jim Coleman. The treatment of the prophetic work of Daniel Patrick Moynihan by blacks and white liberals was equally dismaying to me, even though he was not a friend, as are the other two. After witnessing such displays of academic intolerance and sometimes dishonesty, I should have been prepared when it came my turn to be a target, although it was not for my work in race relations. I found myself becoming indignant when I came under attack as a "collective behaviorist" and alleged proponent of "irrationality" as the cause of social movements.

The debate between a new generation of sociologists studying social movements and the so-called collective behaviorists was so esoteric that it would make no sense to nonsociologists. I suspect that most sociologists were not aware of it. Among those of us who were specialists in the study of social movements and crowds, it became a vigorous, sometimes angry debate lasting for several years. My involvement was not only scholarly but, at times, personal. I became very angry with some individuals and lost any respect I might have had for them as scholars.

Because Ralph Turner and I had, in 1957, produced the first textbook in the field as it had been defined by Chicago sociologists, we became historical figures in a small corner of the discipline. Although we diverged sharply from some of the ideas of our teacher, Herbert Blumer, and his mentor, Robert E. Park, we gave our book the title for this field of study used by them, "collective behavior." In the early 1960s two other textbooks in the field were published. The first, *Collective Dynamics*, was written by two of our friends and fellow students of Blumer, Kurt and Gladys Lang. It was very similar in approach to our work, and I have always felt a twinge of regret that the two books were in competition. In

1963 Neil Smelser, a colleague of Blumer at Berkeley but not one of his students, published *Theory of Collective Behavior*, claiming it would bring coherence to a field that had no theoretical structure. Smelser advanced a bold theoretical scheme designed to explain crowd behavior, including panics, crazes, and hostile outbursts, as well as social movements. The comprehensiveness and complexity of his scheme and the many propositions that he put forth attracted many followers, and Smelser was "in" for a while. Turner and I had some sharp disagreements with his theory and were publicly critical. We also felt some pique at the broad acceptance of the notion that Neil had, as his title implied, been the first to produce a theory of collective behavior. While we had written our book as a text, we felt that it was organized around some basic propositions and did contain a good bit of "theory." Ralph once remarked to me, "I guess if you want people to recognize your work as theoretical you have to entitle it theory so they'll know what you're doing."

Despite this challenge, our work, supplemented by several seminal articles written by Ralph, continued to have many followers, and the textbook itself dominated the field for many years, going into three editions, of 1957, 1972, and 1984. Beginning in 1970, however, with the publication of a widely read article by Elliot Currie and Jerome Skolnick, "A Critical Note on Conceptions of Collective Behavior," we found ourselves subject to an attack that was both theoretical and political. Together with the Langs, Smelser and some social scientists who had written about "mass movements" we were described as "classical theorists" still in thrall to the theories of the reactionary nineteenth-century French author of *The Crowd: A Study of the Popular Mind*, Gustave LeBon. We were charged with treating social movements, such as those of the 1960s, as "irrational outbursts" rather than rational, politically correct assaults on a corrupt, sick society. That we tried to analyze crowd behavior and social movements in the same books was taken as prima facie evidence that we were trying to trivialize the latter. We were even charged with treating social movements as of no more significance than the hula-hoop fad.

As attacks of this sort became more frequent during the 1970s, I was both amused and angered. My first reaction was, "Who, me? Classical?" I thought writers and artists who were classical were either dead or very old. LeBon was dead, but he died before any of the modern so-called irrationalists were born. I knew, moreover, that neither Ralph nor I regarded our theories as fully developed, ready to be shelved among the classics of sociology. We tried to refine them through our teaching and research and in each new edition of our book.

To be called classical was amusing and perhaps a bit flattering. To have one's work misrepresented, as Bill Wilson had, was not. Ralph and I were particularly annoyed at how consistently our critics ignored the fact that, in the very first edition of *Collective Behavior* and in subsequent editions, we had taken a strong stand on the issue of irrationality. While acknowledging that their ideas had enjoyed wide popular acceptance, we were very critical of LeBon and other theorists who had treated the behavior of people in crowds and social movements as resulting from emotion alone or even from some psychopathic state. We went further; we argued that what various scholars seemed to mean by "rational" and "irrational" was so subjective that any behavior could be defined as either. Hence we suggested that "irrationality" was a false and misleading issue and that we would not classify the various forms of collective behavior we studied as either rational or irrational any more than we would other forms of group behavior. For anyone now to accuse us of denigrating social movements by treating them as irrational seemed to me to result from either dishonesty or ignorance.

There was a place for a serious and constructive dialogue about our theories, which did have deep roots in symbolic interactionist theories of social psychology, in contrast to approaches that place more emphasis on social structure, on resources, and on predetermining factors. "Resource mobilization" theory and its variants and various forms of "political process" theories have surely broadened the perspectives of students of social movements. They have not, however, swept all previous theories into the dustbin, as some of their proponents seemed to think. As I read work after work proclaiming that the "classical theories" had now been discredited and replaced, I could not help but feel that there were motives other than the advancement of knowledge behind these extravagant claims and the distortions supporting them.

One motive was clearly political. Our assailants were striving to show that they were a new breed of sociologists. They not only did not pretend to be objective and value free but also made manifest their sympathy for the movements they studied. Thus they portrayed us as partisans who, while claiming to be objective, were actually defenders of the establishments that social movements such as those of the 1960s attacked. Although my analysis of the Black Power movement in *The Impossible Revolution?* had been acclaimed by many blacks as revealing an unusual understanding of the perspective of the participants, my critics seemed to believe that my writings in *Collective Behavior* unmasked me as a conservative, classical collective behaviorist. One diatribe distributed at an Eastern Sociological Society meeting by "insurgent sociologists" revealed their inconsistency. It was 1969, and *The Impossible Revolution?* had just appeared. The flyer attacked collective behaviorists as one segment of conservative sociologists. It criticized Turner by name but made no reference to me, even though by that time "Turner and Killian" were usually mentioned in the same breath. One of the insurgents admitted that my recent book exempted me.

The other motive was, in my opinion, personal as well as professional. After witnessing numerous ostensibly scientific debates in sociology, I have recognized that the discipline is not a cumulative science, if it is a science at all. Each new batch of scholars aspiring to fame begin their "contributions to knowledge" by proclaiming that most if not all of what has been written before on their topic was in error. They may pretend to build their new insights on the foundation of clues provided by a favorite teacher or by a theorist who is currently in favor, as Marx was during the 1960s and 1970s. Even if the ideas advanced by the young turks have been proposed by their predecessors, they give them new names. Hence, to stay abreast of developments in sociology, one has to learn a new vocabulary every ten years or less.

To a deplorable extent this allegedly intellectual endeavor has been a sometimes vicious game of "king of the mountain." As I read much of the new literature on social movements, I felt that more than a few young sociologists were trying to "make their bones" by denigrating my work and that of my contemporaries. One of them sought to validate his work by scheduling interviews with several of us during an American Sociological Association meeting. What he would assert in the article he was writing was that resource mobilization had replaced classical collective behavior theory as the dominant paradigm in the study of social movements. Ever since the publication of Thomas Kuhn's book on biological science, *The Structure of Scientific Revolutions*, sociologists who viewed themselves as scientific revolutionaries had been trying to identify dominant paradigms that they could overthrow. In view of the constant state of theoretical disorder, even chaos, in sociology I regarded this as a ridiculous quest. My interviewer was shocked when I told him that I did not regard resource mobilization as a paradigm but merely as another in the long succession of sociological fads about which Pitirim Sorokin had written in *Fads and Foibles in Sociology*. I, in turn, was incensed when he asked me if I had ever participated in a social movement. One of the watchwords of his school was that the social movements described by the classical theorists did not sound like anything they had ever taken part in, implying that we were just arm-chair theorists.

The article he subsequently wrote turned out as I expected. My statements were either distorted, taken out of context, or ignored. Kurt Lang was another of the interviewees on this occasion. He was so angry when the article appeared that he wrote the author a ten-page letter denouncing what he felt amounted to intellectual dishonesty. He declared that the interviewer should have known better because he had taken one of Kurt's graduate courses in social movements while a student and should have been well acquainted with his ideas.

The whole controversy had an unexpected payoff for me. Shortly after the publication of a journal article purporting to correct previous sociohistorical analyses of the civil rights movement, I took my last sabbatical leave from the University of Massachusetts. The theory proposed in the article seemed to fit so poorly the events I had witnessed and studied in Tallahassee that I decided to look at them again. Since I had a leave for a semester at full salary, Kay and I were able to take up residence in our apartment at Pensacola Beach, just 200 miles from the scene of the Tallahassee bus boycott. In my new research I was aided by the writings that C.U. Smith and I had published in the 1960s, by an oral history done subsequently, and by the opportunity to interview again some of the participants. The results of my research showed, not surprisingly, that Smith and I had not been entirely wrong in our original analysis, even though some revisions were in order. The outcome of my sabbatical research was an article published in the *American Sociological Review* that came to be widely cited in the subsequent literature on social movements.

I found it ironic that one of the points of contention between myself and my critics concerned the role of emotion in human behavior and particularly in collective behavior. They implied that to invoke emotion even as one factor in the development of social movements was to treat the behavior as "irrational" and "impulsive." Yet I probably would not have been impelled to do the research, nor would my writing in the resulting article have been so cogent, had I not been angry. Obviously I cannot deny the charge that my research was to some extent biased by the fact that I was party to a controversy, but I have already shown that I felt my critics' motives were not so pure and rational as they pretended. I thought that this would surely be the last article I would have published in a major journal. I was really weary of what seemed to me to be an unending and fruitless intellectual status game. This was not my "last hurrah," however. My retirement would prove much more active than I planned.

By the time I had enjoyed my last sabbatical, I had already decided to retire at the age of 65. This was even before Massachusetts had made early retirement attractive with the bait of a sizable bonus. I was tired of the never-ending problem of deciding what grades were fair to students, and I was disaffected by academic politics. Every time I faced a class of young people to whom the Great Depression, World War II and even the civil rights movement were ancient history, I felt like an old soldier boring his grandchildren with war stories, for I could not separate sociology from history. On the personal side, the New England snows, the fall foliage, the squash, popovers, and Indian pudding, had lost their novelty and romance. Having had a taste during vacations, I longed for the sun and sand of Florida, for the long springtimes of the South, and a cuisine in which okra, grits, hush puppies, and fried mullet were standard. Indian pudding could never match an icy slice of watermelon or a tree-ripened peach.

My retirement in 1984 was made a joyous occasion by the efforts of my good friends Mike Lewis, Clark Roof, and Jay Demerath. In my honor they organized a weekend of activities celebrating my work and my devotion to both better race relations and my native South. They surprised me by inviting two distinguished white southerners, Will D. Campbell, a battle-scarred civil rights worker and author, and Marshall Frady, a journalist, to speak at a forum entitled "White Southerners and the Enigma of Race." I had read Frady's writings, but I was even more honored by "Brother Will's" participation, for he was a legendary hero to people who loved southerners both black and white. He is the most profoundly devout Christian I have ever known, personifying the theme "Love thine enemies and do good to those who would harm you." During his career, he has extended his love and care both to black victims of prejudice and to the families of Ku Klux Klansmen.

My cup was filled to overflowing on the second day of the celebration. Ralph Turner and C.U. Smith were present to discuss, respectively, my contributions to the study of collective behavior and race relations. After having worked with them for so many years, it was frightening at first but gratifying in the end to hear their appraisals.

The one disappointment of the weekend was that none of the black faculty members whom I knew at the university attended, even though invitations were sent to all of them and I was still listed as adjunct professor in the Department of Afro-American Studies. Such was the gulf that existed between whites and blacks in the University of Massachusetts, which prided itself so on its liberalism.

I was also gratified by the numerous greetings and congratulations that came from sociologists in many quarters of the land. The one I treasure most was a brief letter from Herbert Blumer. I know that he wrote from a wheelchair, for his descent into a terribly debilitated state had already begun. His words were affectionate and his praise lavish, but I cherish them even as I acknowledge the hyperbole. He wrote, " I regard you, without any qualification, as the foremost student in the world in the area of Black-White relations in the United States. You have combined with your penetrating and impressive insights in this area a human quality that makes you a truly great person." A student could hope for no higher accolade from his teacher. But this was not the last word. After the ceremonies, I wrote and told him what had gone on and what I had said in response to Turner's and Smith's evaluation of my work. In an even briefer note he replied, "Your phrase, 'it is people we study, not variables,' is a gem—it should appear on all of our professional letterheads." This I had learned from him, and I wish more sociologists would remember it.

Even after retirement, I did more work in Amherst, for the early-retirement plan included the opportunity for some post-retirement part-time teaching and research. The most rewarding activity was a summer research project done with younger colleagues, Richard Tessler and Gayle Gubman. It was not in the field of ethnic relations but in the area of mental health. We did thirty long, intensive interviews with families of chronically mentally ill persons to explore what their problems were. The deinstitutionalization movement, for which sociologists must take some of the blame, had placed many patients at the mercy of inadequately funded, overloaded community mental health centers. Eventually we managed to publish our results, but the long-term benefit for me was the preparation I received for a later role as a volunteer ombudsman for mental patients in Pensacola, as a member of the Human Rights Advocacy Committee.

Even as I was making the transition from full-time employment to a very active retirement, Ralph and I were concluding work on the third edition of *Collective Behavior*. The final labors were completed during the fall of 1986. Kay, as she had done during work on the previous editions, helped me read proofs and construct the index. At the time I was enjoying a semester as Distinguished Visiting Professor at the University of Delaware. This appointment had been engineered by two colleagues from my days in disaster research, Russell Dynes and Henry Quarantelli, and my very successful former student, Margaret Andersen. Henry and I, both students of Blumer, gave a seminar on collective behavior, and with Margaret I team-taught an undergraduate course in ethnic relations. We joked that while she had once been my teaching assistant, now I was hers.

A pleasant surprise was the discovery that Chuck Stone, a senior editor on the *Philadelphia Evening News* and one-time editor of the *Chicago Defender*, was a member of the English faculty at Delaware. I had known Chuck by his writings on black nationalism in the United States. It turned out that he knew me through my books, so our first face-to-face meeting was like a reunion. I found him just as stimulating and informative as I had anticipated, and Kay and I acquired two delightful friends in him and his wife, Louise.

The highlight of the semester was a visit by Bill Wilson, who gave a public lecture sponsored by the Sociology Department. As busy as he was with a $2.5 million dollar research project on race and poverty, the honorarium that the University of Delaware could offer was not enough to lure him away. He told Margaret Andersen that he would come only if she could obtain a ticket for him to see his former student at Massachusetts, Julius Erving, play basketball with the Philadelphia 76ers. She obtained tickets for Bill, for the two of us, and for our spouses, so we were able to see the great "Dr. J." play in one of his last games. Thus, athletics can occasionally serve academic ends.

After retirement, I received two more honors as a sociologist, both of which required enough expenditure of time and energy to make Kay ask, "When are you really going to retire?" The first was election as chair of the Section on Collective Behavior and Social Movements of the American Sociological Association. That a majority of my colleagues in this field voted for me helped allay my concern that being labeled a "classical theorist" might indeed indicate that I was totally out of date. A section chair has little power other than that of organizing the sessions allotted at the annual meetings. This gave me an opportunity to bring together in one session some of the leading scholars in the field, such as Ralph Turner and Anthony Oberschall, and representatives of the younger generation who were not sure that collective behavior and social movements belong together, including Doug McAdam. The session was harmonious, constructive, and very well-attended. I felt that I had made a worthwhile contribution to peace between two generations of scholars in what had become a highly controversial area of study.

My final honor was election as president of the Southern Sociological Society the first year I became eligible after returning to the region. I found it amusing and somewhat gratifying that my name had been proposed to the Nominating Committee by the Radical Caucus. After my election, Larry Reynolds, who had promoted my candidacy, said to me, "I told the members that we had tried long enough to get a Marxist on the ballot without succeeding, so why not back a candidate who at least is not anti-Marxist?" One of Larry's chief allies was my friendly enemy from Connecticut days, John Leggett.

After my year as president, I had one more article published in a major journal, my presidential address. In 1953 *Social Forces* had carried one of my first articles from my dissertation, "The Adjustment of Southern White Migrants to Northern, Urban Norms." The very important paper that Chuck Smith and I had done, "Negro Protest Leaders in a Southern Community," appeared in the same journal in 1960. I had a sense of closure when "Race Relations in the Nineties: Where Are the Dreams of the Sixties?" appeared in the September 1990, issue of *Social Forces*. Professionally and personally this Cracker was home at last.

Chapter 16   SUMMING UP: PESSIMISM AND A RAY OF HOPE

A Different South—What Was It All About?—Youthful Ambitions—The Dark Side—A Ray of Hope

The South I came home to was very different from the one I had left in 1968. The changes since my childhood introduction to race relations in Georgia were even vaster. It is an urban South, swept out of its rural past by the same winds that have changed the rest of the nation. The rural charm disappeared along with the rural problems that, during the Great Depression, seemed to epitomize the South—according to FDR, "the nation's economic problem number one." The people are far more heterogeneous than was the two-toned population in which I grew to manhood; Latinos of various sorts, Southeast Asians, Koreans, and Asian Indians are familiar compatriots, particularly in a navy community such as Pensacola. So are transplanted Yankees, born anywhere from Boston to California but long since retired to the Sunbelt. It is dismaying to me, a born-and-bred southern Democrat, who rejoiced in Jimmy Carter's election and am still angry over his subsequent defeat, that now so many southerners are Republicans. Even by the time I published the first edition of my book *White Southerners* in 1970, white voters living in the South had become one of the bulwarks of Republican strength in presidential contests.

Sociologists and historians who have devoted much study to the South as a region now debate whether there remains a distinctive southern culture. I stay out of the discussion but feel personally that there is still enough different about the South and many of its people to make me feel that I have indeed come home. There is always a "new South," but enough of the old persists to remind me of the one I once knew and have always loved in spite of its faults.

Along with the growth of the crowded cities, the most visible evidence of change in the region is in race relations. As a Cracker who knew and accepted segregation when it was at its cruelest and most extensive, I now suffer from culture shock when I see the changes that were so violently resisted during the civil rights movement. The "Colored" restrooms and drinking fountains are gone. A few, very few, black families worship regularly in my parish church; there is still a black Episcopal parish in Pensacola. Blacks appear to shop freely with whites, and both are often served by stylishly dressed black salespeople and cashiers. In the past two years I have formed a close friendship with a black man

215

of about my age. Henry Burrell, who grew up in the slums of Detroit, is a veteran of the U.S. Air Force and now is permanent deacon in the Roman Catholic church. We work together as members of the Human Rights Advocacy Committee in northwest Florida. When, after a meeting, Henry and I want to have lunch together, we don't have to wonder where it will be safe for us to go. All we have to decide is what kind of food we want.

As an adjunct professor at the University of West Florida, I have occasionally taught classes in minority relations. Rarely have I encountered a student, even one raised in the South, who retains even the dimmest memory of segregation. These students, white and black, are as intrigued and shocked by my lecture describing "the way it was" as were the audiences to whom I gave the same lecture in Massachusetts. I, in turn, experienced a bit of shock one day when a beautiful young white woman casually informed the class that her husband was a black air force pilot on duty in Korea. I still am subject to a twinge of anxiety when I see an interracial couple on Pensacola Beach, remembering how blacks were beaten when they tried to desegregate the beaches near St. Augustine, Florida, in the early 1960s.

I rejoice that black citizens are so much freer than they were in my childhood and that I have been released from the bonds of a Jim Crow society. But my joy turns to despair when I must confront the fact that behind the facade of freedom in public places exists a structure of inequality that is in some aspects more hideous than that of the past, offering less hope of salvation to the victims.

The statistics sociologists and economists present in their endless outpouring of books and articles tell a story of persistent residential segregation, the resegregation of public schools, and an almost invariant gap between the incomes of white and black families. They confirm the reality of disproportionate rates of delinquency, illegitimacy, and welfare dependence among minority ethnic groups, even though the rates are also increasing in the white population and the white poor still outnumber the black.

But I do not have to study the tables and graphs to find evidence of the enduring consequences of slavery, segregation and exploitation. As I drive along the freeway that bisects Pensacola from south to north, there are places where I can see black slum dwellings on either side. Only a few blocks away I can find the all-black public housing projects where the poor but decent residents live in fear of the drug dealers who prey on their children. With Henry Burrell, I visit the juvenile detention center and see children as young as twelve years old awaiting trial for armed robbery, car theft, or worse felonies. There are young white felons there, too, but I know that society still offers more opportunities for whites if they are reformed than for the blacks. I see machines, from mechanical cottonpickers and ditchdiggers to my wife's washing machine, doing the work that once provided employment for many blacks who, though underpaid, enjoyed the dignity of a job. At the same time, I know that despite nearly a quarter of a century of affirmative action, only a well-qualified minority of black workers have been able to move into the professional and high-tech jobs that each year become more important in our economy. Although the small city of Pensacola is far removed in space and population from Chicago, I can see in my new home in the South the same trends toward greater segregation and inequality that Bill Wilson and his students are discovering in the northern industrial metropolis.

Worse yet, I am condemned by the fact that in spite of the dismantling of de jure segregation, I still live in a white world which is, in a way, more segregated than was my environment in Macon. With the disappearance of domestic servants and black yardmen such as "Black Lewis," I do not have the daily close contact with blacks that I once knew. The domestics have not been replaced by black neighbors, although the law says that they could be. Only once in our lives have we enjoyed the fellowship of a black family in an American neighborhood. That was in Amherst, where an army officer whom I knew at the University of Massachusetts, James Faison, bought a house on our little cul-de-sac. He and his wife, Martha, lived there for a few years before building a grander house in another part of the town. Kay and I would welcome neighbors such as the Faisons again and would go to great lengths to defend their exercise of their rights. But we are not about to embark on a quixotic crusade that would entail inviting a black friend, or a stranger, to endure the tribulations of being a test case.

In the early days of my professional study of race relations, my theoretical views were quite clear to me, and my faith in progress was firm. Once awakened to the dangers of the myth of race and the evils of segregation, I cherished the naive belief that the tide of history was flowing slowly but inexorably toward erasing them. The very concept of race and the divisions rationalized by it were, I had learned, relatively recent developments in the long history of human culture. While I did not anticipate their immediate demise, I was confident that every move, scientific, theological, or legal, to destroy them would be a sure step in the direction of racial democracy, to be realized perhaps even in my lifetime. In my teaching at the University of Oklahoma and at Florida State University, I preached a simple but powerful gospel of assimilation.

Then the mixed and inadequate accomplishments of the civil rights movement, and the unmasking of the deep economic problems that remain little affected by civil rights laws all thrust a haze of doubt into my theoretical view and cast a pall of gloom over my hopes for progress. I still preferred an assimilationist outcome, but I no longer had faith that it would come in my lifetime, if ever. The ethnic divisions and the hostilities that were revived and magnified in the 1960s, not only in the United States but throughout the world, suggested that the tide flowed toward unending conflict, not assimilation or even peaceful, harmonious pluralism.

My record of theoretical and personal devotion to assimilation suggests that I should be an enthusiastic advocate of affirmative action in the form of compensatory discrimination. I cannot, however, join the ranks of my friends who believe that it will lead eventually to the disappearance of color consciousness. The evidence I have assiduously examined leads me to conclude that such a program leads only to a form of "supertokenism" benefiting a fortunate few but changing neither the distribution of power nor the concentration of wealth that together keep poor blacks outside the mainstream and even increase their numbers. At the same time, the issue, wielded as a political weapon, perpetuates and deepens the rift between white and black Americans. I see no inclination on the part of white voters and their elected representatives to support or even propose the radical economic reforms that would be necessary to reverse the decade-long trend for the rich to get richer and the poor, poorer. It is easier for politicians to unite white voters in opposition to new taxes, to welfare programs, and to "quotas" than to inspire them with a vision of a society in which the vast wealth of the nation is distributed more equally.

Equally confusing and discouraging is the disarray among black Americans. There are no contemporary counterparts of Washington and Du Bois or of Martin Luther King, Jr., and Malcolm X, with opposing but inspiring philosophies and calls to action. The current "black establishment," the NAACP, the Urban League, and the greatly shrunken Southern Christian Leadership Conference, year after year advocate measures that have proven inadequate and that depend on the goodwill of whites, a goodwill that is diminishing. A small but growing number of black intellectuals—hardly "leaders"—criticize the shopworn solutions proposed by the established "leaders" and advocate self-help programs reminiscent of the Black Power era. No contemporary social movement has emerged, however. While there are frequent cries of anguish from black Americans, the black protest movement that stretches back to the slave revolts and the Underground Railroad appears to be moribund or, at the least, quiescent.

So, sadly, the vision of racial equality and peace dreamed about by so many blacks and whites in the 1960s has not materialized. Neither has my vision of personal accomplishment. I still remember getting my first history book, as a fourth grader at Winship School, and deciding that what I wanted to be was a history teacher. This was not surprising, since our family life revolved around the schedules of the schools in which my mother taught and I studied. The romance of the stories about the human adventure thrilled me; I read weighty tomes such as *The Glory That Was Greece* and *The Grandeur That Was Rome*, just for fun. As a boy who spent far more time reading than did most of my playmates, I was already on my way to becoming an armchair intellectual.

My early vision of myself as a historian reached no further than continuing my reading and becoming a high school teacher. When I entered college, this was still my ambition but somewhere I developed a crusading spirit. I believed, as historians boasted, that the study of history would not only be edifying but could help people from repeating the mistakes of the past. Then I was seduced by the bolder promises of sociologists. Their primary goal, I believed, was to solve social problems, and they would do it with the aid of scientific methods.

Hence I entered my apprenticeship in sociology as a would-be worldsaver, as I think many young sociologists still do. Mike Lewis and I have joked that if you scratch a sociologist, you are likely to reveal a priest, a rabbi, or a Protestant evangelist. In my own case, my most significant role models were my mother, a teacher; ministers I knew as a very active Episcopal young churchman; and my dead father and his brothers, soldiers all. While I made an early decision to relegate the military role to that of an avocation, I fancied that as a social scientist I could combine the roles of teacher, researcher, and missionary, doing God's work through social science.

My conceptions of reality formed in those youthful days of optimistic idealism have since been battered and distorted by years of study and practice. I have remained an active member of the Episcopal church, supporting its work and worship with my money, my time, and my amateur baritone voice. I continue to receive emotional succor from the beauty of its liturgy, so well known to me from early childhood. Yet I must live with the terrible knowledge that my absolute belief in the Christian myth has given way to agnosticism. Even when I pray, "Lord, I believe—help thou my unbelief," I cannot make the leap of faith required to carry me beyond agnosticism. When I feel most like a hypocrite, a whited sepulchre, I am comforted by the words of the great Episcopal theologian, Canon Bernard Iddings Bell, "No one can be an intelligent Christian unless he has been, and remains, an agnostic." I know enough sociology and anthropology to be convinced that no society can survive without the sacred canopy of religion of which Peter Berger has written, and I still find the Christian myth the most nearly convincing of all myths. But as a true agnostic, I am not even sure that it is a myth—it could be true. That is frightening to one who does not totally believe.

What came to be a lack of absolute commitment to any belief system or to any cause has tortured me. My inconsistencies often perplex friends and confound critics. At times I feel that I have lived most of my life with tongue in cheek. One of Louis Wirth's many quotable and thought-provoking quips was addressed to his race relations classes, "Tolerance is the suspicion that the other fellow might be right." While I rejoice in what I believe to be my unusual ability to take the attitude of the other, as a symbolic interactionist should, action can be profoundly inhibited by an excess of tolerance. There have been times when I wished that I could be a fanatic who ignored the complexity of problems, whether interpersonal or societal.

In my reading I have delved into the sociology of knowledge, the philosophy and psychology of George Herbert Mead and his disciples, and the theories of existentialists and phenomenologists. As a consequence, the only thing I truly believe is that I exist but that neither I nor any other human can know what the real world is. While I do believe that there is a reality out there, the title of Berger and Luckmann's book, *The Social Construction of Reality*, reflects better than any other theory my view of my relationship to it. Hence, even when "facts" seem clear to me and even support what I would like to believe, there lingers the suspicion that those who reject my reality might be right after all. In a field as complex and controversial as ethnic relations, this is a heavy intellectual burden. The fear, hostility, and conflict that prevail between whatever ethnic groups one studies constantly confront the researcher with the danger of becoming a partisan who only contributes to the conflict. I saw this graphically demonstrated in the controversies over the Moynihan report and Coleman's white-flight hypothesis, the vicious attacks on Bill Wilson, and the debates about affirmative action.

That I have become a paradox, torn by doubts and inconsistencies, has reached into many aspects of my life. As a young lieutenant in the Infantry School, I got in a violent argument with my classmates because I tried to explain and defend the position of conscientious objectors. One of my first classes in race relations at the University of Oklahoma included a young couple from New York who were communists. They found my criticisms of American capitalism and its involvement in racial discrimination so trenchant that they demanded to know why I wasn't a Marxist. Yet I have never been able to accept the optimistic faith of my Marxist friends and colleagues, any more than I can share the naive beliefs in the blessings of capitalism held by my conservative neighbors. One of the hardest things for some of my liberal friends to fathom is how I can have such heartfelt sympathy for black Americans as victims of oppression and yet retain such understanding and even love of their white oppressors, particularly my fellow white southerners.

Another casualty of my disenchantment has been my faith in sociology as a science and even as a legitimate discipline. My illusions about the objectivity of any social science were long ago dispelled. I even question whether our professional labors have ever produced more than a modicum of results that were worthwhile to society rather than merely interesting. During much of my teaching career I was scornful of the "social studies" taught in public schools and in schools of education. Now I feel that it is elitism that had led me and my colleagues to boast that we taught "social science," not social studies. When I think of the most insightful and best-written books in race relations, what comes to mind are *The Strange Career of Jim Crow* and *Roll, Jordan, Roll* by C. Vann Woodward and Eugene Genovese, respectively, both historians, and *Common Ground* by J. Anthony Lucas, a journalist. I deplore what often appears to be the headlong rush of sociology into quantification. Many quantitative studies generate alleged facts based on data collected from samples that come nowhere near meeting the requirements of probability statistics taught in methods courses. Mathematical sociologists continue to invent new tests to enable them more skillfully to "massage" data that are of questionable validity no matter how sanctified by being quantified. Graduate students supposedly being trained to do research sit at computers analyzing data sets, but never seeing nor interviewing any of the people they are alleged to be studying.

To me, one of the most disillusioning events of recent decades is the continued perversion of the U.S. census in the name of improving ethnic relations. As early as 1960, I knew, as should most social scientists, that minority groups and the very poor are consistently underenumerated. Yet I continued to believe that with the corrections made by the demographers at the Census Bureau, the census provided the most complete and valid social statistics available. Then the 1980 census, with data gathered primarily by mail questionnaires, included questions on ethnicity (Is this person—?) and, for a sample, a question asking with what ancestry group the person identified. I was deeply disturbed by the similarity of this practice of my own government to the racial classifications imposed by the Nazi regime in Germany and the white government in South Africa. John Rex and Sheila Patterson, in England, learned of my concern and asked me to prepare a paper on the subject, since there was a vigorous debate in the United Kingdom as to whether their next census should include questions on ethnicity. This led me to do a great deal of research on the background of the questions on our own schedule and the sort of data they elicited. It soon became evident that minority groups and government bureaucrats struggling with affirmative action goals and guidelines demanded this official sanctioning of the importance of ethnic identification. Social scientists were another pressure group who, along with businessmen, always wanted the Bureau of the Census to go far beyond the simple constitutional requirement to enumerate the population every ten years. Even before the 1980 census schedules were prepared, the bureau had periodically experimented with collecting data on ethnicity in sample studies between census years. The results showed that the data on ethnic identity were clearly unreliable, not to say of questionable validity. When the answers for the 1980 census came in, it was evident that many citizens found the questions very confusing. In addition, a large number, including me, refused to answer the questions on ancestry, finding them as ridiculous as they certainly were.

I was able to make extensive use of the results of my research, presenting a paper to a seminar at the Centre for Research in Ethnic Relations at Birmingham, England, and then publishing it in *New Community*. John Rex found my analysis so persuasive that he quoted me in testimony before a committee of the House of Commons. Thus I had the unexpected pleasure of seeing my name in a British "blue book," the committee's report. The fact that the arguments of Rex, one of Britain's most astute analysts of ethnic problems, were rejected by the parliamentary committee reinforced my conviction that neither in the United States nor in other nations have sociologists significantly influenced public policy. I once taught my introductory students that sociology, as a science, had as its goals prediction and control. Now I conclude that after a century sociology, "the American science," has generated few accurate predictions and has exercised only negligible control.

A discussion of my analysis of the collection of official data on ethnicity with a group of sociologists at the University of Delaware made me feel even more strongly that while deluding ourselves that we might be broadly influential, we have actually spent most of our time, save for that spent in teaching, in publishing to keep from perishing and to gain status in the eyes of other sociologists. After presenting my evidence of the definite lack of reliability and validity of the ethnic data in the 1980 census, I asked, "What should sociologists do with these data—should we use them or ignore them?" To those sociologists in my audience who answered "Use them—they're all we have," I addressed the question, "Then are you saying that bad data are better than no data?" Some even assented to this, as have quite a few of my colleagues who have subsequently used these very data as the basis for journal articles.

Yet I realize that I myself have been guilty of using data from poorly drawn samples, collected by interviewers whom I saw no more than once, in a training session. So I wonder how often we have deceived laypeople who have struggled to cut through our jargon to winnow out the truths we purport to have discovered. Are we not, when at our most persuasive, just good storytellers rather than scientists? My best writings I have done in the style of a social historian, so at the end of a successful career I wonder if I should have not stayed with my first choice, history.

A third major casualty of my experience has been my optimism and my belief in progress. Although my dire predictions that white America will become more, not less, violent and oppressive in its treatment of blacks have not proved entirely true, I remain in thrall to the pessimism that inspired both editions of *The Impossible Revolution?* I see the good fortune of the black bourgeoisie out-weighed and threatened by the increasingly grim plight of poor, ghetto blacks. I see a growing number of good-spirited white people who assent in theory to racial equality and never say "nigger," yet still rant against "the black welfare cheats having baby after baby and never looking for an honest job." They have no problem with "qualified blacks," but would not want them living in the neighborhood because, "You know, they're all right—but it's the ones that would follow with their drugs and crimes." Formal segregation has ended, but a gulf still divides the two societies, white and black, separate and unequal, of which the Kerner Commission wrote a quarter of a century ago.

In my ethnic relations classes the worst question that a student could ask was, "What is the solution?" The only honest answer I could give was, "I don't think we are going to solve these problems. Things do not always get better or turn out all right." Then I often shocked classes by going on to say, "You see, I don't believe in progress. What we perceive as progress is just social change in which the shape of problems is altered or they are replaced by new ones. The world never gets better in an overall sense, and today, after centuries of so-called civilization, we have the means to bring it all to a flaming, radioactive end."

This is strong medicine for students, and it is more bitter for me. My pessimism is the despair of my wife, who has had to endure both it and my times of severe depression. During one such period, she cried out to me, "Do you really feel that your whole life has been wasted?" My actions answer no, but at times my feeling is yes, perhaps because deep inside me, my reference point remains the unrealistic ambition to do great good, which started me on my career.

Now, unconvinced of the hope of heaven, persuaded that human beings and their societies are not perfectible, knowing that all utopias have ended as dystopias, I am possessed of a vision of doom that should crush me. Yet it does not, and I cannot help but come back to Mike Lewis's rejoinder to my claim to be a pessimist, "No one who continues to write can be totally pessimistic." Strangely, despite my agnosticism, I am convinced that much of my pessimism is derived from my understanding of the Christian Gospels. The only man who is credited with saving the world did so by being crucified. His declaration, "My kingdom is not of this earth," seems a rebuff to the dreams of utopian reformers, as well as to the Hebrew vision of a messianic age. As I understand the message of the Gospels, being a good Christian leads to the cross, not to the crystal cathedral of Robert Shuler.

Christian eschatology is summed up in the prediction of wars and rumors of war in the last days, not of peace on earth. The eschatological assumptions of sociologists, I have long contended, lead them into an unwarranted optimism shared by both radicals and liberals. I wrote in 1971, in "Optimism and Pessimism in Sociological Analysis," that "radical sociologists who look forward to a revolution in which not only the evils of the existing system will be swept away but evil itself will be diminished or abolished are in their way as optimistic as liberal theorists who conclude that the system can and will endure if it is only reformed." So I plead for sociologists to try to describe the plight of humanity with stark realism, rather than with an unacknowledged optimism.

At the same time, I acknowledged that even if sociology and other social sciences did become dismal and pessimistic, they could not destroy the other sources of human hope and courage that sustain people and lead them to seek to make adjustments in what I believe is a cruel world. The myth of Sisyphus makes sense to me. Although he never could get the rock to the top, each time it inevitably rolled back down the hill he tried again. So do most of us.

Throughout my adult life, I have pursued the shallow but alluring goals of professional fame, media recognition and financial success. I have learned, but always imperfectly, that attaining any of them leads only to a taste for more. The fruits of victory may be enjoyed for only a short season before they become dry and stale. So what has it been all about? Where can I find a ray of hope?

As I read the story of the human experience, recounted in myriad ways in the writings of novelists, journalists, philosophers, historians, and even social scientists, what stands out as a constant is the centrality of interpersonal relations. The thrill of young, romantic love; the comfort of enduring affection, such as I have enjoyed for half a century in my own marriage; the happiness of parents at the birth of a baby; the satisfaction of knowing that someone is a true friend; the gratitude shown by a stranger for an act of mercy; the joy of giving—these are the things that endure and sustain us in both the best of times and the worst. Despite my sometimes successful quest for honors, the memories of my career that I treasure most are of individual students telling me that I gave them some new insight into themselves and their fellows; of the people who wrote to tell me that my account of my experiences as a mental patient gave them hope and a feeling that someone understood their plight; of a host of gestures or words that have made me feel closer to some other traveler along life's way. In the field of race relations, what I cherish most are not whatever small contributions I might have made to changing the segregated social order of my society but those instances when I have been able to break through the barrier of race and make a black person feel that I do truly want to be a brother, as hard as that may be for a Cracker, even a reformed one. Whatever has passed and whatever lies ahead, these are the things that count and give me my ray of hope.

Index

225